Powys
Jack and Frances

I

John Cowper Powys and Frances Gregg
at about the time of their first meeting
in 1912

The Letters of John Cowper Powys to Frances Gregg

Volume One

EDITED BY
OLIVER MARLOW WILKINSON
ASSISTED BY CHRISTOPHER WILKINSON

CECIL WOOLF · LONDON

First published in 1994
Letters of John Cowper Powys © Francis L. Powys, 1994
Letters of Frances Gregg, Preface, Introduction
and Editorial Notes © Oliver M. Wilkinson, 1994

Cecil Woolf Publishers, 1 Mornington Place, London NW1 7RP
Tel: 071-387 2394

British Library Cataloguing in Publication Data
    Letters of John Cowper Powys to Frances
    Gregg. — Vol. 1. — (Collected Letters of
    John Cowper Powys)
    I. Title II. Wilkinson, Oliver Marlow
    III. Wilkinson, Christopher IV. Series
    821.912

ISBN 0-900821-99-X

To
my wife,
Margaret,
and to our family,
Jane, Judy, Christopher, Bridget and Roland,
who helped with the detective work
of sorting out the letters here,
and who first typed them

Acknowledgements

The late Kenneth Hopkins, poet, helped from his own personal knowledge of the Powyses, and from his research for his book *The Powys Brothers*.

Lucy Penny (*née* Powys), Alyse Gregory and Marian Powys are all dead now, but our gratitude to them continues for their identification of people and places.

My father, the late Louis Wilkinson ('Louis Marlow') identified – a little against the grain, perhaps, and understandably so – other people and places.

Belinda Humfrey,* of Lampeter University, and Louise de Bruin of the Powys Society made valuable suggestions.

Amy Gibson and Maggie Wilkinson made many valuable corrections.

Jeffrey Kwintner, Walter Kendall, Virginia Smyers, Professor Robert Levens, Anna Freeman, Vera Martin, Guido Franzinetti all added to this book, in one way or another, at different times – and Rosemary C.E. Moore, Clerk to the Montacute Parish Council, and Alan Rochards of Stoke-sub-Harndon gave information about the Powys home ground.

In addition, *The Brothers Powys* by Richard Graves, and *The Life of Llewelyn Powys* by Malcolm Elwin have been particularly useful sources of information.

Great thanks to them for their time, trouble and magnanimity.

O.M. Wilkinson
C.U. Wilkinson

*Editor of 'The Powys Review' and of books on the Powyses.

Contents

Illustrations

Preface

The letters of John Cowper Powys to Frances Gregg were discovered in a sack at the Fortress, Devonport, Plymouth, after Frances's death. During April 1941, there were days and nights of air-raids on Plymouth. Frances Gregg – or Frances Wilkinson, as she had become in 1912; but she still wrote under her maiden name of Frances Gregg – had known well enough that Plymouth was a danger zone, but she had had to get a job to keep her daughter, her mother and herself alive. There were other reasons for that move that become clearer in the letters (volume 2).

In Plymouth, Frances had got a job scrubbing floors at the NAAFI – the Navy, Army and Air Force Institution (forces canteen) – based in the Fortress. In a short while she had been promoted to Superintendent.

On 22 April, a telegram arrived for me, stating that my mother Frances, and my grandmother and sister had all been killed by enemy action. The Royal Navy gave me compassionate leave to deal with the bodies. In Plymouth, I asked the way in what seemed a deserted city of ruin, walking along streets of still smoking wreckage, past the emergency soup kitchens. In the Fortress, Frances's staff sat me down, gave me tea and a meal. They told me that when the air-raid sirens sounded on the night of Monday, 21 April, Frances had put her sack in the safe. When the raid became fierce, she told them that she would have to go to her daughter and mother. They did their best to dissuade her. The streets were blocked, fires were raging, bombs were falling. Frances insisted that she had to go to her mother and daughter.

She walked through the blitz towards the house, in another part of the city, where her daughter and mother were sheltering under the stairs. A bomb fell just as she reached the house. It killed all three women.

Television South-West used the tragedy – one among millions – for the opening of their documentary, 'Hilda's Book', by Frank Wintle, about

the bond between Frances Gregg, Hilda Doolittle ('H.D.' – the poet) and
Ezra Pound. This is another story, but it is touched on in the letters. In
the sack were other papers, including Frances's *The Mystic Leeway* – now
edited by Professor Ben Jones – as well as letters from Ezra Pound,
Theodore Dreiser, W.B. Yeats, 'H.D.' and others.

Many of Frances's early letters to John Cowper Powys – or Jack as she
and her family called him – are missing. Those she wrote to John Cowper
Powys before 1922 were ceremonially burnt by him in – as he told her –
'a place of rocks and butterflies'.

Not many of the letters she wrote to him between 1922 and 1935
exist, either. The few remaining ones, from that time, were found by
Jack's sister, Marian, in a drawer in a house at Patchin Place, New York,
after he had left there for ever. Marian forwarded them to her brother –
who never re-read letters, and who was nonplussed at keeping these. Jack
put them in another drawer, at Phudd Bottom, Hillsdale, Columbia
County: and somehow they survived his journey back to England, then
to Wales.

From 1935 to 1941 both sides of the correspondence exist. The later
letters of Frances, written in the 1930s and early '40s, were found by
Phyllis Playter in a drawer at the little house, 1 Waterloo, Blaenau
Ffestiniog, Wales, where Phyllis lived with John Cowper Powys (and
which is now decorated with a plaque in their honour). Phyllis Playter
was the first person to say that Frances's letters should be published.
When John Cowper Powys gave Frances's letters to me, he said, 'One
day, Livio, my dear – one day, we will write a *really long book* with her
letters! – you and I together!'

When I told him that the book could be even longer, because I had *his*
letters to her, he was shocked. After a moment, he agreed, but with
rather less energy, that that would be a splendid idea.

I am sure that he meant to write that long book with me, but he never
did: pressures of poverty, of other work, of age prevented it.

Perhaps the letters are best left to speak for themselves.

The information given in the Introduction and in the various notes in
the two volumes of this edition was given to me by my mother, Frances,
and by my father, Louis Wilkinson, and by my god-father, John Cowper
Powys – or Jack. I do not often indicate which of the three gave me any
particular piece of information. I cannot remember. I grew up in the
midst of the events; lived in the midst of the Letters. I have no reason to
think any of the information is wrong. If there are any mistakes they are
likely to be the distortion of childhood memories.

Where information was not given by any of the three, and was not within my own experience, I have indicated the source.

It is a wonder that any of the letters survive. Not all of Jack's letters to Frances were in that sack which had been carried by her over land and sea, stored in odd buildings, and in caravans, boats, tents, then had had high explosives, shrapnel, fire-bombs tearing a city to bits all around it. Apart from those in the sack, some of John Cowper Powys's letters were kept by Frances's mother, Julia Vanness Gregg. They were in her steamer trunks that had travelled with her through fire, flood and two world wars.

Some of the original letters are torn, some incomplete, some scrawled over, many are undated. Many of the envelopes have had the stamp and postmark torn off. Yet here in two volumes is the collection, in as complete shape as we can make it, a correspondence that begins in 1912 and ends in 1941: twenty-nine years of great changes, in the times and in the writers.

We have shortened some letters and left out a few: for in a correspondence covering nearly three decades there are repetitions. We have felt it best to give a broad idea of the whole correspondence, at the cost of leaving out some not very important parts of it. (Five dots indicate cuts made by the Editors, to distinguish them from dots used by the correspondents themselves in the actual letters when only three dots are used.)

As far as possible, we have allowed a free flow of the Letters. Reference notes, except where they can be condensed to a few words, are at the end of each volume, together with short biographical notes of the central characters referred to in the Letters. Each letter is headed with its date and its own identity number. Notes, indicated by a number within the text of the letters, can be found in the Reference Section at the end of the book. Shorter notes are printed in square brackets within the Letters themselves. The use of square brackets always indicates editorial intervention.

Readers – having once read through a volume of letters – often dip into them again and again, and at random. For this reason, we have risked repetition in identifying people and places. We have also bent the Notes to our will, in taking advantage sometimes of a name in a letter to describe the condition and work of that person, in the context and sometimes beyond the context of that particular letter. Without this, some of the references would be bald and puzzling.

We have cut out most of the opening and closing phrases of the Letters. Jack often signed with an intertwined 'C' and 'H' (standing for 'Cathy' and 'Hinchcliffe':); later, he signed himself simply 'J'. Frances, too, often signed herself simply 'F'. We have not included Jack's usual last words of love to Frances, and later to her family – nor hers to him – unless these vary.

The only other minor alteration to the Letters has been in the punctuation. Jack is the master of the long sentence. However many times they break off to qualify or digress, he never loses sight of their eventual end; but occasionally, as one thought leads swiftly to another and another and yet another, all of them separated by dashes, before returning to his first thought, the reader is defeated. Many of the dashes have been removed – particularly where they disguise the beginning of a new sentence – and full stops and commas have been inserted. In this way, we have made some passages more accessible than they were.

This collection is intended as much for the general reader as for the researcher. To both kinds of reader, we hope that the Letters will bring as much wonder, excitement and sheer amusement as they have for us.

O.M. Wilkinson
C.U. Wilkinson

Introduction

Frances Gregg's infancy, in the 1880s, was spent in the towns and out-posts of America's Middle West; her childhood in revivalist camp meetings; her later childhood on the edges of a slum in Philadelphia, where she heard negro jazz, saw negro dances, and a lynching. As a young woman she was a friend of some of the greatest writers of the century, and loved two of them, Ezra Pound and John Cowper Powys. Her middle years were different; she travelled with her mother and children in a heavy old car around France; then, for the rest of her life, around England, in the eastern counties, in Wales, and in the southern counties.

During these later years in England, she and her family lived in house-boats, shacks, Elizabethan manors, caravans, old rectories, tents, and in London houses that looked like forgotten wedding-cakes.

Her early poems and stories were published, and some re-published. Later, in her middle thirties onwards, she wrote when she could, but was so often in extreme poverty that she just tried to write 'pot-boilers' to keep her family and herself alive. Occasionally she still wrote as she wish-ed: 'The Apartment House' and 'The Unknown Face',[1] for instance, were both published in anthologies of best American short stories.

Frances first met Jack—John Cowper Powys—in 1912, when she came up to him after one of his lectures in Philadelphia. She gave him one of her poems, 'Perché'.

Frances was a member of Ezra Pound's group of young poets, and her best friend was Hilda Doolittle.[2] Frances's poems were being published in 'The Dial' and in 'The New York Forum', together with Ezra Pound's and H.D.'s.

Jack was delighted with Frances's beauty and character, and almost as impressed by her poem, though in fact he had thought the title, 'Perché', referred to a bird's perch or to a fish, while Frances had used the Italian word meaning 'because'. Whether at cross-purposes or not, he asked to see more of her work, and was invited to tea with her mother.

Jack underestimated Frances and her mother. The first letter, here, is from Jack to Mrs Julia Vanness Gregg; this, with two others to the mother, and a few quotations in the notes, are the only letters of Jack's in the collection that are not written to Frances. This first letter, in contrast to his later letters, shows the sweet, bland condescension of the great man.

Frances's mother did not accept condescension. She certainly did not accept it from an Englishman. She accepted Jack's flattery, though, as of right. She was proud of her Dutch blood; and of her kinship with the Roosevelts. All her life when faced with crisis or danger, as she frequently was, she determined to write to Theodore or Franklin Delano, but she never did; except once, to Franklin, about a small point to do with her passport.

Her mother often infuriated Frances. Frances respected her grandmother more, respected her greatly; but there was a strong bond between all three women. Their determination and desperate ingenuity when in danger was inherited from a long line of pioneering women. 'Women', because the men, their husbands, often died young – as some of the family letters show – in Indian wars, in the American Civil War, or when fighting with Captain Moonlight; leaving the women to continue the adventure of feeding, clothing and educating the children. This may explain the mixture of prudence and recklessness in Frances's later adventures, and in the way she dealt with money.

Frances's grandmother, Gertrude Heartt, had married a Southerner, and had moved to New Orleans, in 1858.[3] Her husband died during the Civil War, and Gertrude then moved her four sons and her daughter up through the lines, back north, and settled for a while in Fort Worth. Gertrude became a registered teacher. She also became a formidable lecturer on temperance, venereal disease and women's rights – this in the 1860s! Her daughter, Julia, became a teacher, too; then married an adventurous Englishman, Oliver Gregg, who went off prospecting and never returned. News reached Julia that he had died of exposure.

From the brief marriage Frances was born. Gertrude moved her daughter Julia and grand-daughter Frances to Philadelphia. As a child of eleven and twelve, even in adolescence, Frances used to climb into a cupboard with a candle, to read Dickens, Shakespeare, Hawthorne, Cervantes . . . She describes this time in her life in her story, 'The House with the Garden', and in other writings of hers that are now being re-published in anthologies.

Frances attended the Philadelphia Art College. She then became a teacher.

Her mother, Julia, started the first school for Italian immigrants. Sometimes the boys were in trouble with the police. Once, a boy died in a police cell. Frances and her mother made inquiries; persisted in them, until they found that hoses had been turned on the boy on a night of sub-zero temperature. The police of Philadelphia were very tough, but Frances and Julia made them admit the facts of the case and established those facts with the Police Authority. From then on, they obtained some immunity for their Italian pupils.

Frances and Julia, and even Gertrude in old age, seemed helpless women, but they were in reality formidable; at least when fighting injustice. They were intelligent fighters, too.

The three women became more prosperous. They moved to a better neighbourhood. The house was in a long row of similar houses, as their other home had been; and in the new house, as in the other one, there were dogs or cats that had been injured, or kittens saved from drowning, and sometimes a starved or ill-treated child. Frances, at one time, began to think of Jack as one of these.

The grandmother died. Frances became the dominant influence. Her mother became what she was always to be, the bane and spur of Frances's life: the sounding board, the indispensable whipping-boy. Frances had realised that she was more intelligent than her mother, but she relied on her mother's obstinate strength. Julia Vanness Gregg was a squarish women built to last for ever. Frances was beautiful but brittle; her heart was suspect. She was abnormally shy, which made the confrontations with authority more terrifying for her than for her mother. When Frances became angry with authority or indignant at any injustice, she was transformed. She looked vulnerable, but that made her the more impressive, as though the weak body had become possessed with immortal rage: a fragile vessel of Olympian fire.

When battles were over, whether they had won their way or not, Frances or her mother would see in retrospect something funny, and begin to laugh. The other would see the point and begin to laugh, too. The laughter would become helpless; not of nerves, not in reaction but in sheer appreciation of ludicrous or outrageous Fate. That was the pattern.

Frances's curiosity overcame her shyness. Even in her early twenties she conquered her nerves enough to join groups of writers, and to make friends with the two who fascinated her. She lost her shyness with them. She adored Ezra Pound with the passion of the innocent. On that innocence Ezra Pound had mercy, telling her that ignorance in love was unfit for the complexity of a poet – or something equally awful – but he meant well. He was certainly attracted to her, wrote poetry about her, advised her about her poetry, and thought her work as good as the poetry of H.D. at that time.[4] He was also concerned about her happiness when Frances was thrust among English contrivers. He actively intervened for her sake.

Frances, without knowing the word 'lesbian', except as a poetic reference, adored Hilda Doolittle. Hilda Doolittle was supposed to be engaged to Ezra Pound. Hilda adored Frances. These were the first formative years of the twentieth century. Frances was indeed ignorant about sex, because her mother had thought such knowledge unsuitable for girls, and still did. Hilda Doolittle was more sophisticated than Frances, and tried to enlighten her, but left a muddled impression. That muddle of mind, compounded or confounded by John Cowper Powys, remained with Frances till her wedding night.

In *The Mystic Leeway*,[5] and in her stories 'Judas at the Gate' and 'Male and Female', Frances describes the young Ezra Pound and H.D. She loved and admired them, but she was not over-awed by them. They had great gifts, certainly, and they worked hard at their art, but they were also *poseurs* who sought acclamation, and received it with a sublime assumption of divinity that Frances found funny. They were unique, too, though; dominating the earth with their originality, establishing their own laws, with some reference to the Classic past; sometimes failing, falling flat in the mud, but brushing it off as though it were gold dust. They were grand and silly enough to be treated as equals. Frances argued violently with them. It was a real friendship. They were the loves of her life.

Ezra Pound and H.D. believed that artists must sacrifice everything to art. Frances believed that artists, or anyone else for that matter, must look after the living first, only after that to turn to art; art even at its best was a scavenger – a glorious scavenger, yes, but battening on real life – and artists had better remember that.

Hilda and Frances and Frances's mother had travelled to France and England in 1911, under the guidance of Ezra Pound, so they knew a little about Europeans. Frances had never known an Englishman well, though, so she thought that John Cowper Powys – Jack – was a typical Englishman. She accepted his eccentricities as normal for the English.

Jack made faces at people in the elevated railway. He still looked distinguished as he did so, but that made it more disconcerting. His appearance was strange and beautiful, even though his clothes were spotted and stained, with buttons missing. (Once, when he was about to climb onto the lecture platform, with his hostess trying anxiously to indicate that his fly-buttons were undone, he told her, 'Madam, I wear them like that!'). When posting a letter, he felt the post-box, and prayed to it. He picked up fallen flowers to save them from further bruising. He hung his hands over the table cloth in case he touched it.

Frances realised soon enough that these were manias rather than the usual habits of the English; realised, too, that there were deeper disturbances. He was possessed on the lecture platform, true enough, but he seemed possessed off it; in thrilling ways sometimes, but in irrational ways as well, that made him seem mad.

Jack did not regard himself as mad. He had pretended to be mad at Sherborne School to escape bullying, but that had been a convincing and necessary stratagem. His attitude towards his eccentricities, and his mind, and Frances's, is shown in a letter of 14 September 1937. Julia, Frances's mother, had written that Frances had left her – suddenly – without warning, except for a note stating that her reason demanded it. Julia thought Frances might be mad. Jack replies:

> . . . . . One thing I *do* feel pretty sure of & that's that she wasn't out of her head – for people like her & myself who have a mad imagination & excited nerves *all the while* are the last *kind* of people to suddenly go off our heads. . . . .

In 1912, Jack did not regard himself as a madman, but as a devil. He wrote a poem to Frances, beginning,

> To thee, to thee only I turn, O my beloved?
> To the rest hard am I as basalt, yes, hard as ebony.
> Weepest thou, little one?
> Weepest thou, my darling?
> Thou wilt tremble with deeper tremblings ere many days are passed.

There is occasional sadism in Jack's letters to Frances, but he kept his vice in hand, or, rather, in his head; he allowed no provocation to sadistic delight in his lectures and writing. His own brain was – as he told Frances – full of sadistic visions, terrible sexual images, and tortures of the grossest kind. He revelled and brooded on them, agonised in them, tortured himself with the tortures he himself had imagined, and gloated on the vilest sights that, at the same time, shamed and isolated him.

Frances had a heightened imagination but in an opposite way from Jack's: she was haunted by suffering. She tried continually to heal. As

Frances grew into adolescence, she was full of conjectures and theories; but, for a time, she was possessed by the realisation of pain inflicted all around her. Lying awake at night, she thought that she heard the cries of the tortured. She learnt as much about medicine and nursing as she could, to relieve real suffering; and in that practicality lost her obsession with nightmares.

Frances was a Christian but in such an original way (see *The Mystic Leeway* by Frances Gregg), that no church would have admitted her if they had known. She had a reputation for mystical and occult powers, too. The poet, Yeats, sought her out for a night of magic. Frances's own attitude to these powers becomes evident in the Letters.

Frances was, as she herself has written, 'as real as a carrot', and practical with the practicality of her forebears. To her, Jack was not a devil, but a muddled infant who should have realised his power, become adult in it, and used it. It was important to dredge the silt of the disgusting compulsions clogging his genius. Genius she saw in him, but genius avoided except when he climbed onto a platform, and pretended to be someone else. A practical woman should be able to deal with what amounted to a waste-bin of fragmented power. She set to work.

Jack was absorbed in Frances's beauty and originality. He became aware of her efforts to take him out of his nursery of horrible toys; he may have shuddered under her correction, but he accepted it. He did not, could not, abandon his cerebral sadism. He still imported cases of pornography with pictures and writings almost as wicked as those in his mind. Now, though, he began to take an intellectual, less personal, interest in his 'case'. He watched himself keenly while indulging himself most. He began to accept himself, in all his vice and weakness, and found, in both, a treasure — as well as a charnel-house. Jack's acceptance of himself, as the no-man, the dud-man begins. He glories in life that creates nobility of the freak, the mean, the 'inferior', the shamed, the emasculated. The ennobling of supposed handicaps begins to flow into his writing; not only into his writing but in every way, in lectures, in praise of every person he meets, hallowing the stumbling of everyman, as he raises the 'inadequate' to the level of the heroic — by *acceptance*. It is not comfort — for comfort is no longer needed — it is a glorifying in the odd ones, the dispossessed, the uncertain tramps of the mind, pilgrims of the eccentric, to whom he gives the authority of princes.

He becomes a magician, a magician whose words make the sure as well as the unsure see life through the extraordinary eyes of a man who seems to embody the most primitive forms of life, consciously; who even seems to know how stick and stone and water are conscious; all this while having, at the same time, one of the most developed brains of evolution, conscious and *self*-conscious to a sophisticated *and* elemental degree.

Frances had to use ingenuity in clearing the decks of his mind for the change – and she was not, could not be, entirely successful; but her evident impatience with waste was as effective as any other way. Some of Frances's letters to Jack are savage. They shock. From the first, though, Frances's place with Jack was corrective. That relationship, once established – and passionately erotic as it was, as well – had to be contin- ued, as part of their later love, and through the changes in that love. Jack, at one point, begs for the lash. This has no more to do with masochism than welcome for the cauterizing iron.

It is best, however, to learn about John Cowper Powys from John Cowper Powys: from his letters here, and from his *Autobiography*,[6] one of the first autobiographies to include the 'unmentionable' – masturbat- ion, and the involuntary creations of our imaginations that so surprise and revolt us; tricks of body and mind; all in a book of beauty and revelation.

In 1912, though, John Cowper Powys was not the author of *A Glastonbury Romance*, *Maiden Castle*, and the rest: he was the author of two slim volumes of verse that hardly anybody had read. Jack was known as a lecturer – a great lecturer; perhaps one of the greatest speakers of all time, as many who heard him said. He possessed himself of the subject of his lecture, emptying himself of himself, as he describes in his *Autobiography*:

It was really a *great new art*. . . . . Under the Rabelaisian encourage- ment of my unique circus-manager [Arnold Shaw] I succeeded in *hollowing myself out* like an elder-stalk with the sap removed, so that my whole personality, every least movement I made, and every least sound I made, and every flicker, wrinkle, and quiver of my face, became expressive of the particular subject I was interpreting. . . . . I worked myself up to such a pitch that I *became* the figure I was analysing. . . . .

I have seen him sitting on the platform before a lecture with his head pressed to his chest, his arms dangling at his sides like a puppet's, to allow his own personality to escape down them. When he rose, his con- jurations rose with him. I heard him in 1919 in San Francisco, when I was four, and I made a scene because I thought he was getting too much attention. I heard him in the 1930s in a London hall, when the great song came from a toothless mouth. He was still great. He rose and moved about the platform, and down into the audience; and his magic contracted that great hall into a little room of divination and his arms opened it out again to the universe.

..... 'I am come that ye may have life and that ye may have it more abundantly.' Those words often came to me when I was with John Cowper Powys in the early years. . . . . ,' writes Louis Marlow (Louis Wilkinson) in *Seven Friends*.[7] 'If I were you,' one of his early admirers told him, 'I should think I was a god.' A god whose persuading intonations were loud and clear, a young god, then, hard-fleshed, keen-boned, lean-bellied, in his human manifestation. . . . . yet, in some aspects, he was not beautiful, with his loose aberrant mouth, his Mousterian or simian forehead, 'villainous low', 'like a girl's', –he has called it both the one and the other–his beaked nose, and the heightened, seemingly artificial, colour of his 'Red Indian' cheeks. . . . .

'. . . . . He did give me an impression of beauty,' Louis Marlow continues, 'notably when he was lecturing, but not only then: and it was a beauty of transfixing power for those who saw and heard him. He was . . . . . full of life, full of beliefs, full of power to communicate his abundance. . . . . '

After 1912, Louis began to develop a hate that was almost as great as his love for Jack, for reasons that are clear in the Letters; but the love was always greater than the hate, even into old age.

Jack lectured in many cities and most of the states of the United States, holding audiences rapt for two hours or more in vast arenas like the Cooper Institute, with his favourite audience of Trade Unionists, Jews and Socialists – the outcasts of that time – and then to cosier meetings like those at the Women's Club in Madison, New Jersey.

He was sometimes at his best in an out-of-the-way barn with a few people and a boy and a dog in the audience. An Admiral Sullivan of the U.S. Navy told me that he and some other boys had thought a 'lecture' was some kind of animal, and that they had sat on the rafters over the figure waving its arms below, and that the experience of hearing that figure, John Cowper Powys, had transformed his life.

Frances and her friend, Amy Hoyt – one of Frances's first friends, even before Hilda Doolittle –had attended several of Jack's lectures. They had been prayed over by their Church congregations for doing so. Jack possessed himself of the subject of his lectures, but he also expressed his own ideas. As some of these advocated physical love outside of marriage,

and disapproved of many moral and social laws and conventions, and also
urged the feeding of the poor, and the acceptance of the outcast as equal,
it seemed to the good church people like a Walpurgis Night broth.

Frances and Amy bowed their heads at the public reproach from their
Christian friends; and continued to attend the lectures. Many others did,
too, including Theodore Dreiser, Ezra Pound, H.D., Edgar Lee Masters,
Isadora Duncan, and others who were famous then or who have become
famous since.

Jack was said to earn a large income from lecturing. He had commit-
ments, but he was far richer than Frances or her mother. The two women
had been taught that it was a crime to leave one single speck of egg in the
shell, taught to hoard everything – bits of string rolled into a ball, scraps
of cloth – and they had been taught to open envelopes by rolling a pencil
under the flap so that it could be used again . . . and again . . . Frances
had felt a 'poor relation' with Ezra Pound and Hilda Doolittle whose
parents were comparatively well-off, but neither with them nor with Jack
did she let that handicap her; not even when she brought Jack to her
mother's home. It was a commonplace house from outside, and a
teacher's world inside, with encyclopaedias, geographic magazines, globes
of the world, and relics of the family's journeys. Frances made sure that
all was ready for the great Lecturer's tea-party.

Jack had first sailed to America in 1904, as the guest of the American
Society for the Extension of University Teaching. It was the hey-day of
the British lecturer in America. Jack had thrived. In 1905, he had
persuaded the Society to bring over a young man, Louis Wilkinson – then
fresh from his final Tripos at Cambridge, and publishing his first novel,
The Puppets' Dallying under the name of 'Louis Marlow'. Louis had
become an excellent lecturer, more accurate than Jack, and with a more
recognisable platform manner; but never trying to imitate Jack's genius.
Together, they had formed their own University Lecturers Association.

Jack did sometimes fall on hard times. Louis Wilkinson says that the
Society prospered on the whole, but that occasionally they found that
they had no lectures at all because Arnold Shaw,[8] whom they had
appointed as Agent, had forgotten to book any. Arnold would work
excessively and admirably for weeks and then, usually at the most
important juncture, would do nothing at all, leaving scores of vital
letters unanswered and losing thousands of dollars.

'It was only our incorrigible and childlike hopefulness that kept our
hearts up in those bad days,' writes John Cowper Powys in the *Autobiography*. 'There were times you must understand when I had only

two lectures a week, on one of which Arnold was supporting *his* family. . . .'

Jack had been a speaker from an early age. As a boy he had called himself the Lord of Hosts, and had addressed his brothers and sisters from a mound. At Sherborne School – when he had been thought a freak, and where his younger brother, Littleton, had not always been able to save him from atrocious bullying – Jack was once allowed to address the whole school in an exultant apologia for his eccentricity. He was received with cheers, and a bunch of violets from his arch-enemy, the boy who had tortured him most.

With a degree from Corpus Christi, Cambridge, Jack had become, officially, a lecturer, and had spoken in Brighton girls' schools where the spirits of the sylphs – as he writes in the *Autobiography* – roused his imagination as their bodies did not. Jack inspired young prostitutes with his talk, too. And they inspired him. He was enthralled by one young prostitute's account of what it was like to go to bed with a man with a wooden leg.

His brother Littleton, with a brilliant mind and athletic power, outdid Jack in Classics and, especially, in sport, for Jack had little physical co-ordination. Littleton, at Sherborne School, moved into a higher form than his elder brother. Their father, the clergyman, displaced Jack as the responsible, eldest son, establishing Littleton in his place. Jack was bitterly hurt; but he never ceased to love Littleton. To his brothers and sisters Jack remained the magician, the Lord of Hosts.

There were eleven brothers and sisters in that Montacute Vicarage in Somerset. One sister, Eleanor, had died at thirteen of what was later called appendicitis. Her death had made some of the other children wonder if the father's good God existed. The father, the reverend Charles Francis Powys – a man of simple, direct manner of speech, and harshly restrained desires – was unshakeable in his faith. He shaped his children in that faith. His children retained his teaching about nature, but most rejected his teaching about God.

The mother, a highly sensitive, exact woman, of the same blood as John Donne and the poet Cowper, greatly influenced her children, especially Jack, and gave them their first knowledge of poetry and philosophy. (All the Powyses – and some of the other people mentioned in the letters – have brief biographical notes in the end pages.)

As a young man, Jack was influenced by Thomas Hardy. Hardy lived fairly near, with his wife, at Max Gate in Dorchester. Jack had called on them once or twice, and had been encouraged by Hardy to continue writing. Jack had invited the Hardys over to the Montacute Vicarage. The Powys children had led Hardy to their castle built in the vicarage garden, and called Mabelulu after a mixture of their names. When Hardy was asked to sign their Visitor's Book, he wrote, 'Thomas Hardy, a wayfarer'.

Amongst Frances's friends was an earnest young American, James Henderson, the son of a rich undertaker. When Frances had come up to Jack with her poem she had brought James Henderson with her.

James wanted to marry Frances. He had been accepted officially as her lover; but, as he knew as little about sex as Frances did, he did not completely suit the role. Frances and James tried earnestly to discover the secret of physical love. What did one *do*? James had tried to find out from his fellow students. His fellow students must have misled him for, in practice, Frances and James found their instruction unconvincing.

As Frances had accepted Jack as a typical Englishman, so she now accepted Jack's love-making as normal. His love was passionately erotic; and Frances responded.

It was Jack's brother, Llewelyn, younger by twelve years, who expressed something like disgust at Jack's idea of love-making. He could not understand, he said, Jack's practice of making love without penetration. There was a great bond between the two brothers, with as deep a love as any in the Powys family, but there was an almost excessive candour, too. Jack answered simply and with complete and unaffected dignity that Llewelyn liked to make love with penetration, and he himself did not, and that was all there was to it.

Jack and Frances argued as fiercely as they made love; and their discussions sometimes reached a pitch of excitement that was like physical love. Jack was enthralled by Frances's body, mind and character; and Frances developed a love of Jack that lasted all her life. That Frances marries someone else within the first few letters needs some explaining.

Jack was already married. In 1905 and 1906, during the six months he usually spent in England, Jack had been seeing a young lady, Margaret Alice Lyon, sister of Harry Lyon, a Cambridge friend. Jack had no intention of marrying Margaret, but one evening his mother had said, 'Young men must not trifle with a young girl's affections'.

Struck to the heart, mortified, Jack rose, ran out of the vicarage, into the night, across country, headlong mile after mile, till he arrived at Margaret Alice Lyon's family house at dawn. He sheltered in the porch; and proposed to the girl as soon as she came down for breakfast.

Jack may have heightened his story for Frances. He was unusually honest, though, and accurate about himself and his family. This account of his wooing must be broadly if not entirely accurate. It does not tally exactly with other versions, but it is not incompatible with them. Jack may not have proposed at once; he may have taken Margaret to a 'wild romantic setting' (as described in *The Brothers Powys* by Richard Graves) where the rocks of Hayton rise above the Devon moorland, before asking her to be his wife.

Jack married for honour's sake, and against his instincts. He had developed a loathing of anything feminine. He did not like even a female animal to be near him. He abhorred the female parts of a flower. He recoiled from women, from the very thought of women, from anything to do with women.[9] This made marriage difficult.

Once married to Margaret Alice, Jack was appalled to find that his worst fears were realised. He was expected to consummate the marriage. ' – To think!' he exclaimed to Louis Wilkinson, ' – to think that – at such a moment – *skill* is needed! – '

It shows the earthy, patient realism of even the most delicate woman – and Margaret Alice seemed delicate, with her deliberate enunciation and sensitive guitar playing – that she got herself into hospital, and had an operation, that was a deflowering, and that allowed Jack to become a father.

It may have been fear of repeating the act, as much as the need to provide for his wife and son, that kept Jack in America for six months of the year.

He was not homosexual; not that he would have been upset if the examination of his feelings had proved to him that he was.

By the time he met Frances, he had lost his revulsion for women. He lusted after women, in his own way. Whether he ever made love again in the normal way cannot be a subject for academic study; no one may ever know. It is certain that when he introduced Frances to Louis Wilkinson, he exclaimed, ' – And – ! – And she is a virgin, my friend! – a virgin!'

That surprised Frances. She thought she had learnt everything about love.

It was because Jack could not marry Frances that he thought it an excellent idea to marry her to his great friend and fellow-lecturer, Louis Wilkinson. It was also a way by which he could keep Frances near him.

Both Frances and Louis had great will-power. It seems astonishing that within only three weeks of meeting they allowed Jack to lead them so suddenly into marriage.

Jack's magical way with words had enchanted them. Jack had praised Louis to Frances, and Frances to Louis, in so heightened, so beguiling a style that they were half in love with one another before they met. A god met a goddess. Frances and Louis were both beautiful and intelligent; so, when they met, Jack's descriptions seemed confirmed.

In 1912, Frances was twenty-seven, and Louis was thirty-one – ages when one thinks more decisively than before about marriage, if one is to marry at all; even if – as in the case of Frances and Louis – one is not marrying the reality, but a phantom, created by Jack.

Frances had prophesied to Hilda Doolittle (H.D.) –who had stayed in Britain after their trip to Europe in 1911 – that she would return to England in 1912, *with a husband.*

There was a practical reason, too, for the suddenness of the marriage. Jack and Louis were about to sail to England after their six months in America. If Frances was to sail with them, it would have to be as Louis' wife.

It was James Henderson who was heart-broken – in his philosophical way.

All Jack's magic and machinations turned in on himself. He became agonisingly jealous.

It had been decided, in consultation between all interested parties, including Frances's mother, and even Frances herself, that the marriage would not be consummated for several months. Jack set out to ensure that the agreement was kept.

Louis Wilkinson was a man of great will, character and imagination. He, too, was the son of a clergyman. His father had resigned his fellowship at Worcester College, Oxford, because he wanted to marry, and dons were not, at that time, allowed to marry. He had to refuse a parish because he refused to subscribe to some of the idiocies of the Thirty-Nine Articles. He had started a school, which Louis and one of the Powyses–Theodore Powys (later, T.F. Powys, the author of *Mr Weston's Good Wine* etc.) – attended. Louis' mother and nurse had indulged Louis in his every wish. This may be the reason why, in later years, he never did anything unless he wanted to; not even writing his novels unless he felt they demanded to be written. He sought no approval, and had little regard for blame. He had a correspondence with Oscar Wilde at a time when Wilde's name was kept from carefully brought up youth. Louis was sent down from Oxford for being a member of the Blue Tulip Club, a society of undergraduates who practised blasphemous parodies of Christian rites. They did so – as Louis explains in *Seven Friends* – as a protest against what they considered the blasphemous imbecilities of organised religion. He went up to Cambridge where Llewelyn Powys became his greatest friend, and where he first met John Cowper Powys.

Louis' main aim was to liberate sexual love from the taboos, rules and conventions that he thought imbecile and harmful. In this he showed great moral courage. He had, in the ordinary traffic of life, an excessive care for his own safety and comfort.

Aleister Crowley, the magician – whom a judge once called 'the wickedest man in the world' – claimed Louis as his greatest friend. They had different aims, but became genial and strange allies, bound together by their wish to destroy conventions, and liberate sexual energy.

Louis, at the time of his marriage to Frances, had had sexual experience not only with women but – out of sympathy with Oscar Wilde – with men. His homosexual phase was only a brief period at Oxford, and that out of a sense of duty.

Louis was an ardent if unconventional suitor. After being accepted by Frances, he mentioned that, of course, she would not expect him to be faithful. Frances told Louis as emphatically that she herself expected to be faithful, that she wanted above all to have children, that all else in marriage was of far less importance.

Louis knew what he was talking about. Frances meant what she said, but had not much idea of the practicalities.

The marriage turned out excellently – at least for several years. That was remarkable under the circumstances. It seems even more remarkable when one sees how Jack and Aleister Crowley and Frances's mother disrupted it. Though Louis Wilkinson had as an undergraduate used sex as an instrument of protest, he had a freedom of mind and body that made him as 'normal' a lover as John Cowper Powys was 'abnormal'. Louis had few, if any, inhibitions; he was a healthy animal. He was also a man of intelligence; humorous, witty and imaginative – and autocratic, if allowed to be. Frances allowed; for Louis could be large-minded and generous in some ways, whilst excessively mean in others. Frances loved him; and did not cease to love him even when she divorced him. She did think, though, that there was an abominable side to the genial nature: she did not allow her love to blind her to that. After they became used to each other as themselves and not as Jack's phantom creations, Louis was as much in love with Frances as she was with him. He was happy with her, with the latitude she allowed him in their marriage, and with the two children she bore him – till Frances acted with a decisive strength that took him unawares.

Letters are often more revealing of the writer than prose, poetry or, even, autobiography. Some things remain a mystery, of course; about Jack, about Frances – and about Louis. Louis had a lack of sympathy with those who suffered when, in his opinion, they had no reason to suffer.

Frances suffered agonisingly about Aleister Crowley. She tried to end his friendship with Louis; and Crowley threatened to have her certified insane; and meant it. Louis saw all this, was well aware of it, yet he did nothing about it. Jack did, as the Letters show.

It may seem, from the description of sex and sadism and experiment, that Jack and Frances were macabre creatures. They were not. Jack, for instance, would not have hurt a fly: that is the literal truth: he was the gentlest of men. Peter Powys-Grey – the son of Jack's sister Marian – told me that there was another side to him: that Jack could be possessed of frightening rage; that he sometimes harmed people by his manipulations. I am sure this is true; but I saw a man who was my godfather, and who was gentle with babies, children and animals, even with fish, even with flowers, even with sticks and stones.

Frances and Jack gave an impression of extreme cleanliness. This may have been because both were somewhat uneasy in the body; as though they thought they had borrowed it for a marvellous journey, and had to return it in good shape before midnight. Jack even seemed surprised that he had been dumped in it at all. As his writings seem most at home with the most primitive forms of life, so he himself gave the impression of a rock with a vegetable furze at the summit; a mound washed by the rain, dried by the wind and sun.

'She's a blamed straight shooter!' wrote Hoffman, one of Jack's rich American friends. Frances had a look and a nature of uncompromising honesty, and it was Hoffman's highest praise, but it does not take into account her femininity – a femininity that Frances might not have admitted, but which is apparent in her photos.

Frances and Jack wanted above all else to affect life, in however small or greater degree: Jack more impersonally as the Magician; Frances as though life was her child.

They were, both of them, naturally timorous and deliberately brave: afraid of shadows as much as of real dangers; overcoming – with great efforts sometimes – their fears of both. They had moments of panic that they controlled; and then they had as many moments of heavenly peace and serenity.

Beyond their fears, they certainly were – like many seemingly timid people – brave. Both would have died rather than give way to threats. Incidents in the Letters show this of Frances. Jack was highly nervous of the Law, and of the Police, yet had the innocent courage to take political action that might have resulted in his persecution and ruin. They became more and more sure of what they were about in life and this gave them certainty, beyond fears, pains and sorrows.

As Jack had begun to understand Frances's ideas, he had written to his brother Llewelyn:

> I tell you, my dear Lulu, Frances has revealed a thousand possibilities. There are divine things well enveloped. I tell you there are wondrous things. . . . .

Now he wrote that Frances was to marry Llewelyn's greatest friend, Louis Wilkinson.

When Louis and Frances set sail for England, it was not a honeymoon trip. John Cowper Powys and his sister Marian were with them. There was also Perceval Roberts, who had been up at Oxford with Louis Wilkinson.

Before anything else, before any of the other letters, this letter below stands as the Prologue and Curtain Up.

Pittsburgh, P.A.
[1912?[10]]

On January 9th this strange being — it is difficult even for the faithful biographer to call her a girl — sought out and marked down for her prey that unfortunate poet whose writings are read in every Lunatic Asylum and every Penitentiary and every House of Ill Fame from Milan to Chicago. It is hardly possible, even now they are both dead, to decide which was really the victim and which the devourer. The world at any rate is well rid of them both; and quiet contented people may thank the just fates, which threw two such enemies of society into one another's murderous clutches. In estimating their strange martyrdom one may perhaps conclude the frailer of the two the conqueror since while his work is only known by those whose fixed ideas and traditional affections have set them beyond the pale of our Utopian State, hers proved the beginning of that wonderful new style, the poetry without words or metre which has enthralled us all. Peace then to their ashes! They were indeed a Bridge to the Future; and, Sacrificer and Sacrificed, their names can no more be separated now than can their poor wave-tossed relics, drowned together beyond recovery and recognition under the tides of the fatal sea that first united them. From the amazing fragments of their letters to one another the biographer is bewildered by a complete change in tone which seems to have occurred about the 9th of January, 1913. Until that day her letters seem to have been bitter and savage beyond all description and his in return like the yells of a chained wild-beast. After that date it is his that are merciless and flippant while hers sound like the echoes of the cries of a lost spirit.

Notes

1. These and other writings of Frances Gregg are included in her bibliography, part of her Biographical Note.
2. Hilda Doolittle later wrote as 'H.D.', and is now celebrated in large volumes of her collected works. See Biographical Note.
3. Letters of the Heartts and Langs.
4. Professor Donald Davie, in *Hilda's Book* – documentary television film by Frank Wintle for South-West Television.
5. *The Mystic Leeway* by Frances Gregg is mentioned throughout. This book – that Frances wrote at John Cowper Powys's urgings – has been edited by Professor Ben Jones for the Carleton University Press.
6. This and all other works of John Cowper Powys and Louis Wilkinson are included in the Bibliography at the end.
7. *Seven Friends* by Louis Marlow (Louis Wilkinson) re-published by the Mandrake Press, 1992. See Bibliography.
8. Arnold Shaw later published some of the first writings of the Powyses and pamphlets by Louis Wilkinson. See Bibliography.
9. *The Brothers Powys* by Richard Graves (London, Routledge & Kegan Paul, 1983).
10. This letter has proved very difficult to date. There is a date at the head of the letter, 'January Ninth 1912' – together with a drawing of two crossed cigarettes ('Richmond Straight Cut' and 'Marquise') but this is to commemorate their first meeting on that date. The presence of the C/H symbol ('Cathy/Heathcliffe' – see Note 3, Letter 6) which Jack did not start using regularly till later in the year, and the Pittsburgh headed paper suggest it was written when Jack was staying there at the beginning of 1913 – a period when he was writing to Frances frantically and often ('What a mania I have for writing to you!'). There is also a further reference to Straight Cut cigarettes in a letter postmarked 'Jan 29. 1913'. It is quite possible that it was written on 9 January 1913 – their first 'anniversary'.

The Letters

'With a host of furious fancies—with a burning spear and a horse of air . . . to the wilderness I wander . . .'
—Tom O'Bedlam

1912

1

JOHN COWPER POWYS TO MRS JULIA VANNESS GREGG
(Frances's mother)

[undated, but probably January 1912]

My dear Mrs Gregg,

I do hope you didn't think I was dreadfully unceremonious in asking myself to lunch with you on Sunday and even arranging the Menu. My reliance upon the well-known reputation of Southern[1] Hospitality must be my excuse. I am so anxious to do what I can to launch your little daughter into that poetical success which she so entirely deserves. She has real genius; and it is a shame her verses should not be more widely known. She is the only poet I have ever met in America and I do want to make friends with her while I have the chance. There aren't so many geniuses in the world that they can be allowed to lapse into obscurity. I find that I shall reach Philadelphia by a night train quite early on Sunday morning. I shall breakfast in the Pennsylvania Station and then, if I may, I shall make my way to your house; somewhere about ten o'clock, maybe. There won't be a chance for you to reply to this so I will chance your not being both out. After all, don't make any porridge for me, as I will have some for breakfast and I am getting a bit tired of it. Eggs, toast and tea will be all I shall want. I know enough of the tragic history of the South not to be in the least surprised at finding high-born and cultured Gentlewomen in the purlieus of West Philadelphia. I do trust I didn't bore either of you by my visit yesterday. I did enjoy it so. One gets so tired of the 'nouveau riches' and the bourgeois parvenue in this country. Your little ménage is an Eldorado — a new America for me.

Yours faithfully,

J.C. Powys

1

2

JACK TO FRANCES

[undated, but probably February 1912]

I leave Rochester[1] at 8.35 tomorrow night and *arrive* at Waynes Junction on Sunday morning — How wicked that you won't be there then. I wonder if I shall find anyone at all awake at your house as early as that — a quarter to eight in the morning it will be — Anyway I'll risk it — but how annoying! You would open the door for me in your sleep if you were there — for in your sleep you are awake and in your waking you are asleep. It is especially annoying because this train seems created for no other purpose than to carry me over the Alleghenies straight to your very door.

How slowly that Sunday morning will pass! Yet — what am I saying? — of course it will not — There will be the luckless lady who gave you birth — if she did or any mortal did — you glaucous-eyed devil's daughter! and if I don't make her cry by saying that I know you are not really her child at all — all will go very nicely.

I have to lecture on Plato[2] tonight. It is not the first time. I think at any rate that I shall be on familiar ground *there* — Would it were not so! Ha! ye delicate evasive ones — Ideas of This & The Other — have ye then at last betrayed me into the dreadful Absolute? Have the 'Many' — the little rivers — the treacherous manifold streams — met then, in their hour? And is this the brackish ultimate? O lovely-coloured mimicries that flamed so bright — were ye all the while, ye treacherous false guides, leading me to this dark sea? And henceforth, is there nothing to be done but to ebb & flow with that strange corpse-queen who lives between the unborn and the dead?

Nothing. So be it! And I am glad that there is not — 'For I love thee, O Eternity!'

Don't forget that I shall have a Box of Candies for you, O Planetary Cat!

X.

3

JACK TO FRANCES

Hotel Schenley, Pittsburgh, Pennsylvania
[February 1912]

'I have a head!' — I know it — only too well — and you do not *stop there*! Do you know what I am thinking about now? Shall I tell you? I am thinking about Egg Jellies — at 5 cents the bag. I have just had a tremendous Bath during which my mind ran upon ashes and sand and also upon the fingers that would inflict this delicate punishment.[1]

I had no wish to eat anything this morning — I seemed tired of everything — so I ordered Country Sausage — and was presented with blobs of Sausage-meat, in three raw goblets, & I actually put a morsel into my mouth — ugh! I had to spit it out. I think that a great many middle-aged Procuresses must have disappeared lately in Chicago. Fancy! after talking of eating *you*, I eat instead a highly-seasoned oleaginous concentration of Miss Perot, Miss Daniells, Mrs Quizzlinnan, and that other thing, with a snout like a little female wild-boar, that we said we would go out shooting! — Loathing! Disgust! Nausea! — an ounce of civet good apothecary! — I must go out and buy some of my girl's red Carbolic toothpaste to clear my imagination with! How our minds run away with us. It must be because you said that you had dreams of indescribable things (not human) that at this moment I see all my dear 'friends' and sweet 'Ladies' — Mrs — and Mrs — and — and — and — and — and — surrounding me in the form of moving entrails and excrement — wonderfully animated — and with eyes on the end of groping tentacles. Pah! I will not touch with the tips of my fingers a single human being until I see Frances again. It gets on my nerves to think that my mouth has actually been touched by that Tape-worm Mrs — and that Maggot —. I wish the real Jack and Frances could be buried directly they separate; and quaint puppets — tagged and wound-up, to nod and leer and propitiate — occupy their places till they meet again!

You demon of mine, you mad solitary sea-cat, why have you infected me with your villainous loathing for nice warm, kind, well-meaning, well-rounded human flesh & blood?

I tell you I wish I could wash my spotted memory clear of every single sexual emotion I have ever had — except for you; (and I'm damned if that word describes anything *we* ever feel) as you would wash mouth, eyes, throat and every pore of my skin with biting saturnian soap!

Even as I write this your being and essence flow over me, like a flood, and I am clean of all — The salt-cold Frances at her priest-like task of pure ablution round Jack's human shores . . . .

X.

4

JACK TO FRANCES

[Postmark: New York, N.Y. Ste. E March 21 — 3.30. 1912.]

I had a mood of the most devastating sadness — sadness and a kind of annihilating shame. It was the first time of my existence that I had been led by pure accident into the position of all positions I dread most — that horrible sensation of being a burden, a weight, an insolent and greedy assumer — something insensitive and irremovable — something *in the way* — a corpse, a coffin — a huge and scoriac descent of brute earth — a shovelling and heaping-up of dead rubble over the little tender stalks! It was when your mother suddenly asked me when I was to see you again and (without thinking) I said, 'Saturday morning' — and James[1] said, 'How selfish you are — you and Louis[2] — are you not carrying her away?' — and then I remembered and said Saturday afternoon and you said, 'We will have our class then,' and swayed a moment with a sudden, little child's thrill of joy — the joy of a child returning to an old playmate — and then your mother said that you would be more and more occupied — and James said the word 'Voyage', and that poor little outer-circle wench hid herself behind the door and felt like a shadow of a shadow — and I went away; and to myself was a Capreae-glutted Tiberius[3] flayed alive by a wistful child's look — and all the way along that road that same image was with me — all the way — that piteous little thrill of joy with which you turned to your old playmate — and his words 'how selfish you are' played horrible tunes upon the car wheels. For the moment I almost — almost — *envied* him — the boy left behind — with that 'What is it to you if I love you' look upon him. — 'Alas! poor faun'. You don't know how much my mind searched for some way out — some way by which I could annihilate the world-devouring assumer as I seemed to myself and escape and join too — free from myself — that moonlit playmate's dance, that slipping aside from the confused armies of the arena, into the laughter of the little wood-paths . . . . .

And then, by chance, in that great hall of the Pennsylvania Station at

New York, when I was standing with Arnold[4] and, like a priest intoning, the Pittsburgh train was being called aloud with the strange finality of sealed covenants and burnt ships, in the official 'Aboard', I saw descending the high granite steps — his golden hair divinely ruffled and exultation transfiguring him — none other than our Louis — like a visible god! Never have I loved him more — and never in so complete a way have I been 'saved'. In a moment all was different. Had I not — I also — got my playmate? The vision of the outraged faun — the vision of Tiberius the absorber — the hurt of that devastating quiver in the silver leaves of our Poplar of France — all, all vanished — all the old clear sun-born unclouded classic amicitia returned again — in my delight in his delight I was restored — in comparison with him, with his royal conquest, was I not also a slave without the gates — a minstrel in the halls? . . . . .

THE TIMES

Tuesday, April 23rd 1912

MARRIAGES

WILKINSON : GREGG — on the 10th April, at St Stephen's Church, Philadelphia, by the Rector, assisted by Dr Rogers of Westchester, Pa., LOUIS UMFREVILLE WILKINSON, of Aldeburgh, Suffolk to FRANCES JOSEFA GREGG, daughter of the late Oliver H. Gregg, of Kentucky, U.S.A.

5

JACK TO JULIA VANNESS GREGG
(Frances's mother)

Cunard R.M.S. 'Caronia'
Wednesday 10th April[1] [1912]

She went down into her cabin with Louis as soon as she could see you no more. I think she cried a good deal, but very quietly. I was miserable and could hardly say a word to May[2] or Roberts[3]. We sat waiting on the chairs we had chosen at the back of the ship and at last she came with Louis and sat down between him and me. She looked as if she would

CUNARD R.M.S. "CARONIA".

Wednesday - 10ᵗ

She went down into her
cabin with Zouis as
soon as she could
see you no more - I
think she cried a good
deal but very quietly.
I was miserable and
could hardly be polite
to May or Roberts -
We sat waiting on the
chairs we had chosen.

never laugh at anything again. She read letters that Louis handed to her and commented wearily and briefly on each. I was miserable; but her sadness isolated her and there was nothing to be said.

This went on until it became intolerable. Then Louis and she walked up and down a little while, while the rest of us waited again. Then they returned and she said, 'I want to walk with Jack'. Oh how glad I was at that moment, Madonna! We did not walk long because lunch-time arrived but I was not miserable after that and she was better.

In the afternoon we sat together and once again she said, 'I want to walk with Jack'. This time I led her off to the very most upper deck where there is a shelter from the wind and it was very warm and sunny. She said that she thought I had seemed queer and aloof during the last days. So I had to try once more to make her understand what nervousness and timidity, and fear of intruding are mixed up with the more highminded elements in me. She did at length understand this, and my distress until she did so helped a little to distract her mind which was a good thing. Louis at length found us on the upper deck and we all had a very friendly and a much happier conversation.

At dinner we all sat late and after dinner we all sat smoking in their cabin. When May and she were alone May talked to her a lot and managed to interest her and went on talking quietly after they were in bed till she became peaceful and drowsy. She has got the upper berth, May the lower.[4] It is a good berth (outside) with a porthole.

Thursday

She and May had breakfast in their cabin and slept peacefully all the morning till lunch time.

After lunch we talked for a long while about Meredith,[5] I attacking him and Louis defending him. Then we sat in the alcove Deck B and drank coffee. Walked with her and Louis together on the upper deck while May and Bobbie slept. After dinner the four of them played bridge (I hated that!) but Frances won 43 cents. She was in good spirits.

Friday

We all had breakfast together at ten o'clock, a long merry breakfast. Then she unpacked or something and Louis was with her and I wandered like a lost spirit on the upper deck hating everyone. Then I tried to keep this diary but was too restless to do it.

I could not get hold of the passing hours. They all resolved themselves into only two divisions; when she was there and when she wasn't there.

At lunch we met and I was happy again. She and I got off together and went down to the steerage deck to the very front of the ship where we stood at the prow and watched the waves breaking. She was in very good spirits. After dinner (curse it!) they played Bridge again — again she won. We went to bed very late. Louis saw her to her cabin and stayed while May went to her bath. I was in Bobbie's room and he too was away. I was very dispirited. Presently Louis returned and said he thought she wanted me — so I went and found her very sad. 'I want my mother,' she said. This is the *Third* time that I have heard her say that. I thought I had only been with her three minutes when Louis came back to carry me off before May returned from her bath — half an hour! he said. A strange melancholy was upon all of us that night. A hot Southern wind was blowing . . . . .

Saturday

We were so late that Louis and Roberts went on sleeping so Frances, May and I had breakfast alone. She was quite happy again and in splendid spirits.

We all three afterwards got to the upper deck where we were found by Louis. After lunch we had a splendid game in our favourite alcove all together writing oracular and prophetic messages in rhyme adapted to each other and then drawing them like Virgilian[6] lots. After tea Louis went away, then May went away and then Bobbie. She and I found a sheltered place right on the bows of the ship on the steerage deck where we could watch the masts and rigging against the sky. We then went together into the little Marconi office and sent that wire to you. We wrote it in the office under the advice and with the help of the official there who was very kind to her.[7] Then we carried it to the purser and handed it to him. At that moment Louis found us and said he would have wished to be included in it. He asked (like a flash), 'How did you sign it?' I said, 'It was entirely my affair. I promised to send it. It was my business. I signed it Jack.' After that there was some little disturbance in the air.

Louis said you have been away 2 hours and we believed him and looked very chidden. But soon I realised that we had only been away three-quarters of an hour. It only seemed like hours and hours measured by the way the sands gleamed as they ran. Then for a little while we were in disgrace and Louis and Bobbie and May leant over the edge of one deck as we walked on the lower one — till suddenly Bobbie (bless his heart for ever!) scrambled through the bars and dropped at our side and held her other arm. This soon shamed old Louis out of his momentary temper and all once more was well. Bobbie has been splendidly obeying your instruction to look after her. She has learnt to love him. She has won him to her side. He has saved several situations. Any change for instance *in regard to the arrangement of berths* would be at once firmly suppressed both by May and by Bobbie who has a cabin to himself. That evening all was harmonious and happy. No Bridge, thank the gods!

We quarrelled and debated as to what 5 poets we five should select as the best of all in order of merit. . . . . Finally we decided as follows and in this order, Shelley, Swinburne,[8] Poe, Keats, Fitzgerald.[9] Frances and I were annoyed at the including of Fitzgerald but since Shelley was first of all we were content. That night once more she was seized with melancholy. Louis had gone down with her and when later we three appeared at her door she went past us and went up alone to the deck. Louis went after her but Bobbie and I guarded the only passage of return so that she should see her Praetorians were ready at her side. She soon returned and May comforted her and she slept. It was the worst night.

Sunday 12 o'clock

I have not seen her yet. I never have the courage to go to her cabin to say good morning. It would be suitable enough as May is there but I cannot do it. I am nervous and self-distrusting in regard to her. Often when she thinks that I want to be away it is only that I dare not assume that she wants me. It is hard to make her understand this and not very wise in me to try to explain it. It has just struck twelve. I have not seen her. She stayed in her cabin this morning. I did not dare to go. Why hasn't she been up in the air? She ought to be on deck. May is with me — together we must do something.

'Here, where I point my sword, lieth the East.'[10]

O Madonna, Madonna I could cry sometimes. Well — well — A merry game my friends, a merry game and a mad world.

Sunday 12.30

She was with Louis all the morning until lunch down below.

In the afternoon we played our game of deciding who were the five most well loved poets. Frances had put Chaucer on her list. Then we decided the five we most hated. After tea Louis had to unpack or shave or something and she and Bobbie and May and I watched the sea for a long while. Never had any of us seen what was then like a sudden gift of the lost secret gods poured upon the sea in our path. Red purple, the colour of gentians, made indescribable catafalque for the fallen sun. Like Caesar's cloak it lay along the waves and in spirit we all walked upon it (borne up by Frances) as the Lord walked upon the sea. We were in a strange mood of exaltation and happiness. We imagined our arriving at an unknown country, over which Frances was Queen. We imagined the landing, the bells, the music, the trumpets and crowds and then the drawn swords that would sweep around her as they would carry her up the thousands of flights of marble steps towards her ancestral home. She said, 'I would not leave you — I would turn back at the top of the stairs.'

That dinner was very happy. They had a piece of music by *Dvorak* (if I spell it right) which she knew.

In the evening also when she was in high spirits we played the same game of selecting the five best prose writers. These were in their order of merit.

1. Charles Lamb
2. Thomas Hardy
3. George Meredith
4. Emily Brontë
5. Walter Pater[11]

That evening she said (and Louis allowed) that she would walk with me on the deck next morning before breakfast.

Monday

We walked together from half past eight to ten. (May had seen that she had a cup of tea first.) Then us four, for Louis was still asleep, had breakfast together.

Then May and I and she sat on the upper deck while Bobbie wrote letters until Louis joined us. That lunch was sad. Unluckily the music played included old Darky tunes which you and she have so many associations for and I could see she could not stand it. For some time she fought bravely against her feelings; but at last, when they got to that particular one about home, she got up and rushed out of the room.

We waited a minute or two — then I went to her and found her struggling to get command over herself standing in the passage that leads to her room. She was digging her nails into the palms of her hands. She was not angry with me for going to her and, brave child that she is, let me lead her back. By that time they had left those tunes and she finished her meal quietly, gradually recovering. The afternoon we played card tricks. She discovered, by her genius for calculation, every one of Louis' and Bobbie's tricks, exactly how they were done.

We talked together of the voyage and neither May nor Bobbie or I or she were at all anxious to see the end. We none of us want to think of the end. Only seven days more together! She showed us rainbows in the water that afternoon — a thing I have never seen before — and we saw emerald-coloured waves tonight. She is now down below with Louis. She and I and Bobbie have been walking together; now she has gone; and I am writing this while Bobbie looks for May. She has been in an absolutely bewitching mood this afternoon. One of her moods after she has been what she calls 'bad' — when she says these things and looks like this — it is enough to break your heart.

But she is happy, Madonna. She is happy, and she is finding ways and

means of managing Louis and indeed of managing us all. Hers is the
power and the glory; world without end! She wore her wedding dress last
night and looked absolutely *royal*. She was shy at first when she entered
the dining room because of her bare arms and she turned that long scarf
round her shoulders to hide them; through that dinner her cheeks were
flushed scarlet. I wish the time would hasten on at this particular
moment! It is now 6.30, half an hour and more (we are always the last)
before I see her again.

O Madonna I am desolate at the thought of not seeing her for five
times seven days. At dinner she was melancholy and her gloom increased
as the evening went on. May told our fortunes on the cards and a curious
sense of fatality weighed upon us all. We went to bed early.

Tuesday

We did not see her at all till lunch. Her throat troubled her a little.
After lunch we sat in an alcove and drew the red curtains round us and
tried table turning. A spirit from the drowned Titanic was there, called
'Laroche'. He said, 'Frightful Disaster, assumed name, foreign affairs,
my love, madness, madness. . . .'[12] . . . . Then we called the Catholic[13]
and asked him who he was most in sympathy with. He said 'Frances'
and then she got tired and removed her hands and he went away. I was
all the while praying that *you* would not appear, because she would
have lost her self-control if you had.

That afternoon after tea Louis went away to read and May and Bobbie
also and we were left alone. It was my happiest afternoon of all the
voyage. She was in splendid spirits.

Bobbie has given her a magic gold ring like a thing out of the Arabian
Nights made of many rings curiously twined together. It is a Talisman.
It could summon spirits from the vasty deep or summon *us*, her liege
servants, from the ends of the earth. That night we were all happy and
wrote poems of each other's deaths and fantastic epitaphs. Hers on
Louis made us all laugh madly.

Wednesday

This morning I walked with her on the upper deck before breakfast. It
was a beautiful morning and her spirits were high and heart brave. I shall
never forget what she said or how she looked. All this morning we wrote
letters. She sometimes opposite to me in the writing room and sometimes
in her cabin. We have just had lunch — she is in very good spirits still —
the 'Mikado' was played and she likes it. Louis is treating her with real
tenderness and consideration and they are constantly laughing with each
other and at each other in a way most delicious to watch.

All therefore goes well, dear mother.

Now I shall stop and post this. Please give my special love to *James* [Henderson] . Bless you, your affectionate son Jack.

P.S. She has gone to have her throat painted by the Doctor — she says that will cure it at once — her spirits are still high and she has got an excellent appetite. She eats more than I have ever seen her eat.

6

TO FRANCES (in Dresden)[1]

The Vicarage, Montacute,[2] Somerset.
[Monday] April 29th.

No word — no sign — from you yet. Well! — I suffered a little (we say a little when we write) . . . . .

I wonder if the child knows what the first days without her have been. I do not think you do know child; I cannot believe you do — else you would have sent me just a card — a sign — anything with your writing on it. Hush! *no*! this isn't scolding — it isn't — it isn't — What is it then? It is only a funny sort of gasping in the throat of a sea-horse. But perhaps tomorrow I shall hear. 'Tomorrow and tomorrow and tomorrow' — Fool! That is not the vein. 'Cathy,[3] I hate you and you deserve Hell-fire for this —'

'Odi et amo — Quare id faciam, fortasses requiris?
Nescio. Sed fieri sentio — et excrucior!'[4]

I have asked Lulu[5] to go to Venice with Bobbie and me (as we agreed I should) and he is extraordinarily delighted at the idea. Poor Lulu! he is jealous of you child. But when he sees you all will be well. Yesterday I did not forget your birthday for one single moment. O I have no spirit to write more now. There is no-one now to break bread for me. I have been near some dangerous moods, Frances. . . .

Lulu and I and Bobbie [Perceval Roberts] will start from London on the 25th. We shall refuse to go via Monte Carlo. If Bobbie insists on that we will have to go separately but I don't think he will.[6]

You and Louis must secure us rooms at your hotel in Venice as soon as you reach it. I think the Hotel *Daniele*[7] would please you best because it alone of all of them opens directly upon the open Lagoon. The Grand Hotel[8] is on the Grand Canal and you don't see so much of the sea from there.

Bobbie and I and Lulu must all have separate rooms *please*. *Please*

get mine next yours and Louis, even if it turns out to be an *even* number.
Lulu *must* have one opening on the Lagoon and with a *large window.*[9] I
shall have to be very careful of him.

Jack to Himself — *letter or no letter.*

I hate 'I love' —

'Heathcliffe' 'Cathy'.

7

JACK TO FRANCES (in Dresden)

Thursday [May 2nd 1912]

At last! And the only letter I have ever had. Child I thank you, I thank
you, I thank you. . . . . . You have held out your hand and I have got it.
It hardly matters to me now what happens for I hold it fast to the end. I
would not allow a single word of what you have said to be changed — the
first letter[1] you have written to me and the only letter I have ever
had. . . . . . Isn't it funny these situations when you can't speak and yet
can't not speak — like those moments on the ship when we didn't know
what next.

. . . . . There is something when Lear and Cordelia meet near the end
about foxes and burning brand[2] that runs in my mind as it did once
before under the bows of the Caronia. . . . . Let the world go — let everything. . . . .

'Heathcliffe/Cathy'

8

JACK TO FRANCES (in Dresden)

Burpham.
Wednesday [May 8th 1912]

I am writing this in the garden here among a wealth of globed peonies
but she who is Melancholia's darling and the daughter of mad joy, they
have caught and held her, and Hyperborean[1] herbs. Look, I send you
Rosemary — 'That's for remembrance — pray you, Love, remember!'

No — fear not — Lulu will raise no barbarian howl as the little image of

Isis passes down those watery streets.[2] But how extraordinarily interesting to see, O my enchantress, how your translunar spells work on him! To me he said as we made our way among the rushes, 'Perhaps I shall carry her away from all of you. Louis will be jealous of me but I know a talisman that can make him do my will.'[3] . . . . .

I have sent Lulu D'Annunzio's book about Venice[4] and I wrote this in it.

> 'Now while the sea-weed drifts
> At the Moon's call,
> Now while Depression lifts
> Lightly her pall,
> Now while cisalpine mists
> Bury their dead,
> And the Dark Mother twists
> Flame with her thread,
> Roses we do not need;
> Pansies or Rue —
> Naught but Pomegranate Seed
> Send I to you!'

It is lonely without the little boy. . . . .[5]

9

JACK TO FRANCES (in Dresden)

Tuesday evening, May 14th [1912]

. . . . . Since about five o'clock a peculiar feeling of happiness has been invading me. . . . . From six to seven. . . . . I walked by myself between hedges of hawthorn and ditches full of wild parsley. There was there a stock-dove or turtle-dove; not an ordinary wood pigeon whose listless-lewd advice to all sinners to 'go one further' must be well known to you, far less that Belial in Uranian Feathers, that Apocryphal Third Person,[1] with whom (Earth and Heaven!) you sometimes play 'hide-and-seek' and 'hunt-the-sleeper', but the real bird of Solomon's Song of the psalms of David — the mate of the Phoenix whose death that strange threnody always placed at the end of every volume of Shakespeare in so solemn and sweet a way invokes.[2] Now this bird you must know, little one, is hardly ever known to be heard earlier with us than June, but something in the hour (Favete linguis — utter no ill-omened word!), some lucky auspice of that particular road, some special benediction of the fairies, some miracle, some call of the unseen moon, worked upon it so well, that, as the wind and the sun went down together, its voice — the very incarnation of all that mortals mean by 'desire at rest' — thrilled through the tree-tops and the tender corn-stalks and the white parsley flowers and vibrated over long shadows upon the roadway, as though the ghost of some supreme touch upon some unearthly violin were realising that quaint Socratic argument about the immortality of the soul and, hanging suspended there, had conquered time and fate and death, in one quivering sob of ecstasy. Some stammering gentle madman among the poets — some 'Bobbie' of the earth-gods — alone could describe the healing this sound worked upon me — 'such harmony is in immortal souls'. Nor has it yet departed. For nine days now has an evil cloud been over me — you have perhaps known it — but I think it has entirely gone now. Well! — I do not know what to say in explanation. I think there was more in it than even that sound. . . . . .

I found myself copying out whole stanzas of Walt Whitman.[3] That perhaps was the beginning of it. Walt Whitman as you know (old in-destructible world-dog) has ever a way of leaping from the pages! and 'who but he understands the sorrows of lovers?'

. . . . . Tomorrow I may go to *Brighton* to buy the circular ticket Louis swears you and he are going to get, returning via Florence and Paris. *Brighton*! What associations that word calls up to me![4] Make Louis smile by repeating it in your most mock-dismayed manner!

I am trying to think when last I was there in any mood not utterly corrupt — by my soul; I do not think since when in Catholic obsession I carried with me the 'Apologia'[5] to the beach! But that must be at least ten years ago — yes, just before the little boy's birth. And that was only the Divine Mood — madman that I was! — and by no means destructive (as I well recall) of the wickedest wishes, among those perilous sea-pearls! But now — Aldebaran[6] itself will not glimmer upon those pebbles with a more silvery detachment. . . . .

So we are to meet at Verona? It might be worse. They tell me there is a hotel actually looking out upon the Roman Amphitheatre. I think that would *suit us* all; whether we sit by the side of Caesar; or cry our salutations from the mouths of the beasts!

Verona? Well! 9.58 am. the twenty-fifth.

10

JACK TO FRANCES

Sunday evening. [May 19th 1912]

. . . . . We each know those insane Atlantic Spaces, those empty moon-lit porphyry-paved courts that intersperse the tiger-hunted jungles of our innermost minds — Ah! we are not more sure of having each other, than we are of having ourselves — so do we, more than all the tides change, flow away. . . . . .

You see we both tend, far more than others, to get enslaved by a certain habit of affection and it is this, I think, really; (though in our concealed rebellion against it we may feel ironical which makes it so hard for us to swing recklessly clear). A certain Russian-like incapacity for *action* counts for something also in the matter — an almost slow-worm like tendency, to follow, in all practical and definite situations, the line of least resistance. You once swore to me that I did not realize how made of iron your will was! Well! I still do not realize it — but I am ready to admit this — The kind of will *we* have (you see you ain't going to be able to get beyond me here, Cathy, my boy-girl) is able to achieve more than much stronger wills are able to achieve, by reason of our imagination — for our imagination, backed by what will we have, has a magnetic power over other people and even over circumstances, which is allied much more nearly to the instinct of animals than any sort of rational force.

In this way, with less strength of will, we have positively diabolical cunning — like the cunning of mad people — and like the cunning in the face of corpses — and like the cunning of Harry Lyon[1] when he has 'supped upon the Sacrament'! O I swear we are born to be one another's plague and Elysium for ever!

. . . . . We flow away from ourselves in mad flight — in the flight of the ebbing tide — but with some inexorable attraction we return — and here, let us say, the magnet that draws us is the moon. Well! with you and me *the will* which is in the business plays the role of the Moon — — and from its magnetic pull, however far our imaginations sweep, arbit-rarily and with despotic sway, it swings us back to one another. That we are *born* for one another must be allowed — that in you (in Frances Josefa) I find what in the lack of which I have grown almost abortive (as one can grow backwards into a horrible abortion) must be allowed.

That in the profound impossible Heathcliffe sense we are insanely one, must be allowed – but, against a fatality of this compelling sort, our free evasive horizon-crazy spirits should revolt to the death – were it not that by putting our most fanciful arbitrary and imaginative wills into it – we monopolize as it were destiny itself, and in the process become creative of actual events – such as all the fatality I speak of left to itself could never produce. This is what little Monsieur Bergson[2] means by his Creative evolution – this is what Nietzsche[3] means by his 'Amor Fati', translated 'Why *I* am a Fatality', this is what our Tarsian [St Paul] has in his mind all the way through his dialectical labyrinths – as you have often told me and as I have often known.

God! when I do start writing this story of mine, little one, I will put into it some world-secrets that will be caviare to all but our own sealed tribe! The nervous irritation paralysing me since this Noah's Ark dove (surely invented by all the ghosts of all the children who have ever died unbaptised!) started its witchery, has been due to the very fatality of the design thereof! For how shall such earth as we are composed of make of itself, without many horrible discords, strings for the music of the spheres? But whether I finish it this Summer or not – I have got the idea and more than the idea of what I will do.

. . . . . So you won't write 'another' – Ha! I like it well that you should say I won't – In fact I like it – (do you see my handwriting grow dangerous at this point very clear and terribly easy to read and like the handwriting of Peter the Great when he first learnt down at Deptford to compose in English and to make ships?)[4]

You won't, you won't, you won't?

Is – that – so?

Sadista?

Well – enough of *that* also?

God! how many little vistas there are where we have to pour libations hurriedly and turn! – 'Well I know this dark tarn of Auber – these ghoul-haunted woodlands of Weir!'[5]

In Verona at 9.58 on the morning of the 25th – that is, by the way, Saturday.

Do you know I have just heard from Bobbie saying that after all he *won't* be with us. . . . . I shall see him as we pass through London tomorrow and he will tell me what he will tell me and he will tell me to tell you what he will tell me to tell you!

HeCathycliff

11

JACK TO FRANCES

(Genoa[1] June 1912)

Sorella Mia

Lulu managed that Mantegna book entirely by himself.[2] I knew nothing of it —nor did Louis—He was very pleased with your card.

'Will this train *never* go!' — Will these seven days never go? Lulu's temparature was two points better this morning—but he is a little annoyed that there is not more improvement.

The sun is hot today. What jangling bells! I'm glad we saw the picture of St Marks at the end.

As for Milan —was ever a place so hated and so loved!

Abbassa Le Forca Sempiterna e viva la Verita Bastarda!![3]

> [*Lines like lightning flashes violently drawn*]

Don't you know me?

> [*More lines like lighning*]

Yesterday ended well—How will these seven days end? —

'My kisses are not sentimental'

Il Parco [the park] ! This is not a letter, this is only the murmur of the water in the court of Castello Sforzesca.[4]

12

JACK TO FRANCES (in 'Deepdene', Aldeburgh, Suffolk)[1]

Montacute
[late June 1912]

. . . . . We rested at Salisbury the spire of which looked more pointed-cold (like Harry Lyon's tongue)[2] than ever we had seen it, and at Sherborne Station old Littleton[3] met us. What weather it was and is — 'I hate your England' we keep saying and *so do we* — cold miasmic damp vapours hang over every wall and leaf — surely the very dead are pushing their way up, to welcome us Home! What! Has even 'Pitt Pond' lost its magic? Carries the name of 'Stoke Wood' no more perfume in the mention?

At Sherborne I smelt the scent of lime trees in the air — *Lime trees!*

Where can I have seen them before? Will this Avenue never end?

Has not this city got any corridors? Has not this ship got any prow? Into our little back room then! and let us 'support art', and dally with vain surmise – ah! me! While Thee the shores and sounding seas –

> The Cat the Rabbit and the Pig
> They limpt through many a wood
> And some were large and some were big
> But ne'er a one was good.[4]

At Sherborne, Littleton was not inclined to assume himself the responsibility of making Lulu stay there under Rickett[5] with a high hand but Lulu and I assumed it ourselves and I went on last night to announce it to the parents. So he is now in Littleton's Sanatorium near Acreman House [Sherborne Prep. School] in bed. So Lulu will have as good a chance as we would wish for him of really scientific – (Castello Sforzesca) diagnosis! He was as well after the journey as before it; and his urine trouble was better when I left him than it had been for long – but his temperature was a little up. The little boy[6] I found completely transformed from a child into a schoolboy. He was pleased with the pistols – he showed me his butterfly collection. He says he can jump into the swimming bath and *sit* at the bottom of it for ten seconds – and has made eleven runs – he has had a fight with Evans Tertius and won it. 'He was cheeky and he went for me'. He says that Carey is his greatest friend, that his jam is nearly finished. He said 'Did you used to say Dash and Damn, Daddy?' His nickname is 'Polo'. His favourite exclamation, 'Good Lord'. He now understands his Latin tenses and on Sundays goes for long walks in the country and wades across little streams and is pursued by angry farmers. He said 'I shall call Daddy "Sir" soon' and he looked at me with such a quizzical whimsical look – half respectful and half patronising. He showed me such a funny little notebook

> For Rep.
>
> 'from *Vocamus* down to *Illacrimabilis*
> End of Term July 29th.
> Mouse-hunt with Jim.
> For chocolate drops twopence halfpenny.

His mother is to arrive on Friday at six. He wishes to meet her alone and commands that I should remain in the gardens near the station.

To the complete surprise of all of us the parents have accepted Lulu's staying at Sherborne with complete resignation. They both of them have now the attitude of having with melancholy and Buddhistic resignation washed their hands of their mad wilful children and all their ways. My father I found more concerned over the fact that the revellers in his orchard (for it was the evening of the 'Temperance Fete') had not gone away with the fall of night — and my mother over the fact that the Algiers vase[7] which I gave her resembled the pictures of Palestine in the time of our Lord.

I will shortly look out Lulu's diary and also one of my poetry books, if I can get hold of it — both if I can.[8]

I seem to see you, child, as I saw that prisoner through the little round hole in the Shereef's [Magistrate's] palace in Tangiers, nothing but two devastating eyes and an outstretched hand. Ha! Rosinante,[9] my grey Mule, up, up, to the rescue, to the rescue! A Sforza! A Sforza!

How much? *Very* much!

13

JACK TO FRANCES (in Aldeburgh)

Acreman House, Sherborne
[Postmarked July 6, 1912]

O child, child, how many are the knots that must be unloosed and, as James [Henderson] would say, 'straightened out' ere the future is moulded to our will! But let the mists descend — let the dragons of the deep clash their scales — let the confused armies of reaction ebb and flow — we are their equal[1] — we will deal with them, we will pierce these sea-walls and let in the wild salt-water — 'about my brain'! Lift your hands — those little fingers full of woofed spells — weave your circles. It shall go hard but that Circe and Odysseus together do not harness those Oxen of the Sun![2] And *she* is on the Sea, our Enchantress of Enchantresses — she the mother of the Oceanides.[3]

Now, if ever, need we courage and wit and a clear forehead! . . . .

Rickett regards the state of Lulu's lungs very seriously . . . . . . He says that unless it were absolutely necessary he certainly would not operate for this stone, as Lulu's lungs are not in a fit state for him to stand an operation. . . . .

. . . . . The worst of it is that he is after all our discussions not really resigned to careful and scientific cures—he rebels at the nurse—he rebels at the orderly method. The presence of the nurse worries him—after his recent freedom with us.

. . . . . He will be very relieved to hear that under no circumstances except 'in extremis' will there be an operation. . . . . . I shall (fear not) talk to him gently — calmly — as you would wish me to, child. . . . . But write to him, even though only a word or two, as often as you can manage it—you can help him more than anyone.

. . . . . I have just been over to see Lulu and we have carefully discussed the problem of the Montacute visit. Our temporary conclusion is as follows if Louis will agree to it. Mrs Wilkinson[4] to stay at Montacute — the rest of us at Willy's farm five miles off.[5] I think there would be no difficulty in securing rooms for you and Louis and your mother in some of the little farms quite close to Willy's, and I could sleep either under the same roof as you or at Willy's and we could all have our meals at Willy's. With what Louis has now lent me I shall have money enough for this, both for the extra rooms, and also to help Willy in buying extra meat etc. so that the food should leave nothing to be desired. Louis unluckily associates the farm with badly cooked meat but please assure him that now Emily[6] is there things are quite different, and if I buy the meat and vegetables I think there will be no fault — and of course cider and cheese and endless cream is always available.[7] . . . . . Then you can see we can go over to Montacute at least on two days out of the seven and on two other days out of the seven Lulu could drive over to us — so that we should not be seriously separated from him. . . . . . Mrs Wilkinson's visit would please my mother. My father would not have a chance of getting into a wolfish mood. We should be much more independent and you and your mother would have exactly the kind of existence you like, and you would see Willy and Katie[8] who are the best of us all. The first week in August would still be the best for them as my mother would probably be agitated about either Mary Shirley[9] or Mrs Wilkinson not having the best room or having to sleep 'down the passage'. The 'passage', by the way, (you will love it) has recently been painted blue—exactly the very colour of those Arab houses. . . . . .

14

JACK TO FRANCES (in Aldeburgh)[1]

July 16th [1912]

I got your letter of yesterday, your letter of the devil's Litany —
'Nam sacrificaverunt filios suos, filiasque suas daemonibus.'[2]
What can I say? At least I think I do not lose track of the working of
your mind. I think Josefa[3] with incredible rapidity and deadly wiles is
digging pits for her enemies and pulling up rope ladders into her cell,
while Frances sits weary and inert 'writing letters in the summer-house'.
I know you too well to make any comments upon what you are doing.
If I were our friend I should be terrified at this 'July wearing the robe
of September', because I should know that when you retreat then you
are most dangerous — you talk of being 'Conquered' you who never
retreat except to spring.[4]

THE TIGER	You are weary, my friend; it seems to me that you limp —
THE TIGRESS	You are a coward. You *dare* not rush upon this village.
THE TIGER	If anyone else —
THE TIGRESS	Hush! What was that? A snake moves in the grass.
THE SNAKE	O most cowardly of Tigers, and O most unhappy of Tigresses, listen for once to the voice of the serpent.
THE TIGER THE TIGRESS	} We hear, O Lord Devil
THE SNAKE	Does the Tigress leave the Tiger because he is less brave than she?
THE TIGRESS	*Yesss*! (*She draws her paw along the Tiger's flank and licks the hurt with her tongue*).
THE SNAKE	'Yes' is Man's language.
THE TIGRESS	Thou knowest.
THE SNAKE	When I am weary. When I am a coward then am I most to be feared.
THE TIGER	Once upon a time, before the accursed feet of —
THE TIGRESS	(*To the Snake*) Let him go on. Whisper in my ear that which you would'st do — (*They whisper long and long and the Snake glides away*.)

THE TIGER	– and so, if only, and as it might have been, they lived together in the deepest den in the world –
THE TIGRESS	(*Rising to her feet*) I am weary unto death. Come, the road is long, the time is short. I am weary. The nights which are ours are not long. I am weary. There is much yet to do. (*She leaps through the brushwood*) Come. I am weary to death.
THE TIGER	What did the Snake say to you?
THE TIGRESS	I am weary; and thou, a coward, tellest long stories – Come!
THE TIGER	I thought – I thought – I thought how sharp her claws are! If it were not for these Lord Devils how perfectly we should understand one another! (*Enter the Huntsman with guns and dogs*.)
THE HUNTSMAN	Now I am sure of them. For such stripes as she has the zoo would give –
THE SNAKE	(*Lifting its head out of the grass*) This admirable Huntsman seems to me to have got into the wrong Jungle. Be careful, little dogs – be very careful little lice-coloured dogs!

. . . . . I shall go to London on Sunday and leave by the morning train so as to reach you by noon. O why, O why, didn't Milan put that thought into our heads before the night upon the Lido.[5] But there is yet—

THE TIGRESS	Hush you Fool! *This* is not a story– enough I am silent.

'Descriver fondo a tutto l'universo
Ne da lingua che chiami mamma e babbo.'

To put into words the ultimate of the universe is
not for a tongue that babbles mamma and papa.

. . . . . What a meeting of the various coloured beasts it will be! A proper background, O a very proper background – How *will* we be able to conduct ourselves under so much scrutiny! And every one knows – Isn't it infernal? One sometimes thinks if only one of *us* were in their skins for a day – 'poor little devils! Let's clear off and give them their wretched four days; they are not so many; to do with what they will!' I must admit it is a kind of consolation to me to think that everyone *does* know – that in reality, below the surface, quite apart from jealousy, we are regarded with a sort of desperate speechless *envy*. And well we may be!

O Sadista, little incestuously loved sister (Shelley would understand that!6) from the top of your head (whether you comb'd your hair last night or not) to the soles of your feet (though you have walked bare-foot thro' every cattle yard of Saxmundham7) I love you –

[*Further lines violently scored out, and again signed*].

15

JACK TO FRANCES (in Aldeburgh)

Thursday, July 18th [1912]

. . . . . When I speak of cowardice1 I refer, you understand, only to my inability to send everyone and everything to hell, to lay my hand on my money and start a completely new existence with every ship burnt. I prefer to use the term 'cowardice' here, lest such a term should lie concealed as a vapid cuttle-fish at the bottom, a thing for you in your searchings to try not to see.

As a matter of fact we resemble each other enough for you to know that mixed with dread of violent and catastrophic upheavals is a . . . . . [*crossed through*] . . . . . but I needn't harp on that string. All I wish you to realise is that it is *not* a matter of 'love' or 'tenderness' or 'the attachment of familiar usage' or 'habit', for at bottom in these things I am incredibly aloof and withdrawn. It is *not* a strong, deep instinctive clinging to old associations and closely formed ties. It is nothing else than the same quite simple and *impersonal* aversion from being the direct cause of definite distress that makes it difficult for us (for us at any rate) to *fish with worms* or eat Paté de Foie Gras.2 Very likely my morbid and imaginative way of *visualising* distressing and agitating situations exaggerates such results. That is where emerges the damned tyranny of these 'others' over us. They always mesmerise us into fancying that we can hurt them far more than ever we really can! I know their little ways! Of course as far as that goes we could avoid 'scenes' by just clearing off and never seeing anybody again – but unluckily we should still have our thrice-accursed imagination left, with power not to lessen, but doubtless to increase, the distress of the result. I know that by giving you these glimpses into my machinery I run many risks. 'If so inherently and abnormal cold to parents child wife, mother sister etc. etc. how can *I* have confidence?'

Well – I can only say that you are for me all those things for which I was born, so absurdly born into such dissimulation, and with you only do I feel free. Until now of all words most have I hated the word 'love'. It has always meant for me pretence pretence pretence. All my life I have been pretending to love and only giving way to my angry remoteness in such concealed war dances behind doors as that which you have lately indulged in. *Now*, when that horrible word suddenly completely changes its character and becomes not any more a suffocating prison but the widest of free horizons, I find myself bound not in the least by my feelings for *them* but by their feelings for me, the result of these years of dissimulation . . . . It is as I have said the difficulty of causing quite definite material practical distress to animals made more or less as we are made. You needn't curse me now for talking as if all depended on me and my damned disposition . . . . . . I know how every moment now as you read this your proud familiar devil is prompting you to curl your fierce New Orleans lip and send me to Hell with a 'When did I ask you, Sir, she said'.

. . . . . 'O how I hate you!' your devil tempts you now, very much, to answer. 'You name the only thing in which you, rather than I, could assume the initiative, and then you say, '*Now* I am at your service my friend. In *everything else* see how brave I can be!' – and then you leave *everything else* (or inevitable necessity leaves everything else) for me to deal with.'

. . . . . We seem to be so heaping up inflammable material for our meeting that it will be wonderful if our tracks through those salt marshes are not marked and charred by smoking grass.

. . . . . It now seems as though we are going to be surrounded by every friend we have! Upon my soul it is so annoyingly grotesque that it becomes laughable. Bernie[3] will be here then. O and Bobbie [Perceval Roberts] too. 'Pon my soul I might have brought the Catholic [John William Williams]. And Tom Jones[4] no doubt would find the Aldeburgh air very invigorating. Pity James [Henderson] can't emerge from some immense overlooked cabin trunk. We might even wire for Ezra [Pound]. Only by the Lord you'd ride your bicycle to the Hebrides then. But evidently at Deep Dene the word is – Go to now; let us make a Feast to invite all our friends so that there shall not be wanting to the Sacrifice.

I had a thirst for you, child, Yesterday, that amounted to misery. I have never I think wanted you, under my hand, so fiercely. How shy

we shall be of one another, when first we meet! O I can see that Gregg
bow[5] of yours! How we shall talk of everybody of everything and all the
while scarce know what we are saying.[6]

16

JACK TO FRANCES (in Aldeburgh)

Saturday. [August 3rd 1912]

. . . . . I only carried off my poetry books[1] because I do so love reading them to you and hearing your direct first impression as it strikes you,
but if you would really sooner have them, I will send them by post at
once.

. . . . . Three weeks today, *Saturday the 24th*, we shall meet then (if
you and Louis agree) at the Wilton Hotel, London (or at the Gloucester
Hotel, Weymouth).

17

JACK TO FRANCES (in Aldeburgh)

Wednesday [August 7th 1912]

Still nothing but rain! Ever since you and I separated nothing but rain!
If they want it to be fine they must not separate us. I am glad to have a
day or two alone with you two. You are right, such physical suffering
is the worst of all things while it lasts. And for you to have watched your
mother hurt like that.[1] Some children can bear their mother's hurts
singularly well; but you reverse these little matters. I suppose she endur-
ed some moments when the suffering was equal to that of child-birth —
equal to what she went through when that dark-haired little devil we
know entered through the gates. . . . . . I shall predict that she'll not be
lame at all, but we shall see.[2]

. . . . . Will you send me, by post, my 'Death of God' poem[3] — you
know, the typewritten one? Ralph[4] wants to read it. And of course he
might publish it. We had the funniest time, child, in pouring rain in that
little Lancing Tavern. Flossie[5] is awful. We pity Bernie,[6] but upon my

soul Ralph's situation is a hundred times worse. She cursed him all the time for being silent and depressed and she didn't allow us a moment to speak; even of horoscopes.[7] Nina[8] is his only consolation and she is like the most sinister of Chinese Idols. Please, child, wait a little before you say anything about not going to Montacute. Perhaps Madonna will be advanced much further towards recovery by that date than you now think. If you realised the black misery it will mean to Lulu if you do not go, you *couldn't* hesitate unless it were absolutely essential for you to be by your mother's side: and I trust that won't be so by that time. You don't know what difficulty I had in getting him into a mood of waiting patiently until the 26th. It'll be the *greatest blow he has ever had* if fate intervenes now, and you don't appear. . . . . . I implore you, child, by all you reverence most; by your most secret obsession; have pity in this case! . . . . .

Often when I am with Lulu I hate him, hate him for his dilapidated and weaponless clinging, but you and I, child, are responsible for him now, and as we carry him into our 'Cat's Cradle' you must not loosen your fingers when the road is most bad. I wonder whether you ever think that if the Gods said, 'Now, for the rest of days, you must live with one or the other and let the unchosen die!' I should choose Lulu? I wonder whether you ever think that really at bottom, I love Lulu more than you? If so, now on this Wednesday, the seventh of August, I tell you that you are *wrong*! And Lulu knows well enough that you are wrong, and if it happened so, which way I should choose. But you and I are not separate in that way. I may stretch out my hand further to Lulu than to my little boy or my mother or anyone else. To you I do not stretch out my hand. Because our fingers have grown together. This hand I stretch out to Lulu is not mine, it is yours. Every kiss henceforth I give anyone — especially the Judas-kisses — are yours as much as mine. . . . . .

I am going to write down a funny word — O my darling, my darling I love you forever! . . . . . 'Go ahead!' as Willy[9] said, 'hate and hate.' That is a good merry game, it only burns the soul — and we have two to fall back on — the better! What White ashes ere we are burned out! Poor little brother farmer Willie! I fear he is having but thin sport with me! I rejoice, by the way, to think that between this last January 1st and the next January 1st during this year 1912, I shall have been with you 144 days and with Mrs Powys[10] 84 days. By the blessed St Mark, child, that doesn't look as if we were mere Platonists!

But behold Jack grows mathematical. He must have been doing sums. He must have been revolving multiples.

$$24 = 13 + 11.$$

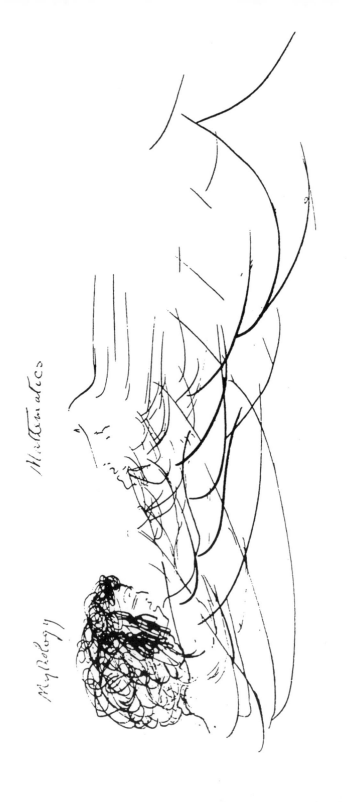

$$24 = 13 + 11.$$
$$26 = 13 + 13.$$
$$25 = 5 + 5 + 5 + 5 + 5!$$

Pyhthagoras is the only Philosopher and once someone *stopped* crying in room 57.[11]

18

[Letter-card] **JACK TO FRANCES** (in Aldeburgh)

Brighton, Aug. 10th [1912]

I have just sent off a little toy to your mother and I will write her to-morrow about a Mirfield Father Novice Mr Salubey[1] is bringing to stay with us and conduct Divine Service in our parish church. Your news of her was disquieting, child. . . . . .

It is hard to say things in letters. I expect people have said *that* before! Poor devils quarrelling helplessly out of pure misery at not being together. Well, *we* don't quarrel. We have common sense. By the way, child, Ralph [Shirley] has got as far in your horoscope as to announce that your sign of the Zodiac is — what do you think? *Virgo*! 'People' he said 'born under this sign judge hardly!' I don't care if they do.

Rain, rain, rain, Brighton therefore is not even Brighton.[2]

19

JACK TO FRANCES (in Aldeburgh)

Thursday morning. August 22nd [1912]
[probably Burpham]

The gods are against us indeed. Poor little Katie.[1] This is an unforeseen blow. Well — Glastonbury must go, and now I shall not see you till Thursday the 29th. I am going off to Montacute at once and shall stay there till next Wednesday, when I shall go to London and stay the night after with Ralph. . . . . It is all very well to talk about influenza. The real cause of all this is our present cursed system which permits no freedom to a child of unhappy and hopeless passions like Katie. They all hoped, as you see (and you can believe how one of them hoped) that she would get better quickly and there would be no need to put off this visit. But she must be bad, poor child, or they would never, as Louis knows, have a trained nurse there. . . . . How the gods hate us! Never mind. We will not yield! Katie *shall* be better. . . . . I love you.

20

JACK TO FRANCES (in Aldeburgh)

[Montacute]
Saturday. August 24th [1912]

Some of us think Katie is worse today, some better. I think she is a little better. She has just had one of her bad fits which ended with her shouting and crying for the 'Walt Whitman' book. This has not been lost; it is in the house, but Gertrude[1] thinks she ought not to have it and perhaps she is right. However Mother was got out of the room and Gertrude let me say to her all of Walt Whitman I could remember by heart and it quieted her. When we were alone she told me that she was better, that her mania for the cross was a disease and that she was tired of signs and symbols and wanted to be out in the air again — wind and sun and her old lovers. She is not mad but dangerously near it and she knows that herself. Gertrude says that the cause of it is not only un-satisfied passion but listening to us all talking — and the reading of Walt Whitman. I see the force of this, but I do not agree. . . . . It is possible, Gertrude says, that Katie's brain has always been small, her emotions fierce, and that she ought long ago to have been separated from such people as most of us are and have lived an absolute placid and common-place life — if possible, looking after children. I wonder if she is right. She blames me for ever having given Katie that fateful Walt Whitman. Certainly she has made a fetish of it. But I still think I was not wrong. I think that *we are too many*. That is the really fatal thing. The result of this has been that Katie with her abnormal sensitiveness and affection-ateness has been bewildered between such opposite wills. At her worst, at the end, at Witcombe, the Cross was everything to her. Willy thought she had drowned herself. She left her room in the very early morning it seems, leaving the pictures, the books, the jewelry and everything arrang-ed in the shape of crosses. But just now she whispered to me that the Cross had helped her when her mind was bad but that in her health, and even when she felt better, she returned to the wind and the sea and Walt Whitman.

. . . . . I don't know what to think. If *only* you and I were in such a position as to give ourselves up to her, it could be done – but there it is – we cannot. . . . . But it is annoying to me to think that I am really, by giving her that book, in any way the cause of all. . . . . . If Gertrude and May [Marian Powys] find in the strain of this more than they can stand, and if they contemplate sending her to an asylum of any sort, I shall certainly ask them to give me a chance with her. I should get her away with only little Emily, our nurse, to some sea-side place and collect shells and seaweeds and so forth with her, and give her the impression of having *escaped*. She has just been saying that she is in a prison – a Church-Prison. We brought her a cat as a distraction but she terrified May by the way she confided all her troubles to this impervious demon and spoke of 'they' who stop her from getting to the Sea. You see how it is, child, we are all swept hither and thither all day long on the storms of her mind. . . . . . We shall meet on Thursday.

21

JACK TO FRANCES (in Aldeburgh)

Sunday. August 25th [1912]

. . . . . Katie woke at 1.30 last night and has been talking perpetually ever since. The nurse says that she would be better if sent away to a home. But I must confess that I am very unwilling for this. I think it would be a risk. She is on the edge of madness. She talks of killing someone if she is not allowed to see Stephen Reynolds.[1] '*She* knows how to escape,' she says of the woman who hanged herself the other day. . . . . Christ! You should hear the tearings and rendings of bluff in every direction! I tell you there is nothing like having madness in the house to bring people to their senses. . . . . .
Evening Monday
In Katie's Room.

I have read to Katie a lot that you said, and it arrived *just at the right moment* and has done her *very much* good. She says – [*All that follows in quotation marks is in Katie's pencilled hand-writing*] – 'By *willing* we can walk upon the sea. I have broken the cross Christ is freed and returned to the deserts a child. The moon and the owls are our sisters. The seagulls and ravens help us. Fear thou not much but hope thou not at all. Nietzsche's madness has not been in vain – love from Katie (S.R.)'[2]

(There is trouble between Ralph and Bernie – *tell Louis this is a secret* – it will end in Bernie's leaving the office – and what will he do?)[3] Just now they were ringing bells desperately. May was helpless, Katie in a paroxysm of anger convulsed like an epileptic and clinging to the iron of her bed. Your letter calmed her instantaneously when we were alone and everyone was turned out of the room. Last night the nurse who is afraid of her lost all control of her. At three o'clock she was ringing the bell wildly for help and my mother and Gertrude had to go. Katie had got on to the window-sill and was threatening to throw herself out. So it looks as if Heathcliffe (with Cathy) will have to get up early tomorrow morning. Poor child. I am passing from Katie to Cathy – it is a wave of cruelty to me to be away from you when you are ill like that. I would have licked your icy feet back into feeling, with a tongue of fire. And the tooth business and your face all swollen – my little child! I cannot stand not being there to tease you and pet you and be kind cruel rough gentle rude tender bitter cruel gentle. . . . .

Lulu is wonderfully well and happy. Yes, you were a true prophet and I was wrong. . . . . Write more messages to Katie.

22

JACK TO FRANCES (in Aldeburgh)

Montacute
[August 27th 1912]

. . . . . She always wakes up after the drug at two or three and terrifies the nurse. . . . . Katie becomes, just as animals do, conscious at once of anyone's fear of her, and rendered by it at once angry and bold.

. . . . . O my friend it is an infernal situation – and you must remember *we* have to think out everything and really carry it out; for the parents only stand aside and let things drift.

Now are there such places as very small private Homes where one single person alone, such as Katie is, can be properly looked after by the right kind of people? Would such places accept a patient who made constant attempts to escape and was constantly falling into violent anger? One good thing is Katie is always fond of strangers; *and hardly ever dislikes anyone.* Above all it would be necessary for a *man* to see a lot of her and guide her thoughts. . . . . . Any man more or less sympathetic & kind would soon win her confidence and quite probably she would fall in love with him and not want to escape or go to Stephen Reynolds. This is a hope.

. . . . . But then if she went say to a small Private Asylum – the obvious restraint and the sight of others with various delusions, would it not make her entirely mad? . . . . .

I wish I could either give up the time to go right away with her – or had the power to kill her and finish it. It is a frightful and disgusting idea to find yourself joining with the armies of the sane and the normal in putting a child like this who is after all only a little mad into padded rooms. I can discern in her that feeling that everyone is against her and I can see that with the cunning of an animal she is only waiting her chance – She has in fact whispered this to me, as her accomplice, again and again.

Her expression varies between looks of savage hate and looks of impassioned and prophetic spirituality.

She is always speaking as though she were Christ – but sometimes it is the Christ with a scourge – only sometimes the Christ with the precious ointment. I can well understand the nurse being terrified of her – for her arms strengthened by work at Willy's farm are as strong as a labourers and her face is sometimes convulsed with rage till it looks like a combination of all the most terrifying wild beasts. I tell you, child, I keep going over in my mind every sort of issue out of this and I cannot see one. I have got Gertrude to write to Stephen Reynolds asking him for a letter to her commanding her to use her will to be calm. But I fear things are really beyond his power to cure. . . . .

And yet in intervals she is wonderful – you would be amazed at the poetry of what she says.

But what can be done? This best of well-balanced worlds is so constructed that at every turn it thwarts the wishes of one born of the spirit and of earth and its answer to all the logic of the imagination is a *padded room*.

23

JACK TO FRANCES (in Aldeburgh)

[Postmarked 'August 30, 1912']

. . . . . You're quite right to clear off to Paris—It gives me a grim satisfaction to think of somebody doing something that they *want* to do! . . . . .
I *may* be able to join you if you stay there long enough . . . . .
This afternoon she was very violent again but in the end all was well.

24

JACK TO FRANCES

Wednesday. [September 18th 1912]

In the train,
en route to Sherborne.[1]

I have proposed to Mrs Powys that we should stay two nights with Lucy.[2] This will lengthen out our return to Burpham (I hate Burpham) until Wednesday next. So that two days after I arrive there I shall be able to say, 'This day week I go to London'. To London in fact now my thoughts are always turning, as for the ensuing twelve weeks they will turn to Philadelphia. . . . .
How silent we both stood at one point in our wanderings through those Fontainbleau rooms. We met then, if ever; and as I think of the occasion I recall, by how slender a majority, on a day arrived at over the dead body, as it almost seemed, of poor Count Rolph,[3] the waves between Murano[4] and Torcello heard the whisper of the imperial libratio and watched Villon's, Hardy's (and was it Ezra's) glory sink uncelebrated away.[5] How curious it is that even now I do not know whether to you also as to me these continually recurring days when we are not together mean a constant tiring joyless unsatisfied longing. I know you are often tragically wretched. I know — who knows it if not I? — that you lacerate yourself and tear yourself to pieces — but whether in the same way you are miserable and for the same cause as I, I cannot tell.

25

JACK TO FRANCES
(Mrs Louis U. Wilkinson, 20 Hadley Gardens, Chiswick, London W.)[1]

[Postmarked 'Queenstown'[2] – 2 pm. – October? 1912]
On Board R.M.S. 'Baltic'.[3]

To my amazement, child, Mrs Powys tells me that she is going to invite you and Louis to go down to see her. What does this mean? It is an extraordinary step. What is it? I expect that you will be able by some intuition to track its motive. I imagine you will not go? How strange that it should arrive simultaneously with 45 Bond St & the trolly to Twickenham[4] – chess is a very curious game. I have just been walking up and down the long covered deck below the ordinary one, the same deck as I once found an unhappy little girl sobbing in the darkness. Her tears tasted very salt, but afterwards, on a coil of rope, she forgot them and stopped being bad.

I have no one to give me half a roll at dinner now or to steal raisins for. How all the Caronia's story returns! . . . . .

I bought a volume of Strindberg in Liverpool which I shall send you when I have read it. It has its place for us as you will see.[5] You and I are *misanthropic in grain.* How all my fellow passengers are to me like walruses and crocodiles! Well do I know why you have to use the word 'betray', even when leading them gently by the hand.

. . . . . A telegram I had from Montacute said that Katie was better. Glad indeed I am to hear that.

. . . . . I have not forgotten any word of our conversation in Ravenscourt Park – 'it is only half past six. Mrs Pegge won't ring for an hour –'. The 9th of October has certainly done one thing that I thought nothing could do. *It has made Jack love Frances more.*

Yet how many things there are that I have promised myself in stories to do to you that are still undone! They shall be done yet! . . . . .

26

JACK TO FRANCES (in Chiswick)[1]

[October 1912]

I wonder what is that very curious noise in the room below me said Father Antony to himself as he tightened his belt over his soutane to allay the craving of pre-communion hunger. It sounds like Robert the Devil clapping his hand. There again! Surely that must be some possessed animal butting his head upon the floor! How very curious! This is certainly the most remarkable house I have entered. Holy Mother of —I mean Shade of Saint Edward! What is that? (He crosses himself). I believe I heard a howl like the howl of Satan. There again! Certainly the devil is not far from me. Apage Satanas! [Away, Satan!] Hush! Let me listen. St Alphonso be my absolution if I put my ear to this chink. It is either Apollyon with a lost soul or a lost child with a lost doll. By the most blessed Trinity no! It is a mad tramp — and he keeps on repeating 'We are safe — we are safe — we are safe.' This is getting serious. No one *has a right* to be safe, and certainly no one has a right to howl with joy when I am not administering the Blessed Sacrament to them. What? Can there then be more than one Blessed Sacrament? This madman also had fasted long.

Stop, my friend, stop, you will make me wish—He is mad and wicked and lost. But are the damned so happy?

They never told me *that* —

1913

27

JACK TO FRANCES
(Mrs Louis U. Wilkinson, 5041 Pulaski Avenue, Philadelphia, Pa.)

Hotel Schenley, Pittsburgh, Pennsylvania
[Postmarked 'Jan 29, 1913. Street Car R.P.O.']

I do hope the eye is better, child. I am sorry.

How we were swept away from one another last night. It was the strangest separation we have yet had — but at the same time the least of separations! Oddly enough it seemed as though that crowd might flow between us and we might part; you to the Reading and I to the Pensy;[1] without their even being able to untie our hands. And shall I tell you a thing? It is not the other Frances I have got with me now — in this little box among the straight cut cigarattes (I open it to let her breathe) — but the real real real one — swollen finger and bad eye and shoes bent sideways and loose petticoat and miserable life and the worst of days and a difficulty to speak and everything!

At this very moment I am opening the box again and combing her hair back with an extinct match. Here is her dressing-case and eau de cologne bottles but where is, Mais ou est le preux Alexandre?[2] She has never forgotten her Notes before! And now I may talk to her, for the real Frances — and she is so little and transparent and has such a funny mouth — does not mind what nonsense I say to her. And I am saying to her such mad things. I mustn't say them loud for fear the other Frances should hear. No, though it is morning, our conversation goes on just the same. *We* are not embarrassed.

I rather think I have done with Mrs R — Observe I am not in her house — I think she is weary of people who talk to straight cut cigarettes — And in good hour she is!

37

28

JACK TO FRANCES (in Philadelphia)

Hotel Schenley, Pittsburgh, Pennsylvania
Thursday [January? 1913]

What a mania I have for writing to you. Isn't it absurd? I tried so hard last night at eight o'clock to telepathize you with sufficient power to force you to stop whatever you were doing and listen to me — but these things are not permitted to us at present I fear. Were I half killed, you w^d know — but short of that it is impossible —

[*enclosed in the letter*]

> God save us, we're a damned lot!
> For the least one of us no chance is
> But among all of us there's not
> Any damned half as deep as Frances.
> Villon lost are you for your name
> Sieur de Voltaire whom wit a lance is
> Jests in deep Hell for just the same
> But neither's damned as deep as Frances.
>
> King for whom horses were too slow
> On cloth of gold whose will to prance is
> Now on Hell's fiery coals must go
> But redder coals are under Frances.
> Sforza of Milan built a Park
> Where Hooded Death with Twilight dances
> He also howls in Hell — but hark —
> He does not howl as loud as Frances.

29

JACK TO FRANCES (in Philadelphia)

[February? 1913]

. . . . . Does it give you pleasure to know that at this moment I am experiencing a suffering of a quite damnable kind because you belong to dear little Louis instead of to me – Why can't I get your *mouth* out of my mind? O and the way your chin curves, & the way – worst of all! (I *know* no one shivers at these little things as much as I do!) the way the Demiurge has managed you – under your chin – & so – downwards!

Ah! Frances – Frances – Louis may have more amorousness for you and more tender affections – Ezra [Pound] may have more concern over your mental creations – James [Henderson] may be the more submissive slave, and Lulu [Llewelyn Powys] the more subtle courtier – but I *know* that of all your lovers Jack, at any rate *now*, when there is no Cathy to break the impact, loves the 'me', the 'self', the inner 'will', the elfish 'psyche', the actual 'person' that Frances is (when she says to herself 'I am what I am') most hopelessly and constantly of all. I have been 'infatuated', as Louis will remind us, before and I have idealized before – But may God swallow me if I have ever been in love before. Sadism is an insipid byplay to this – and I suppress it. How absurd to go on in this vein! I always used to stop & hesitate & be a devil of a time choosing my words when I wrote to you anything but Tiger-talk – but now I could go on telling you about this folly sans stint – hours by the dial. The odd thing is that whereas formerly I would find all manner of literary analogies w^h gave me pleasure to read – now nothing is more flat to me than every species of love poetry – the demons don't seem to be thinking of the same thing at all.

Listen, stop laughing a minute – Hold your head back – Light your pipe, Louis, you devil, with all the matches in the world – Hold your head back –

Well! I have kissed you now! –

I love you!

30

JACK TO FRANCES (in Philadelphia)

Hotel Schenley, Pittsburgh
February 13, St Valentine's Day, 1913

I sent you three Valentines in one envelope. I posted it in the Parcel Box. I hope it will get to you in time. The pansies are for Pansy. The Loving Cup for Frances Josefa and the other one for 'Emily'. Whoever else sends you Valentines I know I shall be the only one to send one to your Doll. Look here, child – I am obsessed with terror lest 'anything should happen' to you before we meet. I am not thinking now of 'Louise' but of unforeseen accidents. For the sake of everything sacred to us both – and by God that narrows the field pretty considerably – for I can only think of one thing that is altogether that! – write me one real love-letter soon soon soon, so that I shall have something to hold on to, whatever occurs. I am sick with a thousand absurd terrors. The maddest thoughts pass through my head. Listen – on this day the 13th. of February, I avow to you that there is nothing in me good or bad, lovely or base, sane or capricious, that is not yours, from this day on, as long as I am I. As it is Valentine's Day I may be permitted to say what I like and what I please. So from Reverence-Nothing Jack to Mock-Everything Frances this queer love-letter may go. So would a polar bear from the North Pole wave its sentiment on its hind legs with one gesticulating Paw to an albatross sitting on the top of the South Pole – glossy and content from having eaten four British officers.

Look at that little picture on the Emily Valentine! That particular position pleases me to think of – Child – Cathy – Devil – what can I call you so as to really indicate this? I am at the moment looking at you more quietly and gently than you can believe and I am good. You are at this moment sitting on your heels half on Jack and half on the sofa, and I am not criticising or thinking but simply drinking up the desolation of your face. You are looking now as you always do at such times like a child who has always lived in a great lonely house and forlorn over-grown garden among sad strange old faded books full of legends and among dead things and things not yet existing. If you make me talk to you I shall tell you nothing but stories about Dean Swift[1] – how he was just fifteen years older than Stella,[2] how he taught her out of old folios, and especially out of Ovid's[3] Metamorphoses – and how she was so brave that once she shot and killed an intruder who broke into her garden. And I shall tell you how at the end their coffins were buried side by side — under that strange epitaph he wrote — ubi saeva indignatio cor lacerare requit.[4] In this kind of way I shall talk to you; I mean I am talking to you — for I am good and you are only a little less sad and shadowy and wistful, than your boy-girl doll — and the faded pictures into which you have put your fancies. But suddenly there is an interruption. Outside a hawk kills a bird or somewhere in a distant room a great clock strikes the hour — or the wind gets up and begins whistling in the chimney — yes; and then all is changed. I am not good any more. I am more bad than I have ever been, in all my days. And the two big eyes of the solitary Frances open very wide and frightened, for they see the change and half guess what is going to happen. It is no use struggling, little one — that great dark velvet dress has only three hooks and they are so easily, so easily loosened and she is so easily — it is no use clinging with your hands — lifted out of it! And now her long arms are bare and as she crouches in the corner of the horsehair sofa she cannot pull down that white petticoat over her ankles because it is a very old one, that she had when she was very very little. And then the Evil one who a little while ago loved her so gently — must needs loosen her hair and shake it free, and press it back, O so far back, from her forehead — and when he has done that — he must lift her up and bend her backwards over the heavy oak table holding her hair in one hand. And then with the other hand he gathers her flesh — between armpit and breast — as one might gather a bunch of wood-anenomes and crushes it in his fingers, as one might crush a handful of wild Thyme or Marjoram, and her body, he can feel it all the way down, pressed between his and the heavy table quivers in little trembling vibrations and little quivering resistances — and her hands cling pitifully to the collar of his coat — and her mouth twitches and her lips move — but he does not kiss her — he only looks at her waiting — while his fingers tighten on what he holds — waiting till the long pent-up tears cannot be held back any more — and when they begin to appear, not one of them (were they ever such big tears!) is allowed to get very far on their way down for he drinks them all — all — all — for that is his peculiar thirst and the only quenching of it. Enough! We are good again now. O stories! stories! stories! O unsatisfied, unsatisfied, unsatisfied! Now as you read this — are you listening? I want you — I am good now and serious — to put your fingers just exactly where I write these letters which you shall see —

J————A————A———— C————K

— no! I will make you stretch your paw wider — turn over again, you must stretch them so that every one covers a letter and you must say I am your Frances for ever! Five letters for each finger! The two A's had to be put in in order to make it five! If you don't do what I tell you I will kill you but while you do it I do not mind if you say 'I hate you I hate you' – in fact I shall rather like to hear you say that. Next time when we meet I will give you cause to say it! Enough! I am tired of play! Surely it is impossible for a person to want to get hold of another person as I do at this moment without it ever happening! It is all very well for us to talk and talk – but in the end the old bitterness returns. We belong to each other, and we are not together. We are Frances *there* and Jack *here* and it is almost unbearable. 3 weeks. Is it impossible to wait so long? O Emily-Doll you do not wait *alone*!

31

JACK TO FRANCES

[*printed*] The Terumseh, London, Canada
12 midnight Monday – Tuesday
[April 1913]

I said I wouldn't write again – but I can't help it – I hate all the world but you.

O you have got me, Cathy, body and soul.

I have been today more unhappy than ever before in my life – Why? – I cannot think – Who can tell the working of the mind? I wonder whether you have been happy or unhappy this day? My mind keeps reverting to April 5th – It is cruel that I should have been cheated out of that voyage with you[1] – and I might so easily have had it – but it is impossible now – and the words of your husband echo thro' my head – 'I wish – *we* wish – to be alone' –

Arnold[2] & his wife and child are going to sail with me – on the 10th. I wonder whether I shall be able to go on quietly enduring these separations? Sometimes I think I shan't be able to –

I shall concentrate my mind on your Séance on Wednesday night –

32

JACK TO FRANCES

On board the French ship 'Lorraine'.[1]
[April 15th 1913]

Weather — somewhat rough but wind and sea driving the ship very fast.
For the first days of this voyage I have been too dispirited to write a line.
I have lifted up my sponge — comme le dernière geste de Jesus sur la
Croix — Vinegar and Hyssop! — a very nice drink for Jack returning chez
soi. I have today used up the first of my Kolynos bought in Evans Drug
Store when a paper parcel contained all the wardrobe of the Borgias[2] —
Ha! The *hand* follows me — I find in the book from which I tear this
piece of paper — two hands stretched like some strange sea-things
clinging to submarine rocks on a volume of the Inferno. The photograph indicates that title clearly — Are both those *hands* of my devil
or is one the mother's? Well! today you are landing, I fancy — Spain!
Lucrezia[3] returns to the land of her tribe — to mirth — etc etc — And
I to France. It was to France you know that the gentle Cesare really
drifted in the end. There is the most motley set of polyglots on this ship
— some genuine ruffians. You have read L'homme qui Rit[4] —(A wave
goes over everything!) I am reading the count of Monte Christo[5] — The
good Dante utters before he descends into the cave — 'Peutêtre — le
dernière mot de la sagesses humain!'

I had forgotten that our Cesare had something to do with the story — it
was from *us* that this little treasure was concealed.

I have only once caught the sound of musicians on this ship so far and,
of course, to fill up my cup of melancholia they were playing 'The Fate
Motive' — what tune more appropriate; when two ships upon the same
sea aim for France and aim for Spain?

Hah! What nonsense I talk — The waves roll high — I weary of this damn
fool of an Avenger — I wish I could get hold of The Three Musketeers[6] — I
think Miladi when she was put to death by her three lovers must have
had hands like these — They look as if the admirable Ezra [Pound] had
tightened the knot that bound them and as if the impenetrable Louis had
held the arms they belonged to — No! she shall not die — I pardon her — à
moi cent-mille diables!

This ship goes fast — It has run today, on the crest of the storm, 436
miles — We shall be in Havre early on Friday morning.

. . . . . Every night I stand at the stern of this cursed ship and practice a sweet little tour de force of arbitrary telepathy under this darkened moon. The Lost Atlantis talks to me De Profundis. It says that cherry trees bear cherries and that in this world we cannot do what we will — Damn you, you drowned continent, your proverbs are musty — The waves went over you before *Our Father became Pope.*

There have been changes since then — Little Louis and Little Frances on their Spanish Tour! How nice it is to live in the happiness of our friends! There was a Louis once — He was my Patroclus[7] — where is he now? In the place of little Louis looms up a monstrous Ravisher — a huge unpardonable Cyclops — a Afrit of frightful Power — Who has done this? You — you you — Fleur de couloir d'ivroire — amant de la Néant, Fleur Hypocrite, Fleur de Silence!

Victim who offerest up Thyself upon every forbidden altar!

. . . . . In the very middle of the Atlantic — it is passed now — it is Tuesday the 15th — when I was too depressed even to write to you — there came a huge black sea-gull — an albatross — and it said that a year ago some one in this very place had cried and its tears fell into the water and were drunk by a silver fish and this bird had waited for a year for the ship to pass again for no fish had tasted quite like that one —

But Albatrosses do not know that Voyages never repeat themselves — but wait, Bird on the Sea — wait —

Eight years ago I crossed this sea with Arnold Shaw[8] — Frances Gregg was then twenty years old — and now she is twenty eight —

How curious to write the words Frances Josefa Gregg — aged 28 —
[*page missing*]

. . . . . wandering very strangely and turned foregone conclusions into staircases to strange thresholds — That elaborate sentence does not imply anything — so let it pass —

. . . . . It is now Wednesday morning — the ship rolls more than I have ever seen — I am writing this close by the stern — Arnold [Shaw] has just been thrown on his back from one side of the deck to the other — The surface of the deck at this moment is almost at right angles with the sea — [*line drawing to illustrate this*] — In spite of all this, so much is the wind and water going to due East, that the Lorraine goes faster than her record — The sensation is I fancy like being on a sailing ship — it will be curious to see at what point the crew begin putting knives into the passengers — I believe that is the conventional prelude to any danger on a French ship — it is a funny affair having a bath under these conditions — but I observe that I do so — & use Frances' soap, too.

I can imagine Commander Monrouryean giving orders at any moment that the ship should advance *sideways* to the wind so as to go faster still

& in that manner to *roll* into Havre. The wireless operator said it was impossible to 'have' the Ivernia—you were too far ahead.

In a sort of way I rather like the diablerie, sentimentale insouciante et naïve, of Monte Christo—but the everlasting conversations with foregone conclusions are too tedious for even children. Dumas you know was a Mulatto — and I fancy there must be something of Uncle Remus à la Masque de Manfred[9] in all this.

You must *describe* to me, you little devil, do you hear? —*describe* — the house, street, entourage, ménage, milieu, mise-en-scène, and all that goes on — Only, as you love me, no more of those little Dresden Bulletins De L'Amour à L'Anglaise with their background of closed doors and unclosed fingers.

Ha! Seagulls again — one two three! That means that those colossal waves are doing their work and we are within half a thousand miles of land—

Do you remember how we selected each our own white bird in the mood of the Sentiment of that Disturber of Homes, the Magnificent Bobby [Perceval Roberts]? He indeed is like a person out of the works of Dumas. You are a person out of Hugo — Louis out of Balzac[10] —and I am as you know (only he was so much more capable!) gently adumbrated in Rodin —

Dieu de Dieu! that was a wave of waves! I swear even now the deck was like this— [*another simple line drawing*]

Has the moment arrived to pray to Our Lady? Is this letter destined to be read by Eternity? 'I shall probably die' as Lulu [Llewelyn Powys] would say — never was such a set of ruffians as there are on this ship — South Americans and white slavers and gamblers and yahoos and valets [*the writing changes from blue crayon, to pencil, to ink, variably*] and Americans and Balzacian misers from Marseilles and some noble bandits of Syracuse — I think the predominant note is very curious — 'Gitos of all lands unite!'

I shall perish soon of absolute starvation, for from my point of view this ship is worse provided for than William the Third — The food is uneatable; but Arnold laps it up like a famished pig.

You can remark how the ship vibrates and lurches from this hand—

I begin to discern that England is in sight—Damn England! France will soon appear—Damn France!

Well — be prudent and be happy — Let me hear where you stay in Tangiers and where in Seville. . . . . For Heaven's sake don't let my Page eat poisonous fish or fruit. It is a reckless child and loves well to pluck death by the beard. How the devil shall I manage to pilot the Shaw family about Paris? I wish I knew a few sentences of French. It is incredible how ignorant I am there and how you have got beyond me with your learning. I have always been unlucky in Paris except when I was with you' – and this will be no exception. Arnold wants to spend every hour of the day rushing from show place to show place – He is especially anxious to visit the Sewers – How shall we find the Sewers? We shall drift along many streets asking everybody we meet and pointing earthwards –

I think next to the sewers his mind reverts most to the Bois de Boulogne – Can you imagine anything more desolating than a drive up that long dusty slope? I explain to him that it is absolutely dangerous to go an inch beyond Tuileries – Apaches, dressed in coats of leather, covered over with spikes, who advance very quietly and hug you to death in silence, haunt every exterior Boulevard. I have resolved to see the grave of Heine[11] – (French sailors I observe wear sabots and have ropes round their waists when they ascend the upper decks).

This entrance to the English Channel – the Scilly islands are now in sight – recalls our last voyage to my mind – It is almost as cold & the charm of this beautiful planet almost as absorbing. (If ropes do anything wrong on French ships they appear to have little clubs especially to beat them).

Now let us for a moment envisage the world and contemplate existence – Existence is that Little Louis should be warm and among Alcazars and Alhambras and. . . . .

[*The rest of this letter is missing*]

33

JACK TO FRANCES (in Spain)

Thursday [April 1913]

I hate Paris. I hate Burpham.

I hate the World –

This is no jest Cathy – You may be satisfied – You may lick the tops of your infernal fingers with your forked tongue – I am hit – I am transfixed with the dart that burns – I have *got beyond the point of enjoying* this little drama – O you demon with the body I do not need *to see* you may curl up now like a lizard in the innermost court of the Alcazar – you may bask in the sun — for you have got me — But it is a flame that has in it no sentiment — *Liar*! What about this black tie that looks as if it belongs to your oldest and thinnest sailor suit?

But it is a flame that has in it no lust — *Liar*! No one — I say none — none — none — none — Stop! Not like that — any way but that! These Lime-Trees are somewhat intoxicating — Louis darling. Lime trees may mean hands or arms or even legs. —

Frances, do you know what I am looking at now over the water by this clair-de-lune? At the *Casquet Rocks*[1] — The time is 9 o'clock — We have no souls you & I — What have we then instead? What can I call for now, to an assignation with me on that rock? The ghosts of your *hands* — that will astonish the sailors of many sailing ships in this part of the Sea — new and terrible sea-phantoms — two devilish hands from the South, and two from the West, all phosphorescent and glittering — thin lines of moonlight trailing behind them. Ha! I have called — you have answered — Finis — it is enough.

Now I have a curious observation to make — Haven't you noticed that when we care most for each other we find — Frances and Jack very grotesque and irrelevant names? . . . . . I mean that some other names seem suspended in space and just at the tip of our tongues.

O I got so tired of Monte Christo and I read Wells's book about the Moon instead.[2] I like the idea of the element not subject to gravitation.

. . . . . What a pity that you and I cannot get hold of some magic potion that has the power of creating absorbing passion in anyone and for anyone — as we please — I say *we* — but you have it already — *Drink Cesare*[3] & By God I *have* drunk —

. . . . . There will be 'a time for such a word' — How curious that I should have fancied I loved you a year ago — I know better now! Or if that *was* love, what the devil is *this*? I can only answer by making our sign —

34

JACK TO FRANCES (in Spain)

[*Printed*:] Hotel des Grans Hommes, 9 Place du Panthéon, 9 Paris
Saturday, 18th [April 1913]
[*The letter is written in blue crayon*]

Have just had a letter from Mrs Powys to say the little boy is ill — I think with scarlet fever — So I will have to go home straight & leave the

Shaws behind in Paris — Arnold will be able to get on all right now. I conveyed him to the Folies Bergères (how do you spell it?) and he said that he had been to *much more lewd places* before now! It was, I confess, extremely like a Drury Lane Pantomime. Arnold's comments were remarkable.

I note this morning that I might have carried my dear little Manager to a much more dangerous entertainment — Isadora Duncan[1] & *her pupils* in Gluck's[2] *Iphigenia*. But it was only for that one night.

This is a very excellent Hotel — full of students — and our little Boulangerie was full of students — eating tarts before going to lecture.

Well — I have not even looked at the cover of 'When a Child Loves & Hates, by a *Gentleman*'[3] — this time. The little ways of such gentlemen are as remote from me as the furthest planet. . . . .

35

JACK TO FRANCES (in Spain)

Monday, April 22 [1913]

Well here am I at Burpham. The little boy seems to have a slight attack of scarlet fever but he is much better and in very good spirits.

. . . . . Never has Burpham seemed so remote and so little belonging in any sense to the normal current of my days.

I suppose Mrs Powys has no idea of all this — and yet surely she *must* have! But I suppose, as long as I remain conventionally *there*, as a kind of invisible scaffold, she really does not think one way or another about it. Hitherto I have always got a certain remote sort of pleasure in returning, if only to see the celandines again; but this time without and within all is cold and damp and chilly and conventional, and the touch of the English soil seems like the touch of English fingers, a sort of clay-cold 'mortmain' laid upon the limbs of existence.

And everything is so cold! The weather, the silence, the rain, the self-centred mock-serious people — O god god god! is this then the cage where I have lived so long amid damp straw in 'ironical submission'? *O damn ironical submission!*

. . . . . Do you know, I bought a Parrot in Paris for Mrs Powys. A parrot seems extraordinarily the right thing to bring to England. . . . .

36

JACK TO FRANCES (in Spain)

[Burpham, Sussex]
April 23 [1913]

I want this to get to you on your
Birthday [April 28th]
—but whether it will or not I do not know.

It is so quaint to me to think of your having actually been here — I can't help wondering whether *under my roof* you did any *unspeakable* things—These are little questions that recur to my mind.

. . . . . Your particular kind of hyacinth is out in this garden. I must secure you one I think; though you know how oddly difficult it is to deliberately go out to pick a definite flower.

It rained all yesterday.

Katie [Powys] is going in a day or two to the Agricultural and Horticultural College of Lady Warwick[1] (at Studleigh in Warwickshire I think). She seems better than before her retreat. I shall go down to Montacute on May 1st.

. . . . . I would give a great deal if Mrs Powys [*Many words violently scrawled out; but by whom it is impossible to say*]

. . . . . were only . . . . I have such respect for her. . . . . .

37

JACK TO FRANCES (in Spain)

April 28 [*Frances's birthday, 1913*]

. . . . . Attic life — or hermit-life that is the kind of thing—but Village life in England —the Lord deliver us from that!

And how horrible it is to go out and meet people you know! I like being greeted by a stray black man in a Restaurant — but not to be able to step outside your door without having to greet some damned neighbour or other—that is intolerable.

. . . . . I have written a long attack on Chesterton[1] — I hope it will be in the New Age.

Roll back you damned English clouds! I love Frances—

38

JACK TO FRANCES (in Rome)

Montacute [Somerset]
May 5 Monday [1913]

. . . . . Your letter written on your birthday and finished by Louis[1] –
or rather I might say the letter written by Louis and begun by you had, I
expect, almost precisely the effect upon me that you intended – neither
more nor less – but so. I need not therefore tire you, child, with any
detailed description of what my thoughts and emotions were. You wrote
– I read – you made a gesture in the air – you wrote upon the sand and
I received your gesture and your writing as they were meant to be received – voilà tout!

Lulu's [Llewelyn Powys's] later stories are really rather good.

. . . . . I have written a long article on Strindberg[2] which we are going
to try and get into something. Isn't it a curious coincidence that brings
Lulu and Ezra [Pound] together in this list?[3]

Bless you

39

JACK TO FRANCES (in Spain)

[Postmarked 'Burpham, Arundel May 17 – 1913']
Wednesday

All goes exactly as you would wish. *Never* has there been such an
excellent rapport between us;[1] never have I, as a matter of fact, arrived
at so clear an understanding of what I have missed seeing.

The little boy will not go back this term so you will find him here
when you come. I think you will like him, I hope you will, better than
has been anticipated. I find him certainly more attractive and I am sure
Lulu is quite absurdly wrong in his estimate of him. He has made close
friends with a child of his own age – a little boy called Jarvis who lives
in the house, that dreadful house, near the Church – and they are perpetually together. . . . .

. . . . . Have I not pressed icicles into my flesh in the hottest squares of

Rome suspending my perplexity as to the meaning thereof; but the meaning grows clearer now, when in consequence, out of the hedges of necessity grow the blue roses of the impossible — Well! I write fantastically but it is out of a singular and very real surprise that I write and the point that you care for is conveyed to you when I say in the plainest and directest manner that things seem destined to go exactly as you predicted they might but as I not only doubted they could but doubted whether if they could I *wished* them to! . . . . .

The amazing thing is that questions arising, w^h w^d under any other (former) conditions have been electric with annoyance now settle themselves like bubbles in a stream.

Bernie [O'Neill] is to come down here for a Sunday on Sunday week and Dora Williams is to come for three or four days tomorrow and on Saturday there is to be a party here of all Mrs Powys' friends, when the eventful and mysterious 'Winifred' will outstay the others in order that Mrs Powys may enjoy to the full the effect upon me (she wouldn't have enjoyed that once, per Bacco!) of my recognition of their relations —

Mrs Powys and I went for a walk together in the coldest wind yesterday. . . . . I left her as we returned through the churchyard at dusk, to enter the Church alone. What went on I wonder in that brief interview with the Christus! Did she thank him, as if for a miracle, that this hollow baroque image of a theatrical Satyr her impossible companion had returned as if hammered into something more endurable by some Michel Angelic[2] blows? . . . . .

40

JACK TO FRANCES
(Mrs Louis Wilkinson, c/o Thomas Cook, Brussels, Belgium)

[Postmarked 'Burpham, Arundel June 27 1913']
Friday

. . . . . She wants to walk in a Suffrage procession — from Littlehampton to Rustington.

I expect it will give you & Louis exquisite pleasure to think of me doing arithmetic

Walking parrots and
walking in

                    processions of mild
                        respectable
                       anti-militant
                     common-sense —
                   Vive La Revolution!

Thus the magnificent and coloured Drama unrolls itself!
. . . . . The little boy . . . . . shoots sparrows and hunts with Whiskers
and is delighted to join with his mother in teasing me. They both watch
me with a delicious sort of nervousness as they tease me — as much as to
say — how far *dare* we go in this new mood of his — how far *dare* we lead
this Pedant round and round the Mulberry Bush without making him go
into his shell? Has he really — their wider and wider opening eyes seem
to say — no crustacean covering any more?
. . . . . Am I grateful to you for those little Roman stripes?[1] Well — I
think I should answer to this that I hope to be so, that I expect to be so,
that I desire to be so? For do we not read that whom the lord loveth he
chasteneth? . . . . .

41

JACK TO FRANCES (in Aldeburgh)

[From Burpham]
[No date; 1913]

. . . . . We had a very long conversation yesterday on the subject of
reserve. Lulu — poor Lulu! — was alluded to as the worst example of the
opposite of this — is it the guile of his candour or the candour of his guile
that most annoys! — 'People should not talk perpetually about themselves — should not be perpetually analysing and dissecting. It may be
interesting but it leads to misunderstandings — it leads to unfairness —
we always "show off" & exaggerate when we do it of ourselves — and
when we do it of others — sympathy dies. There should be caverns
recesses sanctuaries reserves. No one has a right to know everything.
People should be trusted and taken for granted and loved as they are —
sans hidden skeletons. Unreserved people are dangerous people — No one
really confides in them' — I seem to hear many voices in the air during
this discourse and the devil uttered the words 'Nothing is interesting
except psychology.'

. . . . . I went – with her – for a long stroll on the Downs. . . . . The explorer[1] – has tame *sea-gulls* – Over this we very nearly had a row. Think of it! Sea-gulls with clipped wings swallowing bread and potatoes in a back garden. But the little boy with the tact of Talleyrand[2] steered the situation through the rocks – 'What Paddy w^d like for them would be a pond with fish in it and then they would only visit the sea and return of their own accord!' Do sea-gulls Ocean-born sometimes return of their own accord?

The Parrot can now imitate *sheep* – There indeed you have Joyous Wisdom. What kind of an animal is Jack now? – whatever he is he still writes –

42

JACK TO FRANCES
(Mrs Louis U. Wilkinson, Pembroke House, Aldeburgh, Suffolk)[1]

[No date; 1913]

Just got your letter – about stockings tarts immortality and the undesirable English. Mrs Powys is planting Fuchsias which I have given her.

. . . . . I went on Saturday to a lunch party & a garden party and this afternoon there is a party here & it will be very lucky if I escape

Croquet

But I am already rewarded for this – We discuss things in an amazingly different manner from formerly –

Even the question of 'immortality' – its meaning etc – is not dismissed but has justice, or whatever one does to such a thing, done to it. . . . .

We are to march – the little boy too – in a Suffrage procession – did I tell you that? That, at any rate, heaven knows, is symbolical enough! Mrs Powys sends her love to you & hopes that you will be able to endure Burpham for three days. . . . .

Mrs Powys won't let the child kill any birds except sparrows and starlings – these latter it seems (clumsy devils!) are the impossible, miscreated ones, among their tribes – the Powyses, in fact, of the air world. Did I tell you that the little boy plays the acolyte in the consecrated cellar (I am permitted to deny myself this spectacle) of our ecclesiastical neighbour?

I note that there is also a tendency to teach him (these departures often go together) to swim.

I am not quite certain how far I regard either of these, perhaps especially the latter, with perfect equanimity. To swim – yes – but to be buoyed up (we arrived at the *usual* pronunciation en route I think) by prelatical hands – somehow that sticks – a little.

. . . . . Do you know what I have got in my pocket? My fingers on them now?

3 little transparent pebbles

picked up at Aldeburgh when Frances was – what we must – love – as I do now!

'TEAM'

43

JACK TO FRANCES

[Postmarked 'Burpham Arundel July 28 – 1913']
St James Day [July 25th 1913]

. . . . . Yesterday I had another meal alone with the little boy and we discussed the question of the sensations of people swallowed alive by tigers. 'If they came out *in a town*' – out of the tiger's belly that is – 'they would be sure to be *worshipped!*' I was not sorry to note this profound understanding of divinity – to be disgorged by a tiger in a town that certainly is to be a god. It is a pity he won't be there to see me emerge in 'the sweet city with dreaming spires'[1] – This is, then, my second claim to that berth, as Shirley[2] would style it; and the creating of Louis and Frances receives its pronunciation.

He – my son I mean – is now pursuing evolutionary researches. He has placed – but I learn this morning that they have disappeared – a field mouse & a house mouse in a cage – male & female – (I don't believe Louis w^d know them apart) the short ears and the short tail of the one to be modified – in the offspring – by the long ears and long tail of the other. They have however as I say gone off – whether together to the House or together to the Field remains a question admitting a wide solution.

Do you know why Starlings taste unpleasantly? There is 'bitterness' he tells me 'in the brain of this bird' which at the moment of death passes through the whole body – so be careful dear. It is true that Starlings feed on sheep; but that makes it yet more remarkable.

. . . . . Bertie[3] said that you were extraordinarily clever because you understood exactly 'how he liked to be treated'. He said he enjoyed more than anything the delight of battle with you and was ready for the fiercest friendly arena – 'I shouldn't like' he said 'however to annoy Louis by any humorous battle with her'. I explained that it was not generally found necessary for Louis to come to your rescue and that it seemed to me that his peculiar methods of argument might be a relief to you.

As a matter of fact I think that you and Bertie will carry off the occasion for the benefit of everyone.

My only fear is that you may find Theodore[4] something of a stumbling block but who can tell? . . . . .[5]

Hic Jacet
Jack
Whipped to Death
He still kissed the
Rod

44

JACK TO FRANCES

Burpham, Sussex

I think even your indurated (what does that mean?) heart of ice would have been touched by the relief it was to me to get this letter with its unessential recession of *Becauses* disappearing in just such a perspective as Paul Verlaine[1] might have watched his Mongolian visage dissolve – through a hundred repeating mirrors – as he sat curled up and drunk – God's darling little flipperty Poppet!

I have been during the last days trying to sink into myself and think out some line for my story, that will serve me as a means of gaining a kind of standing ground, from which I may get various moods into relation with one another. I am leaning & I let my thoughts coalesce round this point, to some sort of imaginary story of a poet, influenced by various philosophies and amours, and encountering, as the main pivot of the plot, a Frances, more or less like the real one – only with certain tendencies exaggerated – and a few diminished – who shall scourge him into some kind of form – without getting off quite unwounded! If I could only get absorbed in such a thing, so as to be really interested enough to revise & re-write chapter by chapter, I think I might be able to do something in my American journeys. The effort of *beginning* a new thing has always overcome there hitherto – but if I could start with a swing before my lecturing begins I ought I should think to be able to write a few pages, at the least, every day. . . . . .

I think I half-hoped once & again that I was going to be allowed to find ancient wicked absurd obsessions as thrilling as they were, say, ten years ago – but it is no use – I have changed in one very important point in that regard – it annoys me to confess it – but you were right when you hinted that my fate would be to suffer from a frightful desire to be loved – Not by a lot of people – Frances Josefa – but by one – and one I could [*word scratched out*] .

. . . . . I had a memorable walk by myself yesterday wherein I review-ed everything and looked, as you might say, round. I tried to contend against this new and more troublesome invasion of your personality, turning up, as Louis would say, round the corner; across the Downs gloom alone, sombre and unalloyed, hemmed me in; but afterwards I happened upon a bank of those flaunting yellow flowers (that take the place with us of your golden-rod) – and I thought, 'Here are you – John Cowper – an animal, aged 40 (nearly 41), having, largely, if not entirely, wasted your chances, so far, in reveries and fancies and obses-sions – here you are,' I thought, 'in your one planetary existence – and permitting yourself to fall into useless lamentations and fretting – because you can't have that particular other animal – Frances by name, and the devil knows what that name hides! – because you can't know that she 'loves' you and can't play chess with her for ever, and so forth and so forth' – and the yellow flowers considered the question very gravely for some minutes, and then they said, in a husky sort of sub-burnt chuckle, like a gnat whistling through a straw, 'My especially stupid and pedantic friend – If you slough off a little of your solemn subjectivity and look at this business squarely you will discern that the way to win the 'love', as you call it, of this other two-legged phen-omenon (did you say she had legs?) is not to go about, howling round her, like a wolf round a grave, but to get your intellectual muscles to-gether and astonish her by your work – Work! – idiot! – Work! If, as we understand it, she is an intelligent maniac, her 'love', if you *must* have it, can only be attracted to you by making yourself interesting – as we are – by enormous work!' – 'But,' protested Jack in his literal and logical manner, 'according to our Lord's well-known Logos that is the last thing *you* do'. At that the yellow flowers crackled with laughter, like a thousand furze-seeds bursting. 'Intolerable and portentous fool,' they

said, 'Heavy and most sententious clown — Have you then never read
that profound work, by the only sensible writer you possess, called
'Alice through the Looking Glass'? Do you not remember how it is only
by enormous labour — by running, in fact, extremely fast — that Alice
was able, as the Red Queen explained, to remain where she was and
what she was made? We remain what we are made — yellow and somewhat glaring flowers. You (made a writing and struggling animal) are
rapidly dissolving into a heap of disgusting putrefaction. Run, therefore
— Ass! Work! Clodhopper! — and with all your labours think yourself
extremely happy if at the end you find yourself — what Fate has made
you. If this other absurdity (Did you say she had legs?) won't love you,
then — well, she won't love you! (Don't think we care!) But at any rate
you will have the satisfaction of knowing that it is

you she won't, or can't, (we don't blame her by Jupiter!) love — and
not the aforesaid dissolving heap of stinking carrion, which is not even a
long-eared fool, such as you must, however hard you work, always — ho!
ho! for that's what *you* are you know — remain. But run, solemn-face,
run, copy-cat — give up your ridiculous little phosphorescent ironies; and
be, the colossal *struggling* industrious *Fool* — that the gods made you!' —

Thus, from the bank where they grew, spoke to Jack (wanting to be
loved by Frances) that admirable English flower, called — [*word erased*]

. . . . .

45

JACK TO FRANCES
(Mrs Louis U. Wilkinson, c/o Theodore Powys Esq.,
Beth Car, East Chaldon, Winfrith, Dorset)

[Postmarked 'Burpham, Arundel, Aug 4(?) 1913']
Tuesday night

. . . . . Do you know what I am thinking of at this moment? — That I
would willingly foreswear anything else — beyond receiving hand shakes
and Gregg bows — if destiny would let me live with you & Louis forever!
. . . . . You always — you remember? — scolded me for my peculiar, let me
say 'poetical', exaggeration of our relations —

Venetian Lions	—	Lucrezia daggers
Jungle Panthers	—	I needn't finish the list —

I know of course that your Roman anger was largely a revolt against the strain of humouring that particular vein in me, which had become a sort of prison for your spirit. *Now* I find to my immense amazement that it had become a prison also for my love for you – that I was, in my absurd idealism, substituting my own Imagination, or rather Image, for you yourself.

. . . . . My anger against you – and I have hated – has been due to any movement of yours to escape from that idealistic prison I speak of – Now I am *glad* you have burst out! . . . . .

. . . . . Shall I never be able to write you a love-letter direct and to the point? The only ones that I approve of are when I say – 'I should like to do this – or that – or – ' Let Louis fill these expressive blanks! They indicate the encounter of my Saturnian fingers with your silken [*word crossed out*].

You observe the crossed-out word!

. . . . . Come, Jack, my friend, just for once look at the unvarnished truth. . . . . Here is this girl, this Frances, eminently desirable to you, so that you could play chess with her for ever in preference to anything else in the world – and you can only see her at intervals – days here and days there – and then – but that is nothing! She curses you half the time.

That is the situation, dear incompetent dramatic Jack, and not all the imagery in the round earth can alter the quiet solid actual loss, which you have to deal with as best you may!

Now it seems to me I am talking sense at last.

. . . . . I sign *Jack* with an effort but it carries as much & more sincerity than any

46

JACK TO FRANCES

[Printed:] Hotel Lutetia, 43 Boul^d Raspail, Paris
August [1913]

[The first part of the letter is missing]

. . . . . Jack, of course, drinks absinthe with Remy de Gourmont[1] who is content to listen forever to stories about Frances. He says he quite dreads meeting Ezra [Pound], who he seems to regard as a sort of Buffalo Bill.

I wish I could bring myself to practice a little of that Admirable Brutality you recommended!

Mrs Powys & I went to Gounod's Faust[2] at the Opera – she enjoyed it – she said – 'for actual pleasure' (*her* words, my child) more than anything she had ever known in her life! Certainly the Loggia & Foyer there are wonderful – But I thought of the Black Man and wished I had my head once more under your heel.

Chess! That will have to be, I clearly see, my only ground for conquering Frances Josefa – In the larger game I don't seem to have got the right kind of weapons somehow! Some of my thoughts – nice little thoughts! – are very curious – They hover about the girlish envelope of Trenchant Philosophy like so many suicidal moths. . . . .

47

JACK TO FRANCES
(Mrs Louis U. Wilkinson, 26 Divinity Road, Oxford)
[Postmarked 'Burpham Aug 25']

Do let me hear something of your impressions of Theodore and his boys.

I have presented Mrs Powys with all ten volumes of Jean Christophe[1] in French – May it do her good!

. . . . . I have got a volume of Remy de Gourmont called 'Promenades Philosophique'.

Philosophie Naturelle – Religion et Sociologie – Psychology – Reveries – et des pas sur le sable. This last has many little sayings that would please you. For instance – 'Une femme à quelquefois pitié des chagrins qu'elle cause sans remords. A défaut de l'ami attendu, en voici un autre. A défaut de l'amie voici une autre amie! Illusion! – à défaut de l'amie, il n'y a rien.'[2] I cannot follow this, except at the end. But there are a lot more very much to the point. I will lend you the book. Shall I, do you think, in my new book we spoke of, carry only one figure through many scenes and adventures? Does it spoil a thing that people and places should disappear except for the impression they leave? . . . . .

48

JACK TO FRANCES (in Aldeburgh)

[5041 Pulaski Avenue, Philadelphia, Pennsylvania[1]]
[September 1913]

Friday evening.

Well, here I am, writing to you on the horse-hair sofa (an object of furniture in the parlour) while your mother is writing to you at the table. We wonder whether our letters will get the Saturday boat or have to wait till Tuesday. The ship got in on Wednesday morning, and about noon I posted a letter to your mother telling her to expect me by lunchtime on Thursday. But the post is so slow that it did not arrive until after she had left. I got through the window, Teddy[2] recognising me, and waited for her till five o'clock. She had a clairvoyant sense that there was a reason for her returning; otherwise she had been asked to the theatre.

I shall stay with her till late Sunday afternoon, then I shall go to the Brights.[3] That will be as long as she can very well have me, I think, because, without a servant, my being here means extra work and she is tired. I shall not of course let her suffer from the expense. Lola[4] tends to become so very exacting that I really fear I shall have to respect her virtue – the worst of punishments!

I have seen James[5] who looked very well. I rather dread seeing Vera[6] —wouldn't you? I think the little doctor here will cure my cough in time. How lucky I came early enough. Your mother is sweet to me. We are very happy together. Only it distresses me to be such a burden on her hands, and to add to her work. There is another dog here with St Vitus' Dance – the most peculiar dog – when I first arrived I thought its appearance very disconcerting but I have got used to it now. I give my love to Louis. My cough has the effect of paralysing my brain.

My thoughts tend to get like the thoughts you have when you are going very fast in a train to a destination not particularly desired. . . . . I think I am pushed forward to some kind of distant new level in my existence, though what the nature of it is I cannot exactly say. . . . . However! Wherever it leads or does not lead, it has no tendency to lead away from Frances. . . . .

49

JACK TO FRANCES (in Aldeburgh)

[Printed:
B
TA WE PA]
[Postmarked 'Philadelphia, pa. Mount Airy Sta. Sep 24' 1913]

. . . . . I can't write anything interesting – I can only touch the tip of your little finger across the Atlantic –

50

JACK TO FRANCES
(8 Campden Grove, Kensington, London W.)
Oct 1st [1913]

. . . . . Your mother & I both find dear Vera a *little* trying; but I suppose if she really is in a suicidal mood, and really *was* devoted to our friend,[1] there is every reason why she should be somewhat cynical and indifferent. One is apt to be grotesquely exacting and not very tolerant in these cases – A wounded bird – that will work its wings about, and stare and peck – the instinct is to put it out of its misery and save oneself for further bother. . . . .

I have seen Lola [Catesby-Jones] twice – she has now gone South for her holiday – She is in extreme need of a holiday – with a cough that might easily, I fancy – turn to consumption. She at once began cursing me for 'treating her badly' and 'neglecting' her last year; and then started issuing ultimatums. . . . .

Did I tell you that *a shark* followed our ship for several days, easily keeping up with it, swimming on its back, a whitish greenish corpse-like looking thing, with a circular mouth. . . . .

51

JACK TO FRANCES (in Kensington)

[Printed:] The Wentworth Arms, Hamilton, Canada
[No date; 1913]

[The first part of the letter is missing]
..... but consenting – consenting – like a dutiful wife – Ah –
Day after day – day after day –
the same craving
For Frances –
What's the damned Latin for 'how long, O Lord, how
long?' .....

Wouldn't it be interesting if I could kill my love for you? Of course you wouldn't like me to – for my sake – it's so good for me, isn't it? – that's all. Kill it? I love you I love you I love you Only you! There! Put out your tongue at that!

52

JACK TO FRANCES (in Aldeburgh)

[Printed:] Hotel Statler, Buffalo, N.Y.
Oct 15 [1913]

..... I have been a little won back by Remy de Gourmont – but he is the most tantalizing and irritating of men. Just as you are getting interested in some really daring piece of what he is pleased to call his 'Idealism', w[h] is really the most insolent and contemptuous isolation of his tastes his visions his mood from everyone in the world – (His ring almost might have upon it 'I like my choice' like that of the 'urbane little man' of that story on the loft)[1] – he will suddenly swing off upon the 'new spelling', or Sainte-Beuve's[2] revival of Ronsard,[3] or the manner in which moths are born – I suppose these 'Philosophical Studies' were really articles for some newspaper that demand something fresh every Sunday. *Paul Bourget*[4] has given me a certain amount of pleasure and I am surprised at it. For it is undeniable that he has less *genius* than any other writer of equal reputation – and he is an abominable reactionary. He is reactionary however in the patient massive *thick* traditional sense of the conservatism of Balzac & Goethe & not in the finickin, meticulous, eager, *taut* strained manner, so Harry Lyon-like,[5] of Mrs Powys' favourite Henri Bordeaux.[6] Paul Bourget's knowledge of Paris is pleasing – the way he brings in the real streets places cafés churches, that even I can sometimes remember seeing & a certain grave scrupulous rather solemn sense of 'our responsibility as writers', which weighs upon his style, is not as annoying as one might think.

But Villiers de L'Isle-Adam,[7] my infant, there is a master! What bitterness, what contempt, what pride, what anarchistic anti-nomianism,[8] what a bewitching 'tendre' for 'the forbidden'!

I have read two books – 'Le Prêtre Marrié' and 'La Vielle Maitresse' by Barbey D'Aurevilly[9] – & I rather fancy he is of the same kind of mood as this other devil.

But even from him, – L'Isle-Adam – I have been driven since I wrote you last – I have got a grotesque book (out of the New York Library if you please!) called 'L'Eve Future' – all about Mr Edison inventing, making you understand – a mechanical chemical girl – in order to assuage the passion of young Lord Ewald for a beautiful mistress with no brain. Edison's creation has not an intelligence but *The Intelligence*. She is drowned in her beautiful box as my lord carries her back to 'Newcastle-under-Lyme' where his castle is! We get into somewhat quaint regions here; you can believe! –however. . . . .

53

JACK TO FRANCES (in Aldeburgh)

[Printed:] Hotel Statler, Buffalo, N.Y.
[Postmarked 'Oct 22' 1913]

. . . . . I feel like a person who has started on a long journey for a penance, but has forgotten the name of the shrine to which he goes, so do the dreams of the country he has left go with him, and move as he moves, blotting out the rest. . . . .

. . . . . I continue to read Paul Bourget because of a certain power & charm that appeals to me in him and because he is always describing 'writers' and 'artists' and 'connoisseurs' and 'virtuosos' & 'dilettantes' and because he is extremely well aware of the division of the world into Wagners and Mephistopheleses, simple fools and elaborate fools, credulous and sceptical – But O Christ, his sentimentality! . . . . .

I have to lecture on Faust;[1] so I have been reading *right through* — I am sure Frances has never done that — The second part of Faust — what a pantomime — yet what strokes of sardonic insight! I had never realized quite entirely how charmingly addicted to the obsession of our own precious Inner Circle the son of chaos is.

He has his own way with the young Brocken witches but the Classical Walpurgis Night (correct, ridiculous & charming!) fools him up to the hilt. He pursues those delicately youthful Lamiae [female phantoms] and gets completely 'left' — But what a stroke when at the end he makes lecherous overtures to the angels who use deliberately (if you please) their epicene charms, to pre-occupy him, while they carry off the prize he is after. . . . .

54

JACK TO FRANCES (in Aldeburgh)

[Printed:] Hotel Statler, Buffalo, N.Y.
[Postmarked 'Oct 28' 1913]

Ah! mon amie, you ask me for a 'real letter' & then stagger me with these sudden and unforeseen accusations!

But no — I am not to call them 'accusations' but rather a statement of how you stand in regard to me at this hour. Tonerre de dieu! & is that making it better? — to know that in the judgement of the especial Tribunal I most respect I am held 'unflexible, unimaginative & heavy'? . . . . . Well! My feelings at this moment are in a turmoil of indignation & revolt against this estimate.

. . . . . If I knew myself invariably sensitive clairvoyant & sympathetic in all personal relations I should laugh at this letter of yours. The fact that it excites emotion in me, & perturbs me so, is — that you *may* take — a proof that I am not armoured against all attack just there! Certainly insensitive — but never, Cathy, to you — & never since you have known me to anyone about whom I have cared or you w^d wish me to care. It is however to my own knowledge *now*, of how stupid & obtuse I have been in the past, that frightens and agitates me when you write like this. . . . .

. . . . . I have *tried* to see the more delicate movements of my friends' minds. I have *tried* to see them as they are; so as not inadvertently to hurt them — but it seems that I have not succeeded — and yet I thought, in guileless conceit, that I had succeeded quite wonderfully, considering, you know, what I *used to be*! So that you see, Frances-Adrasteia,[1] your words are particularly poignant on this count! They have the weight of a Priest's, who suddenly tells his charge that all the very sins he has taught him to struggle against are the ones he will be damned for! . . . . .

> Bless you, youngest of the
> Destinies, but not the least
> Severe!

To love Frances is like loving the fires of purgatory — as now! For that the Inferno at least is past I thank my gentle Guide! . . . . .

55

JACK TO FRANCES (in Aldeburgh)

[Printed:] Hotel Seneca, Rochester, N.Y.
Nov 5th [1913]

. . . . . Cathy, my persecutor, I beg you (even under the lashes) not to be kind.

Not that kindness is exactly in your veins; but I *have* seen it & shuddered.

I have read again and more than once again your 'inflexible' letter — What devilry to drag Ezra in! But I am ready now to confess that after much introspection I find your charges more justified than I felt at first. . . . .

You must admit, child, that with the blending in you of immense pride and a certain little-girl-like craving for understanding and gentleness, you make it hard for the kind of person that I am. Your own intellect is perpetually fretting against the sensitiveness of your body and, in its very rage against its delicate companion, it turns fiercely upon those for whom that companion may be dear, but who have been betrayed by that very same intellect into treating it carelessly and without nuance. Is there not some truth in the hypothesis (what a word in this connection!) that you are a Dual personality — Let us say Frances & Josefa — and what Josefa wants is to excite, whether feeling it herself or not, the unhappy devotion of this or that lover — and what Frances wants is (quite apart from 'love') the kind of complete intellectual friendship that men sometimes have for one another. Now it is obvious that these two desires very often conflict with one another & produce distress, not only in themselves but in the other person—who has, really, to be at the same time a lover & friend — which is a combination more difficult than any on earth — because love always implies the presence of hatred antagonism jealousy cruelty and the lust either to be punished or to punish — and friendship implies an agreement of interests, purposes, tastes, apathies and antipathies, and a complete understanding.

If, as you say, Ezra is more sympathetic towards you than I — is it not because for him there is only Frances — the Josefa (exquisite devil!) being forgotten or non-existent. Whereas I—how can I help it? —am continually torn between my desire to gratify my love and my hate upon Josefa — and my desire to move freely about, as you so happily say, through the mind & thoughts of Frances. . . . .

56

JACK TO FRANCES
(forwarded to No 6 Church Walk, Kensington, London W.)

[Printed:] Hotel Ohio, Youngstown, Ohio
[Postmarked: 'Nov 13' 1913]

Ha! Little one, ha! My evasive one! — subtlest of all — I am to mark — am I? — that Frances *and* Louis only tease Jack when they call him Materialist — Clodhopper — Thick-skin — Inflexible Toad — & I am not to be jealous when you are happy with Ezra? . . . . .

Christ! It pleases me well to have none but such as you—such subtleties! —to play with, at the game of Marsh-Light & Traveller.

There — and again *there* — and I am still lost — while far away with mischievous laughter and fitful fire — the will-o'the-wisp mocks and beckons.

Now would I give a king's ransom to be present at what really goes on in your evasive head — to watch the puppets really dallying[1] there — the Louis Puppet, the Lulu Puppet, the Jack Puppet — and to see what measure is meted out to them —& how they come & go! Ah! That were worth many years of moral rectitude. . . . .

But this I *can* say — that I am glad that fate would have me fond not only of receiving humiliating blows from hands I care for, but for having set up upon the walls of my palace scrolls that no one —no! *No one* is able to read! . . . . .

57

JACK TO FRANCES (at Church Walk, Kensington)

[Printed:] Hotel Burlington, Burlington, Iowa
Nov 27 [1913]

This is a quaint place to be writing to our Frances in, like one of God's
dear little lambs very far off from the shepherd's fold.

All the way from Hannibal[1] — fancy that particular Sidonian getting
into the head of some worthy man so far from Carthage! —the train ran
along the Mississipi which I can now add to the Po, the Seine, the Arno,
the Tiber and the Yeo as a river into which I have dipped my fairy stick.
It has its qualities tonight at any rate this river, that one learnt in early
days as the biggest in the world — most peculiar mists, twisting and turning up and down its stream like those shadowy elementals of Toledo that
you won't believe in — and woods coming down to the water on the
other side.

I stayed at Fort Wayne with a Locomotive Engineer (of the 'Wabash')
but about him I could ramble on with 'descriptive psychology' à la James
(ours I mean) till you came to the conclusion that you were indeed Circe,
for turning your friends into simple tedious clay. And I sometimes think
you have a slight penchant — a leaning — if no more — in that direction.
It comes from the savagery of your attacks, you know; which leaves us
positively gasping, and with nothing left but 'descriptive psychology',
and a sort of patient despair.

. . . . . What a quaint thing jealousy is! The order of my jealousies is as
follows—

> 1. James least of all —
> 2. Lulu —
> 3. Louis —
> 4. Ezra —

in increasing seriousness.

That demon Maurice[2] has turned down my play as it was and makes
me *revise & revise* — and I know he won't take it —after all. To *revise* —I
think next to being jealous of Frances that is the most horrible of all my
penances. . . . .

Well, it won't be long now before we meet. What boat is it?

58

JACK TO FRANCES (at Church Walk, Kensington)

[December 1913]

I've just got your letter — Its contents sink into whatever of an uncorrupted-corrupted soul is left in Jack — And O I am so longing to see you! I find these last days of expectancy almost more than I can stand. . . . .

I think even Louis will have to admit now that his 'infatuation' theory has broken down — No — things have moved — and moved steadily in one direction —

How my peculiar genius for postponed reaction has stood me in good stead with you! . . . . .

To bow beneath a storm and wait — and wait — Ha! There is much in that — What is so odd is that you have really & truly concentrated everything of the 'Great Marquis' that I have in me upon yourself — so that nothing else attracts. But this is only a trifle — a thing on the surface and absurd thing — is it or is it not? But what matter? I am in such nervous expectancy for you — with such remorseless longing for you.

Sometimes I know I am equal to you and able to deal with you & to meet you.

1914

59

JACK TO FRANCES
(Pulaski Avenue,[1] Philadelphia)

[January 1914]

I miss you today. I miss many long hours which were only minutes to the conscious F & J. I want to tell you that under everything and behind everything *I love you.* Do you hear me? – you girl, you woman, you thing. I love you – I am a fool. I hate this silly novel.[2] It will change its character now I have seen you – it is silly so far. I hate it. I can see my weakness and ponderous pomposity, it annoys me.

Listen Frances – Does it really make any difference to you to know that I cannot be bad to you in my thoughts? It is true – I have been contemptible – I am still, in a way, I know it – & there is something else. There really and truly is.

I miss you, I want to see you. I require you – I shall *never* forget this meeting – never! Never! Something in me is very different. . . . . and I am a little sad. But I love you and shall never let go your hand. Don't think bad thoughts of me. I know I am in some ways a dead weight. *But I love you.* . . . .

60[1]

JACK TO FRANCES (in Philadelphia)

[March 1914]

Come, let us vivisect Jack a little – and see what it is really like, this curious disease – the starved 'Frances-nerve' – jerking and quivering in

69

the hidden cell. Why the devil have I such a memory and such an imagination? One alone would pinch me enough – but both together! Today is Tuesday – only seven days more![2]

Don't forget you sea-devil, you insatiable 'little girl' – little girl! – that the 31st, the 1st, the 2nd, Tuesday, Wednesday, Thursday are my last days of happiness for six weeks & more. There is nothing of course – only don't forget – We shall have that little bit of shopping to do – in Market or Chesnut. That'll be more exquisite to me than you think of – that'll be something. Are you smiling now? Are you tired? Does Jack bother you? Well – you know where you've got your heel – don't you? Press it down! Harder harder! It's only a grotesque face underneath – trample – then you won't see – you know, whether it looks bad or good! It'll look neither soon – if you press hard enough!

Why must I conjure you up? – making myself sick with longing for you? Why can't you stay quiet and let me be alone? Why must you be always stretching out that damned thin wrist towards me – and why need you to have gone to sleep that time when you were ill – just like that? Do you think I didn't count the times you started? The cruel thing is that I *know* that very often you are dull & tired just for the lack of the kind of pleasure you get – O damn you – in playing your little tunes – (aren't they quaint tunes – better than the Rhine-girls know?) – upon Jack's nerves – I *know* that! I know it is growing on you like a drug to have Jack's soul under your fingers – so! May it grow yet! till you – too – suffer – a very little – for lack of that Instrument! I now understand why you've given up violin-playing – there are *other* strings – stretched even more tight – with little pegs to set up & down – misery ecstasy – ecstasy misery – at your caprice!

No – no – you won't run downstairs just yet, you will wait a little and look at ten thousand and one photo cards! Is that the door-bell? Is that dear little Louis come back – a little – just a little sooner – than we expected him? And now we must be led upstairs – protesting just a little. . . . .

61

JACK TO FRANCES (in Philadelphia)

R.M.S. Mauretania
Easter Day [April 12th 1914]

O you exquisite Devil! Was there ever such a letter? You mustn't talk to me like this early in the morning; when the little sea girls are all sing-

ing to their recovered Adonais![1] Where can I go to take you with me?
There is no sink, no sofa, no furnace, no shaky dining-room chair, no
corner between door and door. This is Easter and I *must* have Frances. I
must I must I must! But how? Even if I send you a wireless—it'll be in-
calculable hours before you get it and then you won't be quite alone.
I must have you quite alone this morning. And I *will*! I will – do you
hear, little too-easily-bruised! What a letter –Upon my soul it is the very
best letter I've ever had. . . . . so real and attenuated and witchingly
provocative! So wisp-like and darting! Such thin blue smoke. It has
gone to my head – this wavering eddying arrowy little whisper and it has
unsettled me from head to foot! Will you give me ten minutes? –

(in one moment Madonna!)[2]

(Get down Baby!)[3]

(*Damn that bell!*)

Shall I tell you where I was when the cannon was loaded with violets?
I was just behind you as you turned! Didn't you hear me with your Ears?
Ask the right hand one whether it heard me. No! You are wrong – you
are wrong – so you couldn't tell? (All right, Madonna, she is coming!) O
you have justified all the suffering that ever I have had! It is worth it! All
–all and I love Fate!

You must tell me when you write which, of all the Liturgies that have
made up Jack's Passion Week, has pleased you best! Today is the last –
and we must pretend that all Passion-weeks are over. But they are not –
ah! would they were! No, not ever – and never will be. That is odd,
isn't it? – that I have really and truly been landed for the rest of my life
. . . . . henceforth Jack's little mind will be a study for abnormalists!
Now on this Easter Day with you on the sea far behind and all the
rest, Le Néant[4] – let's have a little Cerebral ceremony. Frances' Second
Marriage! –

'I, Jack, take thee, Frances, to have and to hold – at the sink and
away from the sink – in the cellar and away from the cellar – on the
sofa and off the sofa – when the moon is full and when the moon is
eclipsal and let Death try to part us!'

'I, Frances, take thee, Jack, to tease, tantalise, provoke and madden
and enslave – and let him who knoweth cause or impediment speak now
– or else forever hereafter hold his peace!' So it goes and now – 'Thou,
O Death, canst not enthrall us! Alleluia!'. . . . .

62[1]

JACK TO FRANCES (in Siena)

The *Longest Day* [June 21st 1914]

I am writing this as I sit with my mother. Lulu is bathing & my Father and Gertrude are in church.[2]

So it is certain! What a strange mixture of feelings I have now it is — has to be — really faced at last as a fact.

I'll try to tell, Querida mia,[3] how it seems to me. First of all it has the same queer shock as if you had by a sudden effort of will transformed yourself into a different being, climbing up as it were through a hole in the roof, of our subjective cave — into an ampler region, of clearer air, and quieter, more luminous, spaces.

You know, since the pebble dropt down that *well* I spoke of, you have curiously ranged yourself, alongside of Louis & Lulu, *as no woman at all*, but one of us, as we are, *a mighty compliment!* — Frances with Lulu & Louis and the Catholic — my world of companions, more or less sages — more or less! — where the topics rise and fall like waves, and *women* are the glittering shells of the dead dead fish! In this way it struck me oddly enough — as though you were a Father & not a Mother — the same sort of surprise and interest, as if Lulu or Louis suddenly announced they had begotten a son! I've never of course followed the workings of any woman's mind or been swept along the tide of any woman's ideas as I have with yours — so that when I hear this news of you, who have invaded me so much as a mind, it is just as if quite suddenly in the middle of one of your philosophical attacks upon me you announced that this trifling incident had intervened, as you might have announced that you intended to buy a completely new edition of Paul Verlaine — or with the same detachment as if you — as Louis might or Lulu — had begotten a scion of their wandering loves in some debauching into Wales or Lancashire.

By following your mind, as I have been compelled to do, especially in its more critical workings where your sex has disappeared — and that has, in spite of your suspicions, been — as you must know — often the fact — this sudden very primitive accompaniment to that mental play strikes me just as it would if, when listening to you in absorbed remote attention, I suddenly became aware (as we crossed the salt marshes) that you were carrying a heavy burden that I couldn't relieve you of.

So that is how this is to me in the first shock — as if Louis was your little Liverpool[4] girl and you had just announced to me as a pleasant bye-issue that the result of your 'sweet-usage' had been to *inaugurate a Little Frances in the darling.*

Then a quite distinct feeling (upon which we will not dwell — but I confess it) a sudden angry and irrational jealousy — it is *my girl* & some damned other person has shot in & done this — almost as if it had been a rape — & our friend a *drifting high-road Tramp.*

Then — yet another vein — a definite profound jealousy of Louis as Louis, with an extreme reluctant & irritated recognition of his pleasure *in the situation — his triumph — a triumph over me.* This feeling is oddly associated with the kind of messages in which his mother sends her love to me — (as I sit with *my mother*) — as much as to say — 'in the long run, my son, as you see, is the winner —'

But as the hours, since last night I got Louis' letter, go on — another quite different feeling emerges as likely to be the lasting one — Simply an anxiety for you as yourself — girl as you are — & without any arrière pensées of any sort. . . . . (but my presentiments are all auspicious for you) and that it is really so — really happened at last — this unavoidable danger. . . . . *You — Frances* — are in this particular ship — embarked on this particular journey — & whether or not I raise my hand & wave to you or take off my hat & shout to you or kiss my hand & pray for you — is not the slightest consequence! . . . . .

The sea sounds all the time here — echoed by high cliffs — the re-iteration of its sound is like the forward marching of fate & I shall henceforth always associate this peculiar noise with this news I hear.

I long at this moment to have Frances' hand for a second — It *must* & shall end well.

63

JACK TO FRANCES

[Acreman House,[1] Sherborne]
July 28th [1914]

Old Goethe,[2] indeed a very sly old 'codger' — hits it when he talks in that queer platonic vein at the end of Faust (to the huge entertainment of the devil) — of the curious agitating disturbing unsettling & discomforting effect the feminine spirit must have — like a pinch of salt thrown on the cinder-heap. Jack is those cinders. Frances is that salt. And it only needed this 'new situation' following upon the superb gesture with which you rejected me – to complete what had been done. The summer before Venice I wrote THE DEATH OF GOD & before that the Keats Book.[3] Then *you* came, passing through my senses and soul like a storm with hidden icebergs, & now you draw that wedge away – and my boat, shaking a little, straightens itself on its keel, and I look at the compass – But what is that little strange bird on the mast-top –? That is the Frances in you that must always be my living pilot – however much you sheer off down unknown tracks – and whatever great Polar Bear and queer new Albatrosses – out of the Night – crouch upon your ice-floe. . . . .

Let me sometimes have the sense of your hand in my great-coat pocket – along with the Hibiscus & Geranium leaves.

But don't be vexed or hopeless – My hand is the hand of Jack – with this damned indirect affected jargon – but my soul – I swear it – is the soul of John Cowper Powys with a straight keel at last and his hand – *his own hand* – on the Tiller. . . . .

I don't care whether it pleases you or not – it happens to be the truth – I am just now looking up & down & back and forth – 'in mezzo del cammise di nostra vita'[4] and taking stock of my mental posessions – I am no more afraid of you – (nor Louis or Lulu or Mrs Powys). Herewith I sign myself as that which *has* fallen back – upon Itself! . . . . .

They are singing Holy Holy Holy in their little private Prep-service. I note that today is the Vigil of St Peter. I hope that you will note that it was upon St Peter – never mind that gold-crested Cock – that notre seigneur founded his church – in seculum seculorum.[5]

64

JACK TO FRANCES (in Italy)

[Montacute]
[September 1914]

Have just got Louis' letter in which he describes writing to the Consul in Florence etc.

There are strange rumours going about but the Press Bureau both in France and England reveals very little.

I've got my ticket for the *Mauretania* sailing on the 19th.

Lulu is going to sail next Saturday on the *Dunvegan Castle* on the 5th.[1]

Bertie [Powys] has just been – He is going to join an Officers' Training Corps and if he survives the war he has resolved to remain in the army. He still however refuses to give up his opinion that England ought to have kept out of it.

. . . . . My father *is just the same as ever*.

He expresses his missing my mother in two different moods. When he is quiet and walking through Stoke Wood – and when he is angry because people are late for prayers. He says he will stay on here till he dies & not resign because he does not like the idea of starting a new house without my mother.

Katie[2] (of whom there was a picture in the Daily Mirror entitled 'Her Hand on the Plough', representing her ploughing with two horses) is going to come to Montacute and have a Dairy Farm in the fields and orchard here. The outhouses – piggeries and so forth – are to be done up for her use. Father tends to cling to her and refers often to his desire for her and says she is an 'affectionate girl'.

You will notice by this that things are a little strained between him and Gertrude[3] who dreads greatly the autumn alone with him. She is not only afraid of Father's peculiar temper but has also got afraid lately of the *supernatural* – I suppose of my mother's ghost which she seems to be conscious of. She also says that without the healthy humours of Lulu both house and garden are haunted and penetrated by dark dangerous and evil influences. She says that she will be afraid to be alone except with the two sheep-dogs that Willie left behind – to these she will hold very close and not let them go. It is of *the garden* in the evening that she is particularly afraid.

I shall stay here till Lulu sails and then return to Burpham till my son returns to school on the 16th.

My money having come to an end & there being a general straightening of funds in every direction, there is a tendency for Mrs Powys to be rather agitated and troubled as I have to get what I want from her in small poor quantities. 'I shall get angry soon,' she remarked the other day: at which I regret to say I lost my Olympian calm. The war has the effect of making everybody very nervous and quarrelsome. The papers are engaged in a campaign to drive young men into the army – by ridicule and abuse.

I think this sort of thing is very unfair – conscription would be more dignified.

A young territorial told me that in his opinion they ought to send what territorials they want abroad, and not appeal to them individually to volunteer, as it was agitating—and produced shame and bad blood and quarrelling.

It is really rather pitiful to see the boys in the village as I have done this morning sitting in their open doors with their heads on their hands wrestling with their consciences.

The *fatality* and absolute *necessity* of conscription would put an end to this trouble of mind which is now causing many boys to feel the sensation of disquieting shame. They've raised the age of enlisting – in Kitchener's new army – from 30 to 35. It is enlisting only for this war – to be discharged at the end of it.

They are getting girls to refuse their favours to those who have not enlisted.

I think there would be a certain satisfaction in conscription for the village boys, because then the 'gentlemen' would have to be private soldiers with them, as in France: whereas now there is a tendency for the middle classes to struggle to get officers' places: though I think a good number of city clerks have enlisted in the ranks. If *I'd* been at all spirited what I ought to have done would have been to have gone by ordinary train – still running by the way – to Paris – and there enlisted in some foreigner's legion who would have welcomed anyone, and not, I fancy, fussed much about age or acquirements or appearance!

As it is I can only hope that things will be going very well for the Allies by the time the 19th comes – then I shall be less like a funk or a lunk or a skunk. Apart from these little trifling bye-issues – I note that some Liberal papers express disparagement of the Russians as this and that and the other – This is unpardonable I think – and I observe with pleasure that the New York 'Sun' under the heading 'Cossacks & Culture' indicates that these noble medievalists – like mad knight-errants – are arriving to rescue freedom of the spirit from German materialism.

The Saturday Review also puts this point of view admirably in an article called 'Russia, Our Great Ally'.

America seems to have been very impressed by the bomb-throwing from Zeppelins upon non-combatants at Antwerp – I fancy the destruction of Louvain will also strike their indignation. They will want *some* picturesque European towns left. But it appears that the Germans have been doing their very utmost to win over the public opinion of Frances Josefa's native land.

However they say that 50,000 Americans offered themselves as volunteers to the Canadian expedition.

The humorous tone of the American papers that have been sent to us—

their mixture of wonder surprise annoyance and amusement – as if all Europe was a rather disgraceful Comic Opera – is a refreshing note just at this juncture.

I see that the Hamburg 'Cap-Trafalgar'[4] is on the loose as a war-ship to harass Lulu's Cape Line, but I expect they'll finish it before the Dunvegan Castle gets over there.

Willie [Powys] *may* be fighting the Germans in Nairobi – but if so Lulu will find pretty little Mrs Barry[5] to take care of him.

Lulu had rather bad discoloration this morning but he is absolutely resolved to start at all risks – He thinks that another autumn here w^d end him.

The liners carry 6-in. guns now, I understand – A fight between a Cunard liner and a Hamburg liner would be really exciting.

Such matters do not alarm Lulu or me but we both shiver with terror at the thought of the jagged-edged bayonet w^h the Germans have. Luckily *they* also, they say, are a bit nervous of bayonets – and with reason, by Heaven!

The papers yesterday announced that Indian troops are coming.

65

JACK TO FRANCES (in Italy)

Sept. 6th [1914]

Lulu sailed yesterday on the Dunvegan Castle. He was in a ticklish state of health – terrified lest he should at the last be prevented from getting off – but he is safe now. The sea air will save him – seven weeks voyage.

Gertrude is now alone, at the mercy of C.F.P. [his father].

The Germans getting to Paris is likely to prove dangerous for them – but if not – it is only a bagatelle in this amazing war. It won't end till the Germans have not one single army left – and that may be a long time, mon ami.

Lulu must now be somewhere off Cape Finisterre – where we were when you slept on deck, & you and he saw that sailing ship at dawn.

He had that bit of sea-weed with him as a talisman that was picked up out of the Adriatic when you floated. He has a large and airy single berth opening on the upper deck.

How everything has changed! My mother dead – Lulu gone for seven years / you / as you are / Bertie drilling —May[1] in Singer's Building.

This ship I go on will have [*rough drawing of what resembles a revolver, or it could simply be Jack crossing out the word 'guns' in deference to the censor*] on board they tell me. Frances went through my brain and left there the impression of [a] little field of ashes in the middle of which sticks a spike of ice, which, because ashes are very cold, can never go away[2]. . . . .

66

JACK TO FRANCES (in Italy)

11 Charles Street, New York
Sept. 25th [1914]

Just arrived.[1]

I've talked to Arnold about Louis coming in the Summer. He speaks of California work for him there as well as Chantagua.[2] Arnold is going to live in the country at Valhalla, New York, about an hour from Grand Central: he will come in every week to the office but conduct his affairs from his country house. Lizzie [Arnold's wife] is better but still subject to fits of melancholia. May[3] and I are going there for the weekend. I am rather scared lest we should by chance say anything wanting in tact. You know how we blunder!

There is a German-Austrian paper published in English here called 'The Fatherland' for which Prof. Munsterburg[4] writes. He is also bringing out a pro-German book this week—I wish I had the power to write a reply to it — I've always disliked Prof. Munsterburg —a dull and pedantic fellow — and long-winded as the devil. They make great play on the 'barbarism' of Russia, these American-Germans. As a matter of fact it looks as if, out of a sort of delicate contrariety, the Russians are going to behave with extreme courtesy and leniency in this campaign. The 'note' of the enemy being so definitely a reckless mercilessness, the Allies will (all of them) by the mere logic of ideas — be led more and more to behave gently — and to make the contrasts sharper. So far, in Austrian towns, the Russians have been pleasanter masters than the dispossessed.

The commonplace position that 'war is war and must be awful' is absurd. There is all the difference between a style which is first-rate and a style which is nothing — between the one of making war and the other. The dragging in of Nietzsche is absurd too — he always found the

Bismarkian machine a second-rate affair.

I hope Lulu is safe, as far as the Cape at any rate – He runs risks. Are you all right?

67

JACK TO FRANCES (in Siena)

[New York]
October 26th [1914]

. . . . . I've got a bowl of flowers on this table that some people from the country brought in – people of no consequence but they have left these – Verbenas and Mignonette. It is the first time that I've been really able to recognize that Mignonette has any smell at all. We still harmonize pretty well in this flat – I nearly burst out in fury – quite à la C.F.P. [his father] – the other day when returning tired & cross from Boston at 9 p.m., I found that little May was expecting two elegant young men, strangers to me, who were airily coasting around. Louis would sympathise there – I well suppose! These little jerks to one's few moments of physical contentment. One likes one's bath on those occasions and to drift about afterwards drinking tea in pleasant Nighties and talking upon the mystery of things – who's in – who's out[1] – and so forth. Not very nice to have to scramble hastily through one's meal – with no leisurely margins – in order that things may be spick and span for some young gentlemen's visit! Ought not *every girl* to know by instinct – even a sister May – that the male animal returning from his predatory excursions, wants to find his companion *alone* and in a mood of exclusive fond liking, petting and pandering – not all tricked-out in new ribbons and full of wit and vivacity and with a sweeping-brush – waiting visitors! How unpleasant at any time is this incursion of the stranger within our gates – this demon of a curst intruder, coming so smug upon the mart – but most of all annoying when it takes the form of young men of social advantages and silky tongues.

Don't, you bad, bad Frances, think any wicked thoughts about this little ménage of 82 West 12th Street![2] As a matter of fact – This is true as you are in Siena – I am three days most unnaturally good. Why – I don't know quite – except that what L [Louis Wilkinson] calls my 'laziness' & you call my 'cowardice' and I call my virtue seems to be just at present very inviolable – Or shall we say the Absence of

Provocation! The means to do ill deeds removed indeed immensely far by accident and chance.

It'll be rather amusing if without the least intention I am destined to encounter you again with the evil wishes of nearly a year hung withered like a row of little vicious wind-dried weasels – on the park palings of my noble mind! . . . . .

This letter of yours is just a little frightening all the same – shall I tell you why? – because it is too gentle: because it is the first time you've *ever* written to me without a tang of devilment. . . . . But I like it. It's pathetic how much! The least of your scourging strokes has only just healed – and this is almost as if you kissed the place!

Damn!   That word 'you kissed' has excited strange forbidden ancient feelings. There is not the least reason why now (as I sit in this silly flat in 12th St) I should think about Frances' mouth – and the infernal provocation of it, in this light and the other –   Nor will I – no! no! no! no! I will think of Theodore Dreiser.[3] He, by the way, is coming tonight. May has commissioned me to purchase the following list of objects –

Tongue	15 C
Eggs 6 white 3 brown	40 C
Butter ¼	
Cream	7 cents
Cucumber	3 cents
Lettuce	5 cents
Parsley	2 cents
2 *Steros*	5 cents
2 bananas	
1 kettle	10 cents
Best coffee	10 cents

This it appears is to be the banquet prepared for this admirable man – I don't quarrel with it. It'll be the devil to pick up out of these little shops round here – but why not? What am I fit for, but doing little purchases for a little flat?

But Dreiser is really a remarkable being.

He is really like Dr Samuel Johnson – that *may* prejudice Louis – but it needn't, for on those Anti-Chesterfield sort of points,[4] this good Theodore is quite well-behaved. He's a deep one – I am ready to vouch for it – but he doesn't bother about *pretending to be stupid*, as this critic opines.

He is *naturally* interested in all that runs up – like a great benign Whale drawing in – and spitting out – all the sea-float that drifts his way – Critics, Englishmen, Wife-Tarts, Wars – Furious Abuses – Tomato-Sandwiches and Metaphysical Systems. A good-tempered Gargantua – and a Balzacian hewer in the quarries. It ought to cure me of my 'laziness' to watch his massive manner of work. What cyclopian power! The muscles of his intellect are like the back of an athletic torso.

But anyone with less 'vanity' or 'pride' or 'conceit' or 'egotism' – I've never met in my life. He has, in that sense, the magnanimity of the most sweet-tempered village curé. As they said of Goethe – 'who can resist the unselfishness of the man?'

Have heard from Lulu – from *Ascension* – and *St Helena*. He says he is already *much better*.

1915

68

JACK TO FRANCES (in Siena)

Feb 3rd [1915]

Frances – so you are a mother. Well – well – we shall see now our cards
are re-shuffled once again – and to what effect![1]

I would give much to know what has been going on inside that
forehead of yours, it has been so hard for me even to see as often as I
want – with the hair pushed right back. Are you like that at this moment
with the little new one at your side?

There are so many things I want to ask you but you cannot bear them
now.

As for old Louis, I can see him – who better? or more clearly? – playing his role with the atavistic weight of five thousand centuries – So
must Pharaoh King of Egypt have looked when they brought in his first-
born upon a ruddy shield.

Are you happier than you thought you would be? Have you been
allowed to appropriate this new affair with your usual savage clarity of
mind, or are you all blurred and tired and passive and sleepy and yawn-
ing and stretching and very quiet, and ready to drift on, between such
high safe banks, with your boy on your knee and nothing else apparent
or mattering? And are you glad after all that it is a boy?

. . . . . It is a queer business this business of writing to the only person
one has really been (as they say) 'in love with' to congratulate her on the
birth of a child 'who calls Bartram father'! One ought to rage & howl I
suppose – but somehow I can't. You have always been so weirdly
detached from these 'events' – so strangely indifferent to ravishments
outrage invasion that I cannot feel as I should if it were anyone else.

I don't want to hurt the feelings of the Madonna (our dear St Anne),

82

and you mustn't tell her, but I can discern a thin filmy icy *halo of division* even between you and this child of the Holy Ghost.

But I don't think this will mean that you will pinch him[2] or deny him his rights! It'll only mean that you won't let him drown you with his little Louis-hands or drag you down where you cannot see the moon.

Is he strong and very healthy? I wish I knew about weights & measures in regard to infants — but it's no good your telling me how much he weighs, unless you put in something I know in the other scale! Does he weigh as much as twenty oranges? Or as the folio edition of Ben Jonson?

I suppose the 'Christening' will be over by the time you get this? Is it into the Catholic Church — and by a proper priest? And what are their rules, when the parents are heretics?

Was it worse or not as bad as you expected? I suppose worse. But you cannot remember — and I am to be damned for referring to it.

. . . . . Give my god-child a deep direct all-recalling and all-including kiss. Kiss him on the mouth a fierce gentle long kiss and just make him know that it is from his absurd sentimental satyr God-father — for I love you all and really long to have him in my hands — would you trust him to me?

69

JACK TO FRANCES

Memphis
December 28th [1915]

'Humiliated & Offended'[1] was stolen from me in the train by some one or other of a crew of damned Southerners (not black) with whom I had to travel.

I suppose to take away such things as books is an indication of the refinement of the South — they might have taken so many other things!

I can see the Mississippi from my windows — it is the only nice thing I can see. A German policeman of whom I enquired a hotel jeered at me without response — 'We Germans are beating you English — but I am like you — I am not going back there!' How did he know that?

What did Louis say to me as you swept into a car going the opposite way to what I expected? Never has there been such a parting? I was left in the mud; puzzled, bewildered — but not without a little marsh-fire of a mad & drifting signal.[2]

I miss Oliver.

J.

1916

70[1]

JACK TO FRANCES (in New York)

[1916]

. . . . . Wednesday I am quite free of any lecture and could meet you any time you arrive at the Pennsylvania Station. She [his sister, Marian] is longing to have you with her at the cottage. I expect we could make certain between us that you wd. not be alone any night if you and Livio[2] came by yourselves.

The 6th Thursday – Greenwich Village.

7th – Miss Spence.

8th Saturday – *Birmingham* – Pa sleeper both ways near Altoona

9th Sunday – Greenwich again.

Monday free

Tuesday – Miss Marshall in New York in the morning and

Philadelphia – Witherspoon Hall 4 o'clock in the afternoon, subject RICHARD III.

Remember that May's flat is *17 St Luke's Place.*

Write when you get this tomorrow to May's shop – Devonshire Lace Shop,[3] *60 Washington Square* and let me know. Come on Wednesday, sweetheart. The cottage seems a lovely place and the change of air & the country will fix up your cough.

Oh Frances, Frances, if you are bewildered by these two queer beings *we* have to carry about, what am I? But I am not *quite* the same numbskull & I feel very much disinclined to accept this damned business as being 'loved for myself'! No – no! Stay young – stay eighteen – stay the virgin who gave me birth – stay all that & hold me contemptible & curse me but don't love me 'for myself', for it is only the 'Other' in me who is the real thing.

71[1]

JACK TO FRANCES

[November 1916]

[*Part of a letter*]

. . . As to your stricture upon Rodmoor,[2] my brain isn't capable at this moment of any defence – though I feel obscurely that such a defence may be set up. But I never was able to deal with your fierce attacks. They always leave me – hit – puzzled – bewildered – and with a sort of hopeless wish that there were such a thing as the Judgement Day.

But maybe as time goes on the significance of your criticisms will reveal itself to me.

As for *your* story[3] in the Smart Set – I had that sensation of tears in the eyes & the corners of the mouth turning down, in that last scene. Single lines & expressions pleased me well too.

1917

72[1]

JACK TO FRANCES (in Philadelphia)

Hotel Severin, Indianapolis, Indiana
[January 24th 1917]

Frances – I cannot help just making a sign to you now and again as witness that I am not altogether oblivious of the bitter waters you are making your way through.

This is getting towards Oliver's birthday [January 28th], too. Will you have two birthdays then in this frozen time? Or do you intend to hold out till February, the best of all months to be born in (except April).[2] My brain is half-brain these days – I cannot summon enough energy to write even the worst of my 'lyrical verses' – I seem to have lost a certain rebound.

I'm going to lecture for that scoundrel Maurice Browne[3] this week and next, so may meet your phlegmatic lord – I hope so.

Depressing gloom seizes me by the gullet – However you are certainly in a worse plight than I – so enough lamentation. I only just beg you to try and tide over somehow in hope of better days – surely the bitterness of this regimen of Saturn & Uranus cannot last much longer. Just tide it over if you can – there must be some lotus leaves left somewhere. What a world! But you will be restored to us.

73

JACK TO FRANCES

[March 1917]

Thank the Lord! — and a girl[1] too — as you both wanted. God! I am relieved it is all over before I have to leave.

Nunc dimittis — now I can depart in peace — for my Frances is safe with us.

How mad we are — how impossible to calculate our reactions our reversions our returns! Oh how all the old things come back to me at hearing this news — do you think I forget anything? Do you think I do?

I think the 28th is a good number. Will this be another Frances? Will she ever meet my Littleton?[2]

Can't you imagine the gesture with which Lulu will hear the news? As when, in that garden in Seville in a shaky cab, you said to me, 'Tell him that I love my husband — isn't that enough?'[3]

It is perfectly astounding that you — of all people — should be the mother of two children — and yet no doubt the invisible ones know well what they mean by it —

March 30th

This morning arrives your own letter. Frances you are wonderful. Ah, my companion, this letter is like your old self again — everything about it — handwriting style tone feeling — just as you were when I first knew you. This little daughter of yours — I am glad she is pretty — has given you back in her hands five years — a gift my Oliver never gave — he was too wise for that! But this one is less grasping and being a girl she knows what a gift to give her mother. 'Tis extraordinary to me the air of calm and youth and lovely detachment that is about your letter. You have 'drunk your fill of deep — & liquid rest' and you return with that strange exquisite virginal air that is different from everything. I send you two violets, one for the little one, for she seems to have healed some terribly deep lacerations in you.

. . . . . Ha! the old touch again — unconquerable — full of grace and witchery and the wit which is like nothing else. This letter is like what you used to be when you devastated Lulu and me in the Venetia days. I can see you coming out of the bathing place on the Lido! . . . . .

74

JACK TO FRANCES (in Rockaway Beach)

[October? 1917]

Frances, will you & Louis come and see me here? Come over at least for the day.[1]

. . . . . I do want you to see Helen[2] . . . . . The more I see of her the more I realize that she is in many respects out of my reach, just, though not as far or as much as you have always been. I can see that she is restless and unhappy – but I am helpless – & Maurice [Browne] 's fidelity for all its burning candles somehow misses the mark. He is a pathetic being – but I am not sure that Nelly Browne[3] . . . . . isn't more to be pitied. . . . .

Maurice & Nelly *may* be gone – if so we could put you up for the night easily. Helen anyway will be here.[4]

1918

75

JACK TO FRANCES (in Atlantic City)

[New Jersey]
[early in 1918]

. . . . . My sham poems – curse them – aren't as good as I could wish –
but some of them please me – only I wish I could write a few more that
really did. When I am really pleased myself I can afford to submit most
gently to Frances' criticisms, but when I am not quite so well pleased
then I grow touchy. But certainly I enjoy the actual writing of poetry –
sham or otherwise – as I do not enjoy these cursed essays.[1] Why is that?
. . . . . I know I can write essays all right that have a definite quality – and
have moments of doubt about the poetry.

Look here Frances Josefa Gregg don't you you ever get the idea that
Jack can *ever* under any circumstances be caused to *suffer* by any other
girl than you, for he cannot – and so adieu! I should like to have an hour
with your babies now. Love to that great Regardent & Persifleur &
Raconteur with whom it is your caprice to live – & farewell.

76

JACK TO FRANCES (in Rockaway Beach, U.S.A.)

[Burpham] [1]
[April 1918]

At this moment your letter has carried me right over the half of the
confounded world straight to you – and it is you now who are scared
a bit with that curious delicious alarm & curiosity and unconscious

bewilderment that a girl even with your brain feels when she has made her lover want her to the limit. Yes, you have drawn me to you straight as the very dart of Sagittarius. Now where are you reading this? Is this paper on your lap in the garden? On a dusty road bank? Is it about the 28 of April [Frances's birthday]? Well! wherever it is, surely it is possible for me to get at your lips and kiss you long & long —

There — you see — at a word — when you stop beating me & smile — I feel in a second all the old mania for you. This letter has made me extremely happy.

You see I talk plain words — This is not Jack Welsh rhetoric[2] — it isn't! it isn't! This is Signore Jack hugging Frances under the dusty bank — hugging & hugging her — & hugging till she is utterly out of breath — with naughtiness he hugs her — I admit it — but also — but also because she is

Frances!

77

JACK TO FRANCES (in Rockaway Beach)

3 Greenhill Terrace, Weymouth[1] [Dorset, England]
[July? 1918]

. . . . . I was medically examined in Brighton — Brighton! — a week ago. Evidently this new conscription is for military service only, & if you are discharged from that you are quite free — as Theodore is. The grading A, B, & C has to do with the time to elapse before you are actually called up.[2]

Tom Jones is graded C (or 3) & at present remains at his office. Curiously enough I was remitted or respited for 10 days & then given a letter to the army tubercular specialist at Chichester where I have to be re-examined next Tuesday.

The Brighton doctor said he thought he detected tubercular signs in my lungs & couldn't take the responsibility of passing me straight off. He said I ought to have been more careful after that operation.

But apparently I was not turned down on the strength of having that operation or because of my stomach at all — but on the rather surprising ground of this slight tubercular suspicion.

Well — we shall see! I don't think it at all impossible that I may yet be in khaki.

Littleton Charles[3] has been very worried about this business. He was passed graded A (or 1). The Education Department's recommendation to get him off apparently failed — for it is clear that these different Departments do not always work in harmony — & the military authorities are quite independent of the other bureaus and ministries.

His appeal to the local tribunal at Sherborne failed too — but he appealed, still further up, to the County tribunal — & apparently this final appeal (combined with the Education Department's protest) *have* exempted him — for he now writes that he has received his complete discharge from Dorchester. So there it is! And you may believe (knowing my foolish pride in these little things, or my romantical & ill-balanced vanity!) this business of appealing wd be singularly distasteful to me.

Indeed it is an even question whether, if this Chichester doctor does pass me, I shall have the gall to appeal — I can't tell — it will reproduce my old dilemma & indecision — only on more definite & narrow grounds.

Of course my wife[4] will fight me furiously to do so & regard me as an incredible & cruel dolt if I don't — And maybe *so I shall* be if I don't — yet — it will be the devil of thing for me to do — humiliating, to my fantastic disposition, more than anyone can believe!

I am going to stay with Theodore [Powys] today till Monday. Yesterday I had tea with Hardy in Dorchester. He was 78 last birthday (June 2nd). Apparently he *did* read 'Wood & Stone'.[5] I did not dislike his new wife at all.[6]

Well, my dear, a kiss to Oliver & love to Louis & Betty. Meanwhile — here's my withered hand in your funny hand — a picture for our Toledean.[7]

1919

JACK TO FRANCES (in Philadelphia)

Hotel St Francis [San Francisco]
May 5th [1919]

Well, I've had a sad morning with Sara.[2] Poor wretch! She told me the whole appalling story of her son's death – how she was pinned under the car and heard him groaning near her and couldn't move till she knew he was dead and kept calling and getting no answer. In the end I came to the conclusion that she really had suffered nearly to the limit and that it was brutal in me to do anything but just listen and simply try to understand it.

Then she said to me, 'You have completely changed – you are a different person.'

And then I prayed to my 'Daimon' (who has its forehead concealed) and you said, 'Tell the woman *why* you are different – Tell her why, and let your pride and reserve go to the devil!'

And so I did. And I think it was well that I did, for it seemed to turn the current of her thoughts and it was a test too and a severe test, my girl, of the way you wish me to be; for to say anything about my feelings to her meant that 'poetry' and all that kind of romantic reserve – you know? – had indeed to be thrown aside – and to be just simply – well! like anyone else to whom the gods have allowed happiness to before it was too late. It gave me the oddest feeling but I am glad I did it, though even now it still remains so alien a thing from my constructed self of years that I can scarcely believe that the voice speaking is my own voice.

. . . . . Do you want me to send you 'Marius the Epicurean'[3] for you to read every word of, as I have just done? I believe it will strike you as never before if you will let me.

I never asked you how much you wanted to go to England and exactly all you have felt about this going to England – you must tell me that.

Gertrude [Powys] writes to me that she advises me not to come home as they are all so poor – I do not quite understand it. Does she mean that they couldn't afford to keep me at Weymouth if I came? She says that they are still only allowed one ounce of butter a week. So things don't sound very cheerful over there just now.

Dorothy Powys[4] couldn't find any place in London and is back with them at Weymouth while Bertie sleeps in his office.

. . . . . I have begun revising my book [*The Complex Vision*] .

Kiss me sweetheart – for morning, noon and night I want you.

79

JACK TO FRANCES (in Philadelphia)

c/o S. Field
Thursday, May the eighth [1919]

At last I have got your letter – or letters rather – *three* in one envelope. The relief is extreme. I have the sense of recovering from an anaesthetic – no, I mean from some sort of fever. Oh I don't know what I mean but the relief is beyond words. The panic went far, so you must forgive my telegraphing – I ought not to have – but I couldn't stand any more silence.

. . . . . The 3000 miles between us are like a string which is sewn up one side of a gash – and when you write the string is loosened and the gash can be temporarily closed for a few hours.

Oh the relief that you are not ill – but actually alive!

Stay alive a little while longer, sweetheart, and so will I; for I think if we only stay alive a little longer, what now seems so difficult as to be nearly impossible will change its character – we shall not have been quite trapped.

Do you recall? – it was in that wood we got to, far beyond the station, when we went to hunt for Lulu's cottage – and quite cold and calmly there, with you, and without any fevered impulse and certainly no sort of 'gesture', I discovered that I did want nothing so much as to live with you and your mother and children. I want to have Lulu within reach and I want to have an understanding with my son and I want to make Mrs

Powys happy — but what I want now, in cold unimpulsive deliberate blood, is to live with you *and* your mother and children. To live with you alone (since you *have* her and them) is a fairy story — too remote from reality for me to get any satisfaction now even imagining it. You are what you are with the children and her — I know that; for that is the fact. But as long as I am with you — if you had three mothers and six children — in reality we should be alone together, as heaven knows we are even now alone together, over all these miles. And you know me well enough to know that Livio suits me uncommonly well as long as I hadn't the responsibility of exercising authority over him.

Whether I should be approved of by Betty is more doubtful; but it wouldn't be my fault if I weren't. If only I had money; if only I had money; if only I had money. Then everything would be possible.

. . . . . We are two queer trees flapping at each other with our top branches — but now our roots have twisted themselves together underground. This is no image. This is the fact and that is why when the tops of those trees are blown so far apart by the wind and all their branches creak and the trunks creak, the root, which is now the same, just bleeds.

. . . . . It may of course easily be that this love of ours — I refuse to call it mad — I think it is the sanest thing I, at any rate, have ever known — is destined to have to wait for its satisfaction one year, two years, three years — longer even. It may easily be that you will die or I shall die. We are taking a dangerous risk in any delay. I know it. But I think now we look at the situation almost exactly in the same way — and want almost exactly the same thing. It's not a matter of conscience or code that we have to think about but just plain material obstacles among which are the various unhappinesses which depend on us — but of these last we have to think rationally and not absurdly — and we have to kerb our sense of proportion where such happinesses are concerned. For me to sacrifice your air and breath and freedom to this or the other slight sentiment would be a cowardice which, if I am guilty of, and as you know I *am* capable of incredible cowardice, would brand my soul and maybe wither it. On the other hand — but why go on?

Oh you shall have me 'naked' enough, soul of my soul, you shall have me as I am without restraint — without anything 'guarded'.

I was awake several times during this night and so would you be, the night of the 7th. of May. At 12 (your 3) I was awake thinking and at 4 (your 7) I was awake thinking and between then I woke up and thought. It was a night of thought — but I held you in my arms all the time and now and then I stopped thinking and made love to you and kissed you and kissed you and kissed you — held the back of your head with my hands and kissed you — and then with my mouth upon your right breast I drank up your soul till our souls mixed together. Oh Frances my love I want you so frightfully — I know I am dull, prudent, cowardly, material-istic, self-centred and all the rest but the love you have somehow roused in me is very love itself — love of your body, of your inmost identity, and my dear, my dear, I will honestly try to make it reach out from you to all the others. . . . .

Oh the tangle of it all — the bitter tangle!

Did you think I would 'hate' you for the gall and wormwood of that passage about the Frances-puppet out of her box and back in her box?

Girl! Listen — Has my vice been transformed for nothing? These grotesque self-scourgings who but I can understand them? I feel their lash thro' and thro'; I am the witness — and oh I love you so — against your naked breast — press me to you — hard!

80

JACK TO FRANCES (in Philadelphia)

Hotel St Francis, San Francisco
May 9th [1919]

. . . . . Isn't it sickening that the only real obstacle to our being together — short of my taking you & your babes for good and all — is just simply want of money? If I had my former income out here I could sail with you, stay near you, find you a cottage: everything! I know I am more wordly-prudent, cold, cautious, selfish, unselfish, cowardly, timid, and all the rest of it, than you — but I know also that when once I see a clear aim before me I have a certain power of overturning obstacles. I am not, sweetheart — with all my cowardice and timidity and fear of drastic action — altogether devoid of certain formidableness & obstinacy — if I see things clearly.

. . . . . In my early lecturing days I recollect borrowing from some-where a comment on a different tone of that pretty fool Romeo from his former protestations, when he suddenly heard that his small wench was as they supposed dead and buried — Well! one lives to learn the pinch of one's fine-spun theories. . . . .

Here you & I are — you just at the end of your girlhood and I in the middle of middle age — and we know now that we are made to fit into each other like a classic knife into a classic sheath or like a certain hand to a certain instrument.

. . . . . My audiences are small. Mr Wood.[1]

[*Photograph of Erskine Wood and Sara Bard Field*]

and his guarantors will lose about three hundred unless they pick up quickly. I certainly have not the shadowest chance of making anything over that 100 £ promised to Burpham.

If only I could get work in England!

. . . . . Here in this room is a coat-stand – let me hang up the corduroy dress and the green petticoat – here is a big mirror for you to comb your hair. I'll unlace your boots – Sit on the bed – There! There's the pillow for your head – Oh damn imagination – why does it do so much and yet so little? Do you know I tried to say prayers and found myself praying *to* you instead of about you. Yes – I knelt down. It was quaint.

I've just been reading in the Symposium what that old comedian Aristophanes[2] says about love and I'm damned if he doesn't hit the mark with his one person cut in half or his two half-people hunting about for each other and begging Hephaistos[3] to hammer them together. Socrates'[4] speech comes in all right *afterwards*! But no! – to confess the truth – it falls a bit flat.

. . . . . Shall I confess something? That normal sensuality – what an absurd word, what a heavy word for so simple a thing! – has become a troubling craving for you, for your arms – and I mustn't think of your hands or I can't stand it – for your naked body. Never before have I thought of a thing like that – never before! But you are Frances and I now undress you and kiss you from head to foot – but only to be so gentle with you in the end, my life, my love –

81

JACK TO FRANCES (in Philadelphia)

Hotel St Francis
Sunday [May 1919]

. . . . . Oh it is too good to be true that you really have decided *not* to sail. I shall never be able to make you know the huge wave of happiness that floods me at this news. It certainly revealed to me that there must be at least one of the 'invisible ones' who at this hour has heard my prayer.

Once more my satyr-legs crooked themselves before the unknown –

this time in pure, unalloyed gratitude.

While you are here & I am here, anything is possible – By the lord, I forgot 'the dog'![1] But here & now I solemnly include him – bless his ancestral and woolly heart.

. . . . . After all, when my son is a little older[2] he will have intelligence enough not to wish me to 'ruin my life' and, cowardly clod that I am, in some respects no-one could deny that I am a sort of reed or medium for the gods to blow through – and, to keep this reed clear & unperverted, a little happiness surely is necessary – and no-one could say that you would spoil my soul with easy comfort!

A little happiness – I say 'little' but I tremble to think how much! . . . . .

There! I have got you in that chimney corner. Now your head is leaning back and I am kissing your mouth and have my hands on your neck – on your neck and at the edge of your dress where your neck comes out of your dress – just the tips of my fingers there – but all the feeling I have is magnetizing you, releasing you, making you defenceless – giving yourself up to me – and I am loving, with love, like I did in the wood –

82

JACK TO FRANCES (in Philadelphia)

[May 1919]

. . . . I think the moment has come when we must not delay any longer.

Even for this I must not sacrifice Mrs Powys' and my son's £400 a year – you feel that just as I do. You do not wish me to lose touch with my son and his mother. If she wd. divorce me I should be ready for that – But I know she won't. Well – are you prepared to risk it?

Could you get anything yourself to help our ménage? Could Amelia[1] deal with the babies while you were out, if what you got was not writing you could do at home? Could you, if I gave myself up entirely to you and wrote for money under your direction, so direct my writing that in addition to Mrs Powys' £400 or £500 I could add in my inadequate way to your support?

And about Louis? Shall I write to him? Will he sail alone? What will he want? Will he be ready to give you up if we manage, between us, to support his children? Will he make a magnanimous and generous 'gesture' – old villain! – or will he . . . but this I *cannot* believe for one moment –

want to suggest taking your children? Of course if he took a cruel line like that we should have to submit I suppose – for the children's sake – for they must be dealt with, whatever happens. But I never shall even contemplate his threatening a thing like that.

I pray and pray that you will decide that it is really possible for us to live together except when I have to lecture.

. . . . . I could write essays, articles, short stories, etc., etc., etc., at top speed and you should revise them and type them – and some we'll write the other way round – I'll revise yours.

Our novels would have to wait a bit or we could give brief time to them as well.

These 'practical' letters are the truest love-letters I have ever written!

You must not be jealous if, when I make my yearly voyage to see my son, Lulu goes with me.

Oh, my dear, my dear, the happiness of it is more than I can believe possible.

Of course if with your help I could make money by writing – I should be less dependent upon any kind of organisation that might object to my private life!

But, as Sara [Bard Field] says, most of the places where I lecture do not worry about such things and it will have to be my object to get more and more in touch with the general public; specially of Radicals, Jews, Bolsheviks, etc. and drop the other sort of audiences.

I am against your risking having another child. We must put that out of the question I think, don't you?

. . . . . Would you have any feeling of an uneasy kind about the attitude of your acquaintances and your mother's acquaintances to your being Frances Gregg who lives with Jack Powys?

I hope you have already – or someone for you – secured a lower berth from Chicago to San Francisco on the Overland train[2]. . . . .

83

JACK TO FRANCES (in Philadelphia)

Hotel St Francis
May 20 [1919]

. . . . . My Frances! you must indeed have smiled a little whimsically – I wonder if you'll mention that to me? – at my suggestion that *you* should 'work' in order that *I* might still be able to support my family! And you all the while so seriously ill – a nice kind of lover I am – but I know you'll forgive me.

I shall have orchids for my lady your mother – with little silvery objects small as bits of tiny seeds for Betty to pick up off rosewood floors – and for Livio huge illustrated folios of Undine and Theodoric the Icelander and the Little Duke and the Arabian Nights and the dramatic works of god.

Whatever is yours – Ezra [Pound] even – yes, even Ezra himself – that belongs to you and that you care for and do not wish to be parted from I am prepared to make 'permanent arrangements' to include.

As I wrote, a window – some window – was open and a peculiar smell of new-mown hay came in. . . . .

Sara [Bard Field] has just gone to the Hospital – I pray it may be for only a short time but the doctors do not really seem able to tell what is wrong with her.

You will be enchanted with the scenery and the climate here – I have in mind a lovely retreat where Livio will be in his element and where you will get well very quick.

Come soon, my dear love, for I want you. If you don't come soon I shall get thin! . . . . .

J.

I am extremely interested in those clippings about your grandmother[1] – She now becomes a real person to me.

84

JACK TO FRANCES (in Philadelphia)

May 20th [1919]

Telegram:[1]

HAVE BEEN LOS ANGELES HENCE DELAY REPLYING LOUIS OF COURSE SISTER IT IS WORTH TO ME IF ONLY TILL JULY PLEASE COME SOON AS POSSIBLE SO TO MAKE IT LONG AS POSSIBLE THIS CLIMATE WILL DO BOTH YOU AND OLIVER GOOD WHY NOT START QUITE SOON IN A FEW DAYS.

85

JACK TO FRANCES (in Philadelphia)

May 23rd [1919]

. . . . . Oh God – you who I prove in my philosophical book[1] cannot possibly exist – bring Frances and Livio safely here! Come back to existence just for that & then you can die again for eternity. . . . .

Love kills enjoyment of love and becomes an ancient craving like the exhaustion of physical hunger. . . . .

But things look promising as to my being able to keep you properly here without any economic struggle. My work seems to be growing.[2] . . . . .

86

JACK TO FRANCES (in Philadelphia)

New York
[November 6th 1919]

. . . . . Remember – these last days are *mine*. If you came on Monday by twelve o'clock we could go together to the Cunard office in New York . . . only let me know in advance about how much money I must secure from Arnold for you, so that we shall have it in our hands on Monday to pay the difference – and get the cabin. . . . .

87

JACK TO FRANCES (in Philadelphia)

[November 1919]

. . . . . It occurs to me to point out to you that afterwards at sea you might be sorry if you had not snatched at this chance of our being together – try & get a perspective on it. It is really more important that you & I should have a week of complete harmony, to look back upon it to help us endure existence, than you should jump on a box for the fifth time or put Teddy into a new straight-jacket or decide whether this broken perambulator or this broken noah's ark ought to be tied up with red ribbon or purple ribbon.

. . . . . So come on Monday, my dear — my dear!

88

JACK TO FRANCES (in Philadelphia)

[November 1919]

. . . . . I miss the taste of salt and the darkened sky and the slippery clouds.

Well — there it is — But I can of course only, as I say, get an intimation of what I'm going to feel when you really have sailed. I may feel quite differently — I don't know — but I swear you shall not, *shall not*, get ill — it shall not be.

I hope I shall hear from May some good news of you & I should be over-joyed if I found you were really already in her cottage — but I fear that is too good.

89

JACK TO FRANCES (in Philadelphia)

See enclosed   17 St Luke's Place
postal order.   [Postmarked 'New York. November 7' 1919]

. . . . . I couldn't send more than 30$ & this is a pinch at this moment because Arnold gave 50 for my journey tomorrow & back, & it runs it close, but I can get them maybe to pay in cash & I've got my ticket there all right anyhow.

. . . . . Oh, it'll be lovely having you safe in May's cottage.

. . . . . I will wait at the top of those *iron* stairs where you come up from the train — but if by any chance we miss — for there are *several* iron stairs — look about for me a little at the top — and then, if you don't see me, make a porter carry your things to *Information Counter* in the great main hall where the ticket offices are.[1]

J.

I may get a glimpse of Gilbert Cannan[2] tonight. He has made great friends with Pete[3] —but otherwise has avoided publicity unlike Dunsany[4] and Hugh Walpole[5] who are also here. He seems to have been very nice to Dorothy[6] too.

90[1]

JACK TO FRANCES

Monday. December 1st [1919]

I collected Betty's doll out of the garden — also her Jack in The Box from the 'Licite'.[2] You didn't leave many odds and ends behind — only a piece of frayed bordering of a dress or petticoat. James [Henderson] called up in the evening, w[h] was very good of him, to tell me how you had gone & that all was well. I read in the paper however on the Sunday morning of the Adriatic being in collision off the Statue of Liberty — but your ship was not mentioned. All that Liveright[3] wanted was to talk to me about his own affairs — he has an idea of getting *Freud*[4] over here to lecture. I turned him over of course to Arnold [Shaw] — Freud w[d] be a good card in America I should imagine — & if Arnold manages him, in association with Liveright, he ought to benefit considerably I should fancy.

. . . . . There is certainly a ghost in May's cottage now — it scolds. It laughs disdainfully. It covers its head. It stands at the window. I do not vex it. I give it bits of things to amuse it while I am away.

Love to Louis.

91

JACK TO FRANCES (in London)

[December 1919]

When you actually read these words, sitting with bare arms perhaps — oh so well do I know that look of your arms — do just love me very much for this single moment.

Oh Frances darling don't be too cynical and unbelieving — This is a true thing that I am telling you now that I am sad for you and homesick for you — your queer hands. Better are they to me and will be always than all else — are they like withered oak leaves? — so are mine — I wish they were even now entangled. I feel a wicked desire for you now —such as to the end of my life I shall feel. How that wicked desire had interrupted our conversations ere now! May it do so again. I can't help it — you are the one thing that will always attract me like that more than all. But at this moment my desire for you that way is made gentle and sad by my longing for you the other way, the good way, and there it is!

Come, my darling, my true and only choice, don't let my blundering spoil your recognition that I love you. . . . .

You have said before now that you wanted just a huge lot of love of the simplest kind —well! here it is. . . . .

Frances —	I love you.
Jack —	I love you.
Frances —	Is that all?
Jack —	*Now*—do you believe me?
Frances —	I have no breath left —
Jack —	Isn't it odd that we should want each other so and then have gone and spoilt so much?
Frances —	We are mad —both of us—and very silly —
Jack —	I will never again say that I have no heart. It's easy to say that when I've got you in the next room —But now — I think I must after all have a tiny bit of heart and it is down your neck somewhere; or under your waistband.
Frances —	You are a fool —
Jack —	I can't be quite such a fool as I look or I should never have got you!
Frances —	Have you got me?
Jack —	I've got something.
Frances —	It isn't me!
Jack —	You know very well it is! You are a Coquette. You are very much of a girl in spite of your forehead —
Frances —	Kiss me —
Jack —	A good kiss?
Frances —	Oh! I don't know —

. . . . Has all our rending and tearing left us still vague as to where we stand with regard to any common idea? I cannot tell. But I know I greatly miss those talks of ours that made the way, wherever it was, vanish into nothing. Probably it is out of those talks —in Germantown — in Venice — in Rockaway —that something has emerged to which we both respond – but so to speak respond *under fire* from bitter darts of other moods, when we were not talking like that. . . . .

Bless you –

92

JACK TO FRANCES (in London)

Xmas Eve. 11.30pm. [1919]

It is snowing heavily, quite deep now – I have May's room to myself for four or five nights as she has gone to the country. . . . .

I see that Andreyev[1] is dead, having laid his curse on the Revolution. I send you a 'New Republic' with a notice on him and also the best analysis of Wilson[2] I have ever read.

I went with Fania this afternoon to her Gorki Play[3] – 'A Night's Lodging' – which was certainly the best thing I have ever seen on the stage in America. But the audience was very small. I am going to have my Xmas dinner with Dorothy [de Poillier] tomorrow. I have just had a letter from Sara [Bard Field] which says, 'I love Frances more deeply than either she or you understand.' I think I leave for the Middle West about the 2nd of Jan. Of course as far as I am capable of being 'in love' with anyone I am in love with you – but I know only too well how little is the satisfaction to be got out of that, considering my unlucky disposition. But we may just as well note it, by the way! Dorothy has half a bottle of gin – she has asked Helen & Conroy[4] to come in to-morrow afternoon before they go out into the country to share drinking it – *That* marriage seems extraordinarily harmonious!

May is certainly lucky to have found this little room. As I now look at my watch it is exactly 12 o'clock – so it is already Xmas Day! Get Mrs Wilkinson[5] to repeat to you the words of that carol called 'King Wenceslas' and above all note its tune. Yes, it is queer how numbed and dazed and frozen my senses are as far as amorous desire of any sort is concerned. I feel as if I were already a very old man in that matter.

May sent Dr Thomas[6] to see me about that dizziness and he says it is due to abnormally low blood-pressure – whatever that means.

93

JACK TO FRANCES

17 St Luke's Place
Dec 30th. [1919]

Don't forget to tell me every kind of detail about your new existence. Is the house near or on Hampstead Heath, & what kind of place is Hampstead Heath? And have you got into touch with Hilda [Doolittle] yet? And have you got any time or any mood for going on with your novel?

I am sending Maugham's book[1] w^h will interest you *profoundly*. He has advanced a lot since 'Human Bondage'. . . . .

1920

94

Toledo, Ohio
[January 13th 1920]

I've just got your letter about the house. Thank the Lord! It really sounds far beyond my expectation.[1] If you've got garden enough to plant in that's all you can manage now if you're to be the gardener. Are there bulbs in it, snowdrops and crocuses? And daffodils? And have you a lilac bush? But the open fields you speak of sound excellent – and a stream, too. Well! I am *delighted* beyond words – Frances . . . . . I wonder what bird that was? Wait till you hear the first blackbird. They have yellow beaks, and a song more sadly happy or happily sad than any other music – the nearest approach I suppose to the sound of a real flute of all bird's notes. The thrush's song is like the nightingale and comparatively traditional and ordinary . . . . . I suppose there may even be minnows in that brook you speak of. . . . . .

But this business of your cough is bad. . . . . Pray heaven Bernie [O'Neill] by this time has lessened it. . . . . How excellent that you really are going to have a maid. From Suffolk? Well! I dare say she will not then be surprised at the little ways of the Master. . . . . .[2]

I am hugely amused at Lulu's [Llewelyn Powys's] siege of you at once. . . . .

I am reading the last volume of Dorothy Richardson's long novel[3] which begins with Pointed Roofs. She is English, but Knopf publishes her books over here. This book, 'The Tunnel', in its opening chapters, follows *your* method so very closely – the same hesitant scrupulous obscurity–you must see it. Yes, I have become quiet, reserved, self-centred –a little *dull*, may-be. Like old Falstaff when Prince Hal became king!

107

. . . . . Tap Betty's head with your head. Hug Livio. Kiss Amelia – and tell old Louis to b - - - r himself. But I am pleased with him over this house.

95

JACK TO FRANCES (in Hampstead)

The Stratford Hotel, Chicago
Jan 26th [1920]

. . . . . I've just been to see Raymond Johnson (who did my picture, you know)[1] and he has some wonderful pictures in his studio. One he calls 'Shylock' but it is really an imaginative concentration of all the most formidable qualities of all the Jews in the world since Abraham. I want him to change the name. What historic Jew is there who played the part of a Machiavellian Grand Vizier to some Jewish Conqueror? Judas Maccabaeus?[2]

He also has a picture of a pile of rocks by themselves on the top of a hill covered with snow that is a masterpiece to me. . . . .

That El Greco in this art gallery is a tiresome uninteresting picture.[3]

. . . . . Arnold was well advised to get this Mr Spring[4] into the office
. . . . .

96

JACK TO FRANCES (in Hampstead)

Hotel Mercury, Evansville, Indiana
Jan 27th [1920]

. . . . . I am anxiously awaiting your account of that first encounter with Ezra [Pound].

I must certainly have been called back with a magical jerk from the hills you speak of, by these two letters of yours, for I can see nothing but your head and Livio's and Betty's nodding mischievously and mysteriously at me from behind a row of willows on the edge of the Ohio River. Maybe that picture of me that Betty kisses and beats has a real magnetic link with me, and when she beats it I am prodded and pinched and knocked about in these places and when she kisses it I am allowed to find a quiet path or a silent corner. If she put it down her neck no doubt I should think of moss and celandines and be given tea that wasn't Oolong or Formosa.

[*page missing*]

. . . . . According to your picture of yourself (from my point of view) your bones are still covered – but alas! I suspect that the reality may be more like this –

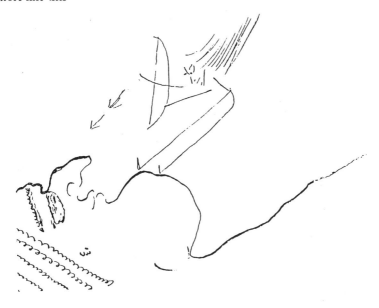

God! you have given me a picture of Hilda.[1] She must have been over-powered or overshadowed by Bobby [Perceval Roberts] and the general confusion when I saw her on that wild morning of your departure from Victoria,[2] for I do not recall her beauty. Personally I still hold the queer view – if you'll let me say it – that you are *yourself* from head to foot *far* more beautiful than any Hilda. But it is not exactly what I want to think of just now, this business of comparison – for I know well enough how you have killed my appreciation of other women. You have killed – oh well: let it go. But you may say to yourself that, whether it's 'beauty' or not, the covering of your bones is what makes other persons something different. I think the stuff, out of which they managed to make you, cost a little more or was bought – those 'goods' – at a better shop. The texture is more refined.

I am worried about Louis being bored and discomforted by that office.[3]

97

JACK TO FRANCES (in Hampstead)

[*c.* February 17th 1920]

[*The opening page is missing*]
. . . . . God! girl, but it's awful weather here now — you're well out of this continual cold & snow, though I fear the rain is almost as bad for you; though, once upon a time, you did write about lying along the rain remembering Egypt.

I am working my way slowly out of the cart-tracks, trailing my crushed leg behind me — in other words Mr Spring's appearance in the office is already beginning to effect wonders. It's the best stroke Arnold's ever done getting him in — all glory to hunch-backs! Yes — things are beginning to pick up splendidly, my swallow-tailed sea-hawk.[1]
. . . . . I must, by cook or by hook, get Littleton[2] up to Corpus in October.
. . . . . I have more or less fixed up the novel in my mind — and it now remains to really and truly begin it . . . . .

98

JACK TO FRANCES (in Hampstead)

[*Printed*:] Hotel Seneca, Rochester N.Y.
[*c.* March 1920]

[*The opening page is missing*]
. . . . . Isn't it Rochefoucauld[1] who says that girls prefer to be people's *last* loves to their first. Well I begin very clearly to see as I get older — that you have spoilt me for ever for all others. They are so dull — my girl — so dull & not one of them can even understand their own business. They can't even *provoke* — far less lead on, unmask & *betray*! & they have no *spirit*, no curiosity — no childishness — no naturalness & no *bitterness*!
. . . . . I ought to land in England about the 28th of April. What *does*

that date suggest??[2] A kiss to *Oliver* —Ha! Ha!

99

JACK TO FRANCES (in Church Walk, Kensington, London)

Sept 6 [1920]

. . . . . 'They're none of them a patch on Frances' —said Lulu[1] yesterday — 'They all pale before Frances'. So you see my bad taste in not being entirely and absolutely faithful to you is not let off!

But at the same time Lulu makes love to everybody within reach. He disparages Helen[2] — perhaps because her 'enceinte' condition renders her 'hors de combat'. He likes Lola [Catesby Jones] very much — She has been kind to him & has lent him a type-writer to learn on.

He likes Dorothy de Poillier[3] and makes love to her after his manner . . . . .

I want to see the boot lace again—I want to see the holes in the stockings — I want to see that very nice thin dress again that you never w^d put on just because I liked it . . . . .

. . . . . This long separation is the devil —I can't understand it — But now I have your hand —

Love to Louis —

100

JACK TO FRANCES (in Church Walk, Kensington)

439 W. 21 St.
[September 14th 1920]

. . . . . I have *not once* felt malice to you — since I said good-bye that day and I teased you & loved you.

. . . . . Two of these Jewish lectures are successful — the Rand School & the Labor Temple — the rest can hardly be called that, though their expense is carried by the two I have named. I have an advanced copy of the C.V. [*The Complex Vision*] but it isn't out till the 25 or Oct 1st — There are 18 errata.

The word 'Perapity' once for 'Personality'. Perapity! It is all the same —

and ob! in place of Om! for the muttering to the unknown —

'Ob! Ob!' do you hear me crying that in my bath as I dip my face in deep & hot water w^h used to tickle Livio so?

I do pray the children are well. . . . .

Here now — listen — on this day, Sept 14, a month from when she sailed — I announce to you *that I know you for what you are*.

Now then, don't go thinking any more that you've never had a lover who knew you really for the thing you know yourself to be. I know it's mad that I should have acted as I have, you being what you are. . . . .

101

JACK TO FRANCES (in Church Walk, Kensington)

439, W. 21st. N.Y.
Oct 4 [1920]

I am so impressed by the way Lulu is always reverting to you and keeping up my standard of human or at least feminine personality by reference to you. . . . .

102

JACK TO FRANCES (in Church Walk, Kensington)

Hotel Hermitage, Nashville, Tennessee
[October 1920]

I've been dreaming about you with extraordinary vividness lately. What is up?[1] I hope all is well with you?. . . . .

There's an allusion to Louis in Ellis's[2] 'Life of Meredith'.[3] Lulu is reviewing that book. It doesn't make you *like* George Meredith very much. I've got another volume of D[orothy]. Richardson for you. . . . .

You must have been going thro' some mental and physical agitation these last days. I have not been left alone by your spirit night or day lately. I hope all is right; or as right as it usually is? Of course, Bernie [O'Neill] is attracted to you — but awfully shy of you. I know that well enough.

I have decided to call this Sussex and New York novel — 'After my

Fashion'⁴ — I don't know whether it will be taken yet. Its chief fault is longwindedness. It isn't fantastic — at all. It is in a quieter vein. Marian [Powys] is making a terrific plunge in moving her shop up town — but she has a wonderful head for business. . . . .

I am going before long to Joplin.⁵ God! I must be careful what I say! Fancy your taking Joplin seriously for a moment. Heigh ho! What a funny world. Here is a very wicked kiss for you — with a different one added to it, like a sigh. Well I certainly hope you are now and then happy. John the son of Charles.

103

JACK TO FRANCES (in Kensington)

Lake Erie College, Painesville, Ohio
Nov 10 [1920]

. . . . . I think you still like *getting* letters — you queer one — or am I mistaken?. . . . .

. . . . . Do you know I think we have suffered from the fact that our peculiar link with each other has been so damned simple — just a deep dark-blue thread — among all the other colours. . . . . We are just so fatally land and sea, earth and water, the perilous chemical opposites that always mean *foam* when they meet — but sometimes also that line of — what do they call it? — *windrift* of little broken shells. Well enough of that — We are not by the sea at this moment. This is that wooden inland pier at Rockaway and you are in your corduroy dress — and I hug you very hard —

104

JACK TO FRANCES (in Paris)¹

The Stratford Hotel, Chicago
Nov 22 [1920]

. . . . . You told me as we walked thro' Hyde Park together when we first met this last summer how you loved London and what you loved in it — just when we came, it was, to that sudden open-air play, do you remember?. . . . ,

Do you like the French? . . . . . Have you penetrated that curious barrier that they always set up? The possessive instinct of the English may well be as you would call it 'cloddish', but what of that instinct in the French – eh?

And I should like to know, you beautiful queer one, whether ever it happens that you have a moment's home-sickness for America?[2] . . . . . Oh and I want so very much to know what you think of the books of *Marcel Proust.*[3] I've just come across him and am reading him with *much difficulty*[4] but a lot of interest. The books are so beautifully printed – They ought to be very deep, thrilling and calculated, to be worthy of this charming setting . . . . . so far the soul of it has escaped me.

I bought *L'Enfer*[5] & read it this week. Naturally I am too 'degenerate' or as you would say – any bad word that you think I should like least – to do justice to this mania for embraces carried *quite* so far – 'All is well, though man oft doubts, & ever best' etc etc. But that passage about the 'sonnerie' of the angelus bells contrasted with the clock striking *eight* pleased me very greatly, and so did all those poetical and profound comments on the little broken cries of the various lovers – such as 'toujours', 'jamais', 'néant' and so forth – especially that 'if they knew' and 'when, when will it be allowed in the sun?' of those two ambiguous ones who *may* be two girls – *That* piece, & the old man with the priest, were what interested me most. But the whole book interested me – That sudden swing round to *Kant*,[6] for example, after the piling up of space upon space. . . . .

105

JACK TO FRANCES
(redirected to Poste Restante, Beaune, Cote d'Or)[1]

The Stratford Hotel, Chicago
Nov 29 [1920]

. . . . . I try to think, really think, of a new book that *shall* be good . . . but you know I don't believe I can think *in vacuo* like that.

I suppose the only thing for me to do is to start writing – at *anything* and then as I go on put into it what experiences and intimations and feelings are gouged out of me by some demon in the actual process of putting down words.

. . . . . Yes, I keep trying to think of a line, of a start, that once entered on, will send a dredge down into the deepest part of my mind and fish something up, *anything* as long as it isn't just lust or just dullness. I can see from where I write now two little human figures – a man and a woman walking by the edge of the lake – there! they've disappeared now. In *an old park* solitaire et glassée Tous forms have tout à l'heurs passées. Littleton Alfred [his son] seems very happy at Cambridge. . . . . I am longing to get a letter from him. I want a letter from him very much. I will observe with interest how Livio and you understand each other as time goes on. Of course a mother and son have a great advantage over a father and son. Perhaps if I just start *anything* and pour out all my malice, misery, disgust, all my desires, all my cravings, all my fainting will towards the good, all the rest of it – I shall be driven on somehow. Here I sit at this writing-table and stare at darkness, fog, smoke, grey water like dirty ice and infinite mud and wish that I had the power to drive on doggedly heedless of all surroundings – in the real mood of 'Ich kann nicht anders'.[2] I have been looking at Rembrandt's[3] picture in this Chicago Art Museum of 'A young Girl at a Window'. . . . . I suppose you don't by any chance remember that picture?

It seems to bring to my mind long days of happy deep continuous obstinate labour, towards an end that is superior to all opinions.

Two men are following one another now along that dingy lake-line – now the train smoke hides them too. It does me good when you write that I am 'the silent companion of your days'. Oh I am, I am, my dear; I am that!. . . . .

106

JACK TO FRANCES (in Beaune)

The Stratford Hotel, Chicago
Dec 13th [1920]

. . . . . I feel a bit anxious because it's a long time now since I heard from your mother. In fact it was you yourself I heard last from in a letter which I guard. Do you remember that line of yours about 'guarding your dead by the water' and that other about 'lying on the rain' – no! – *'along the rain'*? What a queer thing memory is! Whenever I write to you so many fantastic things recur – trees, always trees. Once we buried something under a tree, and when we last met we picked oak leaves. Merlin and Vivian – but *she* put him into a hollow tree for ever and ever – where

she could only go – no one else – and gibe at him and gibber at him.[1]
Now & then, Frances, do you know, I feel homesick and afraid of everything. It is the remote memory of those early days when my mother
kept me too long in her bed. . . . .

Mrs W.L. George[2] has suddenly died; that means George goes straight
home and Arnold [Shaw] loses 1500 dollars. I don't know how he'll
manage. Mrs George was with her husband – a charming lady – and he
was lecturing lightly on Love & Marriage. It does not appear very lucky
to lecture on love – Don't be alarmed however! . . . . .

107

JACK TO FRANCES (in Beaune)

439 W. 21
Dec 23 [1920]

The most interesting news is that Lulu's found a girl who thrills him as
he's never been thrilled except by Frances and Marion Linton.[1]

This is Edna St Vincent Millay[2] – a poet. Fortunately for Lulu's health
and work she is leaving next week for Frances – I mean for *France*. For
myself, I adore her poetry, but think nothing of her personality. But I
certainly do like her poetry very much indeed. But she has thrown a
complete spell over Lulu. He trembles and shakes. He feels sick. He loses
his appetite. He talks of nothing else.

. . . . . Dodd and Mead have turned down my novel, being disappointed
at the sale of *The Complex Vision*. Maurice Browne[3] is in New York
trying to get a start on his own. I hope he will. Pete[4] has broken away
from the Theatre Guild – and has a new company on his own with
Duncan[5] – Isadora's brother. Dorothy Cheston[6] is still in England playing the leading *boy* in the Elizabethan play, 'The Knight of the Burning
Pestle'. Marian is struggling along desperately with her new shop in 57th
St. but I think she will just manage to pay her way. It's an awful rent
though. Whenever my son doesn't write to me *I* write to *my* father.

. . . . . Lulu and I are waiting for May's return. He has just finished an
article on the poetry of E. St V. Millay which is charmingly written.

Yes, it's Xmas Eve and I keep wanting to say to you something. I
don't know what. . . . . that you are the 'silent companion' of many of
my thoughts. Bah! what is the use of my saying such things? Noel! Noel!
Born is the *King of Israel*! *Is* he born? That is the point. . . . .

1921

108

JACK TO FRANCES (in Beaune)

N.Y.
Jan 31st [1921]

I saw the new moon through glass. Since then agitation has followed on agitation. The headquarters police . . . . . told us that they had come across the track of Private Detectives representing parties unknown and they advised us to beware of black-mail and to refuse to give information to anyone. They gave us a phone number so as to be able to summon them at need. They recognised clearly enough that J.B.[1] had been using my name without my knowledge. They seemed to have tried just to scare her and if that is successful they will drop the matter. So I trust she *is* scared and will write no more letters and will appear at no more lectures. . . . . It looks as if she would escape falling into the hands of medical authorities which is her chief danger.

Her brother, they say, is a senator . . . why the devil doesn't he look after her a bit I don't know.

Arnold is in fear of bankruptcy . . . . . When his debts oppress his mind he has a tendency just to collapse and cease his activities. . . . .

I have suddenly developed a most troublesome boil at the back of my neck, so I have had to borrow one of Lulu's softest collars. This is not calculated to increase my urbanity. Lecturing with a stiff neck is no happy thing. But it might be worse. . . . .

109

JACK TO FRANCES (in Beaune)

439 W. 21
Feb 15 [1921]

. . . . . We certainly have knocked our heads so hard together that the little bits of our skulls have got lodged contrariwise. . . . .

I never have known when I have been hurting you — I dare say I never shall. . . . . .

. . . . . I have a notion that a girl's love is a thing completely different from anything else in Nature, and altogether more formidable and mysterious than the love of the best of men — I don't think it is a thing that men in the least comprehend — I mean men far more subtle and tender than I can ever hope to be. . . . . I suppose it is a balance of all those other feminine things where women fall short. . . . . I don't think men ever are able to realize the loneliness of human beings just because of the tendency to childish clinging — and I think that women, because they are mothers, are more aware of loneliness because *they* include without being included.

Girls never *can* say what it is they want from their lover and I think it is a cessation of this loneliness — they want to be really and truly 'possessed', they want to 'belong' as I suppose they very seldom do 'belong', except where their mate or their lover is able to be both detached and possessive in the way they are themselves.

In every two people, one has got to face the outer chaos so that the other can have something to lean its back against, and every maternal instinct growls like a tigress over the head that's resting under its pointed chin. . . . .

I don't feel as if I *hadn't* lived with you. . . . . I want to love you so that you are lost and happy and healed. . . . .

I had to go to the court — next to 'Tombs' prison — to witness on behalf of Joyce's *Ulysses*[1] in the Little Review, for that evil scavenger Sumner[2] is prosecuting Margaret Anderson.[3] I think she will be convicted, but it will indeed be a triumph over the devil if she isn't — but I fear she *will* be, and be in danger of imprisonment.

The editor of The Dial,[4] who was there too, heard Sumner say to a friend of his who asked who's that? 'The English Degenerate, John Powys', but I suddenly became aware of real crafty legal blood in my veins; and I wished I could conduct her case in place of her lawyer who I

greatly fear will mishandle it. I was, anyway, quite well pleased with the
manner in w^h I kept my head . . . and I need my Frances to take down
my pride a peg or two! . . . . .

110

JACK TO FRANCES (in Beaune)

439, West 21
March 10 [1921]

I am off – for California!
Sara [Bard Field] . . . . . says that if I can raise enough money to get
Lulu to San Francisco she will be entirely responsible for him as soon as
he is there and will get him back (quite *cured* she says) in the Fall. Isn't
she an amazing women . . . ? She has had a frightful time . . . an
operation and a sort of comatose sleep for nine days till everyone gave
her up . . . but here she is alive still . . . but with a look of purged imper-
sonality on her face that even your raking criticism would be struck by,
I think. Of course Lulu and she are already the closest friends – so also
Lulu and Katharine.[1] It remains to see what Erskine Wood has to say –
eh? . . . . .
Lulu at the moment is more infatuated with Genefride[2] than anyone
since Edna [St Vincent Millay] went. He is still a bit critical of my
interest for Dorothy de Poillier which is, he says, 'a tame affair'. I was
struck by the fact that he remarked in the Blue Tea Room the other day:
'Something – sometimes – now and then . . . I feel *Contempt* for you,
Jack.'
I sort of think I have heard those two syllables before now! ha? . . . . .
I think he was a bit disappointed that I am not quite as
thrilled by our journey together to California as I once was when I went
to Venice. But he **is** thrilled at it himself – the babyish kid that he is – I
have *never* seen him so happy. It's really pretty and pathetic to see his
excitement. *Nothing* could suit him better. So I am glad it has worked
out so and it *is* sweet of Sara really . . . and certainly it will be wonderful
if it does really *cure* him. It *may*. I remember how good it did you . . .
your legs . . . I suppose they are reverted altogether now to your usual
aged 13 . . . . .
But it is amusing to listen to Lulu and Sara talking – Sara's abandoned
Western idealism and Lulu's Dorsetshire cynicism. But they will get on

splendidly — because they both say *everything* — you know? — in the way Jack never altogether can! . . . . .

Louis, you say, will be with you by the end of April — ? Well — if I come I shall see him too; so there it is! It would be — ha! — more *'appropriate'* if I could have reached you before April's end! But I cannot possibly do that, alas! . . . . .

Ech! but I recall too well the thrilled look on your face when we drove up to those queer San Francisco hills. And I have not forgotten another, still another look, when you first arrived on the Berkeley side of the water with Livio and we sat on the deck of that ferry-boat — or yet *another look* when I would insist on walking 'in the middle of the road'.

O Frances! O Jack! Oh you little fools!

111

JACK TO FRANCES (in Beaune)

Alta Mira, Sausalito, California
March 29th [1921]

Well! — do you think I didn't think of the shy Frances with a hushed trembling lip and a startled face looking at the Pacific from between Livio and Jack? Do you think I didn't think of meeting her at the Kentfield station the day she found her lungs were healed and she was late and tired? . . . . .

Do you remember that huge moon we saw with your mother one twilight, up our hill, past that *oak-tree* where Livio got cross the first day?

Lulu is *very* content. He will stay all the summer here. He has a verandah . . . . . He admires the old man [Erskine Wood] who is looking a lot older. I think he finds things a bit of a strain now and then, with his wife still in the background and Sara [Bard Field] in such shaky health. But Sara walks without any difficulty now . . . . .

. . . . . I could reach you about *June 17th* . . . . .

The old man said last night that the only lasting love he had known all his life was his and Sara's!

Somehow I don't feel as if their affair . . . but that may be my damned conceit — and I think I'm conceited over a certain way we treat each other. They bore each other sometimes. By God, we've never done *that*! Ech! I can quarrel with you. I can hate you. But I cannot grow weary of you. And for me you cannot grow old. That is a queer fact. It may be your imagination or it may be mine.

But really, you mad girl who has bruised the serpent's heel in Jack, it isn't only our crazy fancy, all this. It really is remarkable how our 'love' refuses to become a dull, quiet, settled, wise friendship! It began as a recognition of a strange reciprocal childishness and sophistication; these elements mingled oddly together; just like our love and malice — our hate and our tenderness — and we shall be the old Frances-Jack to the end.

112

JACK TO FRANCES (in Beaune)

San Francisco
May 6 [1921]

I am in the whirlpools of agitations and the confusions of pullings both ways! Wood and Sara and Lulu and Jessica Colbert[1] — all want me to sign up a contract with Jessica for a year's lecturing on the Pacific Coast . . . from Seattle to San Diego and to chuck Arnold altogether. Oh! Oh! Oh! I feel like a fish with a hook in its mouth . . . and yet it is all lovely of them and kind and affectionate — and in my best interest . . . What a blow to Arnold — what an awful blow. I dreamed of him last night and he straightened himself out stiff in my arms and sobbed like a baby! Isn't that the devil? He *has* a mouth like a baby — made for lollipops — and here I smack him across that infantile absurd mouth with the back of my horny hand!

Frances — existence is one too many for my particular type of wit. I can deal with dead books, dead pictures, dead leaves . . . dead girls you will be tempted to add! — but *living* people in *real* life — oh how a cold panic of incompetent wretchedness overtakes me then!

Come, you accursed Complex Vision![2] — have you nothing to help me with? Then go to hell and spin like a top for-ever -- I give you up and go whining to Frances, with her single Vision, for the word to clear the air! Yes — I *will* whine to you — I will — I will — and I will hug you and kiss you and *make* you stop looking like a thing of scorn and despising me. I will make you kiss me in quite — but I must catch the boat!

113

JACK TO FRANCES (in Beaune)

Hotel Alta Mira, Sausalito
May 12th [1921]

Alas! Alas! Alas! the news I relate today is sad enough. I am *not* coming home at all! Instead of 1200$ I have only so far made 400$, and it will not be till I have to leave to pick up the three weeks lecturing Arnold has got for me — from May 19 to June 9 in New York — that my little hall here in Grant Ave will be anything like full. Jessica Colbert had no capital to advertise with and hence it is a matter of slowly building these classes up like I did before.

I have told Arnold he must get *some* sort of a job through July and August at least — but that I hope I may be able to supplement a trifle whatever he does get so as to enable him to give time to my autumn schedule.

It is the receipt of some really miserable letters from Mrs Powys that has decided me to return to California after my visit to New York, instead of sailing for France and England.

She is in a terribly nervous state and has had continual Doctor's bills and now has to go to Bath with her sister to try the cure there.

My son talks of getting a tutorship in his vacation to help things out — so obviously it's up to me not to throw myself on their hands unemployed and idle. I really can't stomach the thought of any risk of having to borrow money again. I owe enough as it is.

So I shall return out here by the middle of June, by which time Colonel Wood and Noel Sullivan[1] and Jessica Colbert swear that they can work up some really good classes. Then I shall be able to send home weekly sums, also send her from New York whatever I should have taken with me. There will of course be the long trip — but there would have been the ship in the other case — and here at least I am sure of being able to keep myself and send her regular sums even if they are not large — and it will be all the difference between being at work and not being at work — and — finally — as doubtless you will have already remarked — Lulu is here.

Well I kiss you. I send a faint sign of the kisses I *would* have given you.

114

JACK TO FRANCES (in Beaune)

Holly Oaks Hotel, Sausalito
[June 1921]

You would be so amused at the way both Sara and Lulu tend to hold you up before me as a kind of angel of last judgement if ever I show signs of bad behaviour to them. . . . .

Never was a person more instantaneously punished for behaving scandalously than I was over that unlucky contract . . . it was just as if I had signed away my soul and immediately afterwards Birnam Wood rushed to Dunsinane!

Well . . . the old man is back . . . but we have not seen him yet . . . We are letting him and Sara enjoy their re-encounter undisturbed. . . . . This immediate winter Arnold is to have Oct Nov Dec Jan so that in that respect Jessica Colbert did yield . . . But I am not very pleased to see that she is announcing in her printed notices that I am to be out here till June 1st![1] — when the hell am I going to get home? That'll leave only practically July and August and a bit of Sept . . . too short a time! Too short a time!

. . . . . It is full moon tonight anyhow and I saw a Pelican the other day.

I am so glad you've found someone,[2] sweetheart, queer enough for you to love in that neighbourhood. . . . . Give Amelia[3] my love, will you, and a kiss, as you may decide suitablest, or just a stroking of her cheek . . . and assure her I do wish her well and I am very very glad she is with you again. Tell her that I here and now predict she will have a beautiful boy whose name shall be famous . . .

. . . . . God bless you. Thank the Lord you are fairly happy where you are.

115

JACK TO FRANCES (in Beaune)

Holly Oaks Hotel[1]
July 10 [1921]

. . . . . Jessica wants *new* subjects and with Lulu's help has compiled a new list for me, including Caesar, Confucius, Helen of Troy, Joan of Ark and Queen Elizabeth – I don't like this – and at the best what can I know after two days reading Froude and Suetonius, of Julius Caesar?[2] Is not this exactly what the word 'charlatanism' means?

Well! let it go.

Oh do you know, I saw in a paper that the existence of 'Thyroidism' had been brought forward by a lawyer as an excuse and palliation in some criminal case? I amused Sara by pointing that out. Colonel Wood wishes to take Sara to a place he has bought in the country 60 miles from here – a hill-top to which they have made a road, but it can only be approached by motor-car and the road is precipitous and Sara shows disinclination . . . for which Lulu scolds her, as not being nice or kind to the old man.

We look out on the bay from the window of this room. The water and hills are really interesting in the morning and evening, though the ferry boats and trains are rather teasing. Opposite is that island called Angel Island, shaped like Raphael's Mount of Transfiguration . . .

Often and often do Lulu and I recall those times with you in Venice and other times with you. You are a living figure here by our side. The other night Sara and Lulu joined in one of those concentrated attacks upon me which I seem constantly to provoke. Why am I the only scoundrel who excites such attacks? Other wretches are left in peace in their bad character! I threatened them with taking your advice, and stopping 'propitiating' anybody anytime; but just going, doing, saying, what I really wanted, liked and thought . . . This alarming prospect pulled them up a bit.

For the last few nights Lulu has been troubled by rheumatism in the back – but it is all right today. He always had to sit up and be massaged a bit about 3.30 or 4.30 am. Nothing could have exceeded my tender consideration until one night I forgot myself and uttered the unfeeling response to his groans of 'Don't make so much noise'! He will not soon forget this! But he is immensely better as far as his consumption goes.[3] California is, I really believe, beginning to cure him. But he is getting very restless over his literary career. Nothing will stop him returning with me to New York. But he will come back here with me on Feb 1st – then if we cannot afford both of us to come home in the summer he will stay out here while I go and return.

Try and write again to me after a while, Frances. This is not a scolding for not writing – I know you – but it is just to tell you that the time has come for you to write again.

Heaven bless you and take care of you till once more we meet again. What will it be like when we do meet, eh?

. . . . . Kiss Betty from me and tell Livio I don't forget him: but remember how he played Indians.

116

JACK TO FRANCES (in Beaune)

Sausalito Cal
Aug 3rd [1921]

. . . . . My son, so I hear, has done fairly well in his May exam – in French and Spanish. . . . .
. . . Lulu insists on going to New York with me about Sept 20 now . . . . . for he finds that it is in New York alone that he can really make headway with his writings . . . and he is absolutely bent – as against the prayers of Willy and Gertrude [Powys] – and the very strongly expressed opinions of Marian – and all that I myself can say or do – to risk his health for the sake of his career . . . I can see that if he didn't go to New York he would again fall into that mood he was in at Weymouth – so unnatural to him – losing all his gaiety and aplomb. He repeats, 'My blood's on my own head' . . . . . Please say every kind of little prayer that you think will be of any good . . . that he won't kill himself by this venture . . . but he is *not* cured, you know – not anything like cured. I confess I had not realised how much determination and iron he had in him until this question sprang up . . . . . The more I'm with him the more I realise how deep, how down into the very depths of his bones is his passion to succeed in his writing and it certainly looks as if it was almost impossible to do that out here . . .
. . . . . If Lulu *did* get over with me and you and I and Louis . . . . . Probably we should all be happier – though less hot-headed – than we were when we went to Torcello, and you and Lulu looked down that well and we discussed all sorts of things as we crossed that water and drank the wine that Louis procured from the wharf where that equestrian statue is . . . And now after only two years my son will have finished Cambridge and be finding some job. And Livio I guess is becoming awfully definite about what he will be later . . . You know, I suppose, that this has been over here a record year of heat – not here but everywhere else – terrible! & in England too.
You'll be glad to hear that last summer's rotten novel [*After My Fashion*] of mine cannot find a publisher – all the better! But it is annoy-

ing to me that I wasted all that time over the damned thing.

Well, Frances, I am at this second with you, hunting for your coat —
was it you or I who found it?

117

JACK TO FRANCES (in Beaune)

Sausalito
Aug 11th [1921]

. . . . . Sara always keeps speaking of you as the most intellectual girl
she has ever met . . . And Lulu is constantly saying that you are the only
one of all the objects of my concern and regard who answers to his ideal
of what is suited to me!

Pardieu, Frances, how do you relish that role? Well — after all — Sara
and Lulu are remarkable people; she is an idealist and he an extreme
realist — and there they are acknowledging that they've never been so hit
to the heart by anyone's identity as by yours . . . and I don't think they
keep this up with me with any naughty or jealous intent — or with a
secret wish to crush all spirit out of me with your uniqueness and power.
I think it is a genuine & very deep thing in both instances . . . Well! *you*,
of course, suspect — but you are such a bundle of suspicions anyhow! —
that this perpetual cult, in which you become something between a lunar
Aphrodite and a solar Astarte, fills the evil mind of your wilful Mr
Welsh[1] with malicious thoughts. No! no! Frances — my good and bad
towards you remains between us entirely unaffected one way or the
other by anything of that kind . . . and indeed the maniacal reserve with
which I protect our private rapports and mis-rapports from any, even the
most affectionate and innocent, meddling, ought to pay you back a bit
for those numerous occasions wherein my insane secretiveness with
regard to less drastic dents on my consciousness has roused *your* indignation. The truth is that we've only to be together for ten minutes and
we should be found launched out into some furious metaphysical row
between one kind of world-chemistry or another — all the Frances and
Jack 'points' of discussion clamoring hopelessly, like flocks of belated
starlings, behind our wild-geese voyage.

Won't it be queer if Lulu really does come with me to visit you next
summer? You are wrong if you think your impression on *his* mind has
diminished one bit — and let me tell you that impression has nothing at

all to do with your physical advantages over others – it is your mind, your mind – even with our arch-amorist! . . . . .

118

JACK TO FRANCES (in Beaune)

Sausalito
[August 1921]

Think sometimes just kindly and very simply of me as you would do of a poisoned goat or a mad elephant.

. . . . . I suppose you meditate long and long on how lovely it would be if I were only not quite so unsatisfactory . . . Well, it *might* be, I don't know.

. . . . . You must remember that I cried for you once, and for you and that acting of Pete [Rollo Peters] once – and otherwise never in my life except for my mother's burying and my son's birth. These things I know are long ago – but they did happen – I am Oedipus[1] – I didn't know how, my mother was the person I understood best and each year I know it more. She is, she was, the one female I can completely and absolutely understand – in her wickedness and in her goodness. I am only talking of understanding. I should awfully like to have a long conversation with Mrs Wilkinson[2] about her . . . I suppose Mrs Wilkinson was the only friend she ever had . . . my father had not one friend – what parents to have! . . . . .

God bless you Frances – take care of yourself.

119

JACK TO FRANCES (in Beaune)

Holly Oaks Hotel
Aug 19th [1921]

. . . . . Your eidolon, or psyche, or whatever it is that is a wanderer, though it does stay in one place by the law of gravity, seems to be actually now peering at me over the edge of this life of St Francis[1] which I have to read – mocking, mocking and yet furious and yet gentle and yet Frances, her very self . . .

It's so quaint, sweetheart, how I am afraid of you. Is it that you alone, of all the world, have 'found me out'? . . . . . That produces a quaint kind of fear, like the fear of thunder in some minds . . . . . It's queer, you see, you have not the faintest shadowiest sort of ghost of a flicker of *fear* of me – have you, you queer one, come, confess it? And yet men – or am I wrong? – like greatly well to be a *little* feared, like the poor old God! So hurry up, Frances, and *fear Jack*!

Ech! I talk nonsense . . . but maybe, you know, seriously? – sweetheart . . . lots of our misunderstandings and difficulties may lie in the fact that you have a more powerful a more formidable a more drastic *mind* than I, whereas when men are attracted, are absorbed, are – this and the other . . . you know! – they like to feel the stronger of the two. Now I am damned if ever I can feel stronger than you and I never shall feel it . . . but I know in many ways too well that I am tougher – or perhaps more misty and cloudy . . . for it comes to the same thing . . . You, sweetheart, my dear and my dear, are so terribly *brittle* . . . strong and yet brittle . . . it *is* odd – so odd . . . But you mustn't die – to 'prove points'!

. . . . . I wonder why it is that you have written in a different tone, in these last two letters – this one and the one before which was – bad bad bad girl – as long ago as April or May.

Is this kind of wine-growing land you are in softening something of marble in your strange pride? . . . Or do you really feel a kind of sense that life is so short that Frances and Jack might just as well take hands and say nice things and let the devil fly away with their metaphysical disputes?

No – you are happier, Frances – *that* is what it is – and less lonely – and so you can say things that you *couldn't* say before . . . aren't I right? Anyway, I am not going to spoil this response to your letter by making wicked love to you. . . . .

The Lord keep you. J.

. . . . . This is one of the letters that a person doesn't forget – not even Signore Jack – but I do so long, when you talk with me like this, and give me your hand, to be able to write down on a piece of paper such things as are not permissible to write down.

But I do thank the heavenly powers, Frances, that that country suits you as it does – and that you have Amelia and this other queer being [Mlle Jaflin] of whom I cannot see even a shadowy outline . . . Is she a very old French woman, or not a human person at all but a crow or a fox or a cat?

Lulu and I tell each other stories about sailing together straight for you . . . . . We have given up our flat in New York so he will have to live alone on a balcony or a roof . . . as Marian sleeps in her shop with a pistol under her pillow.[2]

Do you realise that Lulu has never read 'The Two Brothers'[3] in the Forum? I wish I had a copy. I used to have one . . . did you steal it away? . . . . . The gods preserve you from harm and distress.

Here is a kiss for under your chin that goes like a crescent moon.

F.F.F.F.F.

120

JACK TO FRANCES (in Beaune)

Holly Oaks
Sept 14th [1921]

Dante's 600th anniversary of his death.

You know I sometimes think that lots of our queer rages against each other come from our being most damnably and unluckily *alike* . . . . . You recall that 'sorella' fellow under the statue in the Milan Square?[1] — and the 'my sister' stunt here too could hardly otherwise have been so unassailably successful!

These two weeks I have a terrific lot of work crowding these classes in, one on the top of the other, at the rate of two a day; if I hadn't to share 50/50 with Jessica [Colbert] I should really and truly be making some fine money just at this moment — and even as it is I am no longer in the least pinched and have my son's autumn term's expenses safe in Banco.

I am keeping this paper from blowing away by the use of a bone . . . the thigh bone of a rat, I think . . .

Oh, by the way, I have to lecture on the Negroes and there is one privileged one allowed to attend; 'but only one,' says Jessica C. Whether that one will receive from Mr Welsh[2] a bouquet of beautiful roses remains to be seen!

I was hugely entertained by Louis's letter about his encounter with Ezra [Pound] in Paris. That letter really was a top-knotch one, in his charmingest vein! — and of course the one point of absolute sympathy between Louis and me will always be any sort of school-boy bullying and scoring off of the refined and winnowed and raked-out Ezra!

Well — I will now tell you about my projected book . . . but alas!

only two chapters written so far . . . . .

It's a running *commentary*, you know the style of thing, eh? —appreciation —*sans* 'scholarship'! of Homer . . . of the Iliad and Odyssey both . . . with Lang's[3] prose translations . . . And as I go on I am trying my own hand at fragmentary translations into English hexameters . . . you know? à la *Evangeline*??[4] 'Still are the forests primaeval; the whispering shades and the alders . . .' —and so on—only missing out the 'forget-me-nots of the angels' accent; as not quite in harmony with the wrath of Achilles.

. . . . . Otherwise I have been, at Lulu's inexhaustible encouragement and under his not by any means altogether flattering criticism, writing 'poetry' again. This I suppose will not please you; for I know you think Jack's 'poetry' is a false trail and leading only to mirages of self-complacent illusion . . . I really don't know, in this, whether you or Lulu are right. I think he does enjoy a certain sort of Matthew-Arnold-reflection-of-Miltonic-echoes and a certain kind of an original 'note' in these poetic debouchings here and there, a 'note' that may or may not spring from a real imaginative impression of things, in what I put into them, rather old-fashioned and often inaccurate rhymes. . . . . You would have me write very different things from the things Lulu would have me write. . . . . I believe that you are agreed about the particular weaknesses in my character. . . . . 'Sincerity' is of course the thing—even at the risk of giving people immediate shocks and troubling them. . . . . To be able to bear the immediate shock of being disapproved of!

That is it . . . that is it . . . as when you scolded me for not expressing what I felt at that brutal story . . . Do you recall the occasion and how we spoke of it in Mrs Klang's[5] potato patch? —of Robert Minor[6] returned from Russia??

. . . . . Kisses, flickering and faint I daresay, to you as they are bleached and rain-soaked and weather-stained on their long journey to you.

121

JACK TO FRANCES (in Beaune)

Better stick to *Marian's* address: 54 West 57th Street
Oct 11 [1921]

Here we are in 148 Waverley Place though Lulu may decide to move as we get *no sun*, but he has a roof for nights . . .

I was woken up by the Angelus bell of St Joseph's just round the corner – God! I cursed the Blessed One and the birth of the redeemer . . . at six o'clock – a very Greenwich Village Angelus clang! clang! clang! And then I couldn't get out of the room because Lulu's Fox Prison Lock with Iron Bar doesn't open from inside and he was on the roof . . . and there I had to lie and hear our neighbouring lodger, an angry Major, fasten himself into the bathroom . . . Even when you're in the bathroom . . . only lukewarm water so far . . . I shall have to go out for baths . . .

But it isn't a bad room and it is absolutely bare and Lulu and I can be as untidy as we like . . .

I am prostrate with exhaustion at this particular moment from buying things at the 10 cent store . . . We keep knives and spoons and just two plates and two cups and saucers . . . on the chest of drawers. But the room has been prepared and the floor varnished . . . and it is an airy room . . . and very near Washington Square . . .

I have seen Pete [Rollo Peters], Margaret,[1] Rob Parker,[2] Helen [Conroy], Reginald Pole,[3] and Lola [Catesby Jones], and tonight I have to dine with Fania! All the world is amazed at the fact that the exquisite Pete is out of a job and that Fania, on the contrary, has translated three Russian plays that may . . . *all* of them . . . be accepted . . .

Conroy and Helen Conroy are in the same play but not in the same house; but I believe they still dine together of an evening . . .

Reginald Pole . . . he is, I fear, only a name to you . . . but you would really like him the best of all . . . has got a company and a theatre to rehearse in . . .

Maurice Browne is in Seattle still. Rob Parker has they say separated from Ethel what's her name . . . Kirah,[4] with her tall Statiscian [*sic*], we met this morning again at the French Pastry Shop . . .

So there's some gossip for you, but I suppose among your Burgundian Vines all these people have become shadows of less than no import . . . . .

. . . . . I am as bad as ever in what you call my devoluted affection of wishing I were dead! You see I have such an incorrigible tendency to demand that mysterious thing which we call 'being happy', and of course the world is arranged with a different object . . . and now and again I get so awfully tired and collapsed – you know? So that I cannot really walk and walk and walk as I like . . .

My father finds he walks with less assurance these days; and speech has almost left him but he can chuckle still, I daresay . . . . . and rub his hands – and so cannot I – but I am 49 – in a year fifty . . . and he is eighty next birthday, poor old man! I don't suppose a single human being loves him enough to wish him not to die . . . and yet his heart is sound and he may live for two years yet and more . . . is that tragic? No, I don't suppose so. But it's a kind of impressive fact – that things can end in that way . . . . . How, with the certainty of complete annihilation . . . I suppose it *is* a certainty . . . but maybe not . . . any of us get to the finish of any single day, heaven alone knows! Pushed on from behind I reckon. I have just bought a tea-pot for a dollar and now I hate it – what's to be done? . . .

. . . .

An interval . . . later . . . Lulu has gone to see Helen [Conroy], and Signore Jack is very solemnly drinking tea by himself made from an alcohol lamp . . . . . and meditating on Frances by the light of two candles. Damn! I am not fond of going out, anywhere – I like best drinking tea in my own room . . . and if Frances wants to slip up those stairs – why not? But there is only one chair. But still . . . . .

Another morning – I doubt if Lulu will stay in this house . . . never any sun . . . and we suspect the drains of being unsanitary and there are too many chimneys round Lulu's roof. The landlady swept us in here too quickly! . . . . . Papering the place 10 dollars – and 40 dollars a month's rent in advance . . . but no lease, thank the Lord! We *were* a pair of idiots to select this place . . . but the hotels are so terribly expensive and we were in such a hurry to be settled[5] . . . well, it can't be helped . . . . .

I believe it was in New York rooms that Lulu first developed his consumption[6] . . . . .

Marian has not got her rent yet[7] for this month but she is in good spirits at having got thro' the summer at all. She owes 1200 dollars – 600 of which is directly owing to people who will have to be paid within a year . . . but high finance is nothing to our independent Marian.

John Fanshawe[8] is awfully down and out . . . with a clerk's job of 16 dollars a week . . . his wife supported by her father and his children . . . He is too good and generous and naive for this little world! . . . . . Fania alone makes headway. I saw her last night and she has deluged me with Russian translations. She really does translate astonishingly well. She is going up hill fast . . . She and Marian seem both much more capable of making the world use them well than either Pete or John.

Jessica wants to go to England with me next May . . . did I tell you that? . . . . . Oh dear! what a difficult and exhausting world!

. . . . . I hope Lulu will be fairly cautious not to have too many amorous adventures!

I leave for the Middle West in a day or two –

122

JACK TO FRANCES (in Beaune)

[mid-October 1921]

[*Fragment only*]

. . . . . time it was in a field outside a town in Alabama – where there were sad, very old butterflies – a butterflies' almshouse or hospital – and when I saw the bits on the ground I nearly picked them up again! I can't stand leaving things like that.

I see your handwriting – on the grass in Alabama – in the butterflies' cemetery. It was queer – it gave me an odd feeling. I was glad to have that letter. It is important for me to have a letter once a month anyhow – that is four to one – as I write to you every week.

I don't think I should like to give a letter of yours to the lake at Chicago. So that if you write to me when I am there I shall know it more than by heart – possibly it'll have gone to my head – before I find a burial ground suitable for it – or 'a burning-ground of Siva'.[1]

I left Lulu[2] in good health – but I've had no letter from him since. I had hoped for one here – but none has come. How unpleasant it is expecting letters that don't arrive! but I don't . . . . .

123

JACK TO FRANCES (in Beaune)

The Colonial, Springfield
Oct 30th [1921]

Well, I have passed on to the next town – I like Missouri country well enough . . . . . But oh dear me! I couldn't have torn up a letter from you there – Alabama was better.

But it's so difficult to forgive you for that absurd reaction of yours over my last visit to that town – But of course I suppose I merit it. You couldn't possibly *know* how ridiculous any conceivable approach to philandering with this young woman [Phyllis Playter] would be to me. I just exploit her with material kindness and she exploits with equal unconcern the fact that I am an Englishman and a variety from the more local kind of oil-men. But I think I was damned cautious this time not to pay out old imperial coins—with Caesar's superscriptions on them . . . . .

Do you know I am very much impressed by the novels of Edith Wharton?[1]

The House of Mirth

The Custom of the Country

The Fruit of the Tree

She is old-fashioned—and so on—but good lord! she has such a firm hand and does lay brick to brick with solid architectural effect. It's 'form' with her—she must be an austere woman—not 'colour'.

At this moment I recall how thrilled you were when we drove through the streets of San Francisco. You certainly have had your moments of Betty-like[2] pleasure.

I like better to recall your expression at such times than when you have been angry. I don't know which look you have at this moment. Yet a different one I suppose —the reading-a-letter-of-Jack look and I can see *that* also.

How *can* you say such things as that I have ever *reminded* you of the passing of the time? What mad untrue ideas you do get! Do you not yet know that the one person you'll never be old to is Jack — but that's because I'm always ahead of you.

124

JACK TO FRANCES (in Beaune)

[Printed:] Hotel Severin, Indianapolis, Indiana

Nov 1 [1921]

I hope you are all right . . . I've got a sudden vision of you . . . angry, devastated, with a streaming flood of tears, out of which that pale face, I know by heart, gleams white like a fragment of an ice-berg in a driving storm of sleet . . . is this all nonsense and absurd?[1] Please note *Nov 1st* and try & recall, when you get this . . . whenever and wherever you do . . . But I see your chin; and those steel-blue-thunder-dark glints in your eyes, against a face of ashes, and a queer swollen fury, like black adder's gall, surging up your thin neck! And I take you and I hold you tight & I like you well and you are Frances — mad, strange, reckless, unaccountable . . . biting the very bone of this Dynosaur of a universe! But never ever are you quite out of that subconscious mind which underlies everything —nor ever will be I suppose . . . there you are still . . . in my deepest pocket of spirit . . . with your lips all bruised and twitching and scornful and your hands, that are as if I had made them myself, all twisting and clenched . . .

Eh – you thing, you girl, you wild one – don't you go away with the notion that your Signore Jack has a memory of india rubber! I have a memory of adamant and you have scratched at it so deep that you can almost feel the letters in the dark. But it is all beyond my analysis, what I feel for you – such a whirling tumultuous wood-flood under the dead leaves . . . oh and sometimes I wish that the great accusing day of my life had come and were *over*! No – no – it is the truth when I tell you that I don't understand my feelings for you any more than I shall understand yours for me . . . Maybe at *this* very moment . . . weary of being tossed to and fro over those silly moors for . . . how many years? . . . our old symbolic pair . . . that poor 'H' and poorer 'C' . . . that Louis used to think stood for hellish copulation . . . are sitting on two limestone rocks eating hips and haws, and poking crooked thorn-sticks into the roots of bracken; and putting out their tongues at each other! . . . Well . . . they *are* looking at each other still . . . and I guess they will be 'until the coming of the cockmolecules' as it says in that bible of solemnities about otters and fish . . . yes I guess they will be . . . until these two skulls

are lying in two graves . . . I suppose it won't be the *same grave* . . . or will Livio have orders to cremate you and shall I have to eat ashes instead of dust??

What a history ours has been all told, all told . . . ! Your insane object-ive realism . . . with your many maniacal plungings into chemistry . . . into the actual materials of things . . . and your lodged belief that chemistry is spiritual – is the only spiritual thing[2] – flash of Mira-mira eyes! and my engrained and hopeless and treacherous sensationalism mingled with a genuine love of certain beautiful and magical things that are a little beyond *just* that. But it is all 'beyond' me as they say . . . it is all too queer . . . However there are days when I have to speak to you . . . when I have to have Frances and take her long crooked fingers and love them and love them and love them, till she cries!

Listen – you mother of Livio and Betty – you daughter of that bad one that good one that indifferent one with malice-pot – that bewildered Madonna of the Lost Keys – you wife and a good wife of our naughty Louis – you admirer of Mr Pound – are you listening? Where are you reading this – with some local comic-cuts of Beaune, all tipsy with trodden grapes? Or in the garden with some little half-dead plants watered too much by too much rain? It doesn't matter – but where you *do* read it . . . just stretch out one arm as far as you can reach . . . out of the window . . . out of your bath . . . and *know* if you live, your bad Jack lives . . . that he is really kissing that hand . . . with no pretended sigh, at the tricks of our cosmic chemistry!

Be happy now and then, Frances . . . for you have written your name on the sands just out of reach of that old tide . . .

Be happy sometimes, my dear!

125

JACK TO FRANCES (in Beaune)

148 Waverley Place
Dec 23rd [1921]

. . . . . It would certainly be wonderful to have a Frances to talk to who didn't hit quite so hard . . . but would that be Frances at all? *Perhaps not* . . . and for that reason I am now today writing to you to beg for a good familiar old-time *thrashing*! So send it – to me – for after so long a silence every letter you put into every word . . . and every word you put into every sentence . . . ought to smite with the fury of . . . I can't think what, but something pretty stinging . . .

Tell me something about this French girl [Mlle Jaflin] . . . Do you care for her as if she were a sick cat? Or that little beaten boy[1] . . . who is out of that person's hands now, they say, and fit and goblinish as ever? Or do you love her as you do me – to my puzzled and turbulent knowledge – savagely, *in your way*? Am I jealous? Not yet . . . not yet . . . But if you're together still, when you and I at last really meet, I may be . . . I wonder.

. . . . . You are always like a person in high fever . . . I am the slick priest who says, 'There! There! There!' and turns to the weather . . . But I am never in a fever – I'm like a bloody great fish . . . Don't you ever feel a longing to tell everything to a great cool fish watching the shadows of gnats, and opening and shutting its mouth?

But I am a fish that has known what it is to have been pulled out of his serene element . . . and has vague queer memories of mosses and grass . . . and I keep coming towards that grass again and I would like to talk thro' the water to that face looking down . . . well! There it is! . . . . .

I had a letter from my son . . . the first one for a year . . . and he says I don't write to him . . . and that is true . . . but his not doing it is laziness, and *my* not doing it is shyness . . . Well! perhaps not altogether . . . But he has broken the ice . . . and I can see he is not going to be a bit shy of me . . . not a bit! . . . but amused, interested, indulgent, ironical . . .

1922

126

c/o Mademoiselle Lea Jafflin
Bligny-sous-Beaune, par Beaune
Cote d'Or, France
[May 1922]

Dearest Jack,

Write to me again, and more often even if I don't answer your letters. I am having rather a bad time with this affair with Louis. I don't know how it may end. We are taking steps towards a divorce now, but that will take a year to put through. My income now is [£] 200, and will be considerably less after the divorce. I dont earn a thing by writing. Editors write me the most glowing appreciation of my work but they don't accept anything.

Look here, my Jack. Will you let me clear up one point now? Your letters have been apologizing, in a way, for not sending money.[1] You have done enough, and far too much, already for us, and I never want you to do anything again. I expect to earn my living someway. And I do assure you that when I am on my own again, unmarried, I should be made absolutely miserable by your ever sending us money. Please, do understand it, and don't go on with these queer little funny apologies. You are not responsible for us, my dear.

The book of poems[2] came. Louis had opened the package at Chiswick[3] and forgot to send it on until the other day. If it is the one that came from Llewelyn, thank him for me, please. What I should like to have is his book.[4]

Your poems, I thought, had been shaped up by another hand. But perhaps I am wrong. Very sympathetically, and understandingly touched

138

up, however. They seem very good – no, I dont really like them. However that can't be helped.

By the way, it was never your *genius* I doubted, it was your control of it. Of course I should have liked you to write something out of the very depths of your being, that would have been a comfort to people, queer lonely people like me, for years and years to come. You seemed to me only to tickle your own vanity with shams of books. Dostoevsky[5] was nearest to what I wanted. Heaven knows that is troubled enough, and exciting, and twisted and nightmarish, – and yet, they come from such depths that there is refuge in them. While you, – but you know all this too well, don't you?

Do you know a girl called Edna St Vincent Millay? That is an abominable name that would be apt to put you off anybody. But I really believe she is, she must be, rather a thrilling person. There was a picture of her in Vanity Fair. I never liked a girl's face so much. It has all the age-long innocence of the world in it. Not virginal, I dont mean that. It is a steady face, full of knowledge, full of acceptance of life. A face for Michelangelo[6] and not for Botticelli.[7] Anyhow it is a face I like. I wish she were your 'someone'. I have seen some of her writing, a good deal of it rather mischievous, wilful stuff, but some of it that has an authentic ring. If she has ever written any stories I wish I could get hold of them. I may go back to America next year and I mean to know her. I suppose she is too young though to be patient.[8]

Are you coming over this year? And is there any chance of seeing you? I should be content with a day, or half a day, or an hour. I should so like to walk over a marsh, and hear our two voices shouting about the unimportant verities, an hour out of the clutter of reality would do me worlds of good. Love,

Frances –

Oliver sends his love to you. He never forgets you.
We're leaving here at the end of June. – I don't know where we are going.

127

JACK TO FRANCES (in France)

4 Patchin Place, New York City, New York
June 8 [1922]

Note this is my permanent address![1]
. . . . . I don't know what to say about this business of your getting a

divorce . . . but I know only too well how little £200 is! . . . . . I have left Mrs Powys literally with nothing for six weeks . . . I have had to go for help to my brother Littleton. He now telegraphs to me 'am dealing with the situation', so I fancy he must be taking some of my patrimony —what I should have if my father died — and doling it out to Mrs Powys. She must have gone to her sister's[2] leaving her grocery bills behind her . . .

. . . . . If my son passes his final exam he will be through his education now. I have also had a bit of a bolt from the blue in the form of a bad knee for which I only just escaped a hospital operation . . . but it's much better now thank Heaven . . . but I had to have a visit from the doctor and lost a lecture. If my brother can fix up my family for the summer I ought to be able to keep myself going here, tho' Arnold does not seem ready to fuss himself about getting me any small class to help me through three months. But under Lulu's direction — and it must have been *his* censorship you detected in Samphire — I have hopes of being able to get some essay or other or a few perhaps! taken by some New York papers . . . I can assure you I shan't try short stories any more . . . It was Lulu who had an 'affair' — long over now — with Edna St Vincent Millay! *He* adored that name! She wrote a sonnet about him, printed in Vanity Fair — beginning 'Your face is like the chamber of a king'. He took me once to see her. No, I haven't seen my 'someone' [Phyllis Playter] for nearly a year now . . . but I shall soon again I think . . . and I'll tell you more when more is to be told . . .

P.S. Lulu's success and reputation grows and grows and grows! I am glad to see it so . . . . .

128

FRANCES TO JACK (in America)

[Cap Ferret, par Arcachon, Gironde, France]
October 8 [1922]

Dear Jack,

I was so glad that you wrote to my mother. She would have been bitterly disappointed if your letters had ceased with the cessation of munificence.[1] She is tremendously flattered and pleased and soothed by your letters to her. You kept up your donations longer than it was needed, but they were of infinite pleasure to her, and of real service to me, because I could concentrate my income upon the children and Amelia and her brat and myself—five of us on 250 pounds a year leaves a scanty enough margin. My mother took her entire last year's pension, which, thanks to your generosity she had not touched, and bought us a motor car with it. Isn't that exquisite? Shake that into the faces of your evil spirits when you feel melancholy in the mornings. This improvidence has been naturally of infinite delight to the rest of us. It doesn't quite fill the gap that Teddy left in the family,[2] but it is almost as much of a delight and a torment. It was a second-hand affair of course, and by the grace of God and the decency of an agent who must have been struck by our look of vagrants with untold riches in our hands, and touched by our pitiable ignorance, it is not, as it might so easily have been, used up and worthless. It goes so well with the family, it's gray, and usually dusty, and has so mild an air of battered and timeworn gentility. To me it is a sheer delight. I run it — over the hills and plains of France—nearly two thousand kilometres so far, well over a thousand miles. And across cities as well, Limoges, and Bordeaux and Biarritz and Lourdes. It is madness for me to do it, being utterly, as I am, inexperienced, but I delight in it. Nothing can be too hazardous to please me. I have more than hairbreadth escapes — and mixed in with the whirr under my heels, there is a kind of secret chant by which I try to incite the Lord to try to smite us out of existence, so that I may test my wits against His. Never has a car been driven by a madder chauffeur.[3]

It is due to you, of course, that I have what is the most thrilling toy I have ever had since you abandoned me.

I have gotten over my love for you, but not over something else unnameable and deeper than the love was. I mean that you are there in my consciousness, I am sure, forever. But I have certainly gotten over the love affair, as I have gotten over the fear of death, and a certain dreadful kind of wistfulness. I am like a world in the making, harder, more self-centred, and more repellent.

I wish that May would send me a picture of her baby.[4] I am taking Louis's little girl Deirdre[5] to bring up. She must be about the same age as Peter. Do cajole May into giving me some of her news.

Isn't it your birthday today? Or is it the 8th of November?[6] Does little Peter still look like you? I always thought a baby who looked like you would be a handsome baby —in the days, dear Jack, when I thought such thoughts.

. . . . . Louis spent another day with us on his way home. He was looking astonishingly beautiful, but I thought with just a slight Teutonic blur. You know that shade of something over-sweet and soft that I so dislike in the Germans. I of course flew into a temper and denounced his Dulcinea[7] whom he insists upon endowing with all the virtues because of her initial virtue in the art of love. I thought of you. I was so exactly as you most disliked me. In a cold fury of logic that would give no single point for the blindness of affection. Oh well!

129

JACK TO FRANCES (in Cap Ferret)

[envelope printed:] Hotel Victoria, Bush and Stockton Sts. San Francisco
Dec 17th Sunday [1922]

. . . . . I enclose a violet, a December one, from Mrs Klang's[1] garden and also a piece of that precious 'Myrten' bush of hers[2] that we let die, but that, by some extraordinary miracle, is now flourishing again!

I learn that little Walter[3] with a different care-taker is very happy and regarded at his school as an extremely 'bright' boy . . . so there we have our Myrten blooming and our idiot boy sane and normal and happy! . . .

I didn't go straight to the Hoffman's[4] house . . . you may believe . . . I had a quiet little curious walk first with Frances' ghost. I look at 'F. Point' in that funny marsh-land by the station where we saw the owl and the sea-hawk . . . . . I followed that road where there's a sign 'Neil the Painter' that we used to reach by the path by that house with a green verandah . . . . . where once we found a dead snake. I looked at that hill above the house where we once saw—with Madonna—an enormously round and yellow full moon. I went a little on the road where I went once with Livio alone where he told me that children knew that cows climbed trees. I stood by the railings looking down on the Italian's farm. Everything was drenched with rain and everything was very green. I looked at that little Post Office in the station where you scolded me for fussing about putting on stamps carefully—& snatched Lulu's letter from Africa . . . . . I saw that little path going to the edge of the river from the station-road . . . . . And I walked down the middle of the road with my ghost . . . and the ghost road didn't scold me for doing that this time! Heigh ho!

I am now waiting in my room for a visit from a madman — a hobo — an I.W.W. [Industrial Worker of the World] . . . a megalomaniac who says he is greater than Nietzsche before he went off his head . . . but *not* afterwards! Whether the hotel people will 'kick' at his visits before long,

I don't know . . . He causes me much alarm . . . but he says he has no one else who understands what he says—and on my soul I don't wonder—for he does some odd things — What is the word for telling long, eternal stories with yourself as the hero? . . . . . My eccentric visitor says his thoughts come too quick to put them down! It must be that cave lodged in my skull in the shape of an F. that he has some telepathic knowledge of and wants to hide in . . . There . . . he has just telephoned. He's coming . . . I am just a very tiny bit alarmed . . .

He's gone! He was really sweet to me at the end, promised not to come again until Sunday week . . . but he left me pretty exhausted . . . He makes hideous faces. But he has a certain flickering of his eyelids . . . indescribable . . . that is curiously pathetic. He attracts me when he screws up his crazy eyes . . . and also when he smiles . . . a perfectly delicious smile . . . I could really kiss him then . . . And yet his skin is sallow and greasy, and he is unshaven even after being shaved . . . that bluish look! but in spite of it all . . . I have a funny sneaking tenderness for the chap . . . There's a certain appeal . . . I think he must be like the Pied Piper of Hamelin . . .

I feel as if I would follow him sometimes into the side of a mountain . . . It'll be New Year's Eve when he returns. But I won't —I positively won't — have him till midnight that night . . . Do they yell and howl in San Francisco, I wonder?

Maurice Browne and Nelly [Ellen van Volkenberg] have invited me for Xmas Day to their flat, but I shall shorten even that pleasure and friendliness . . . Oh dear me! —I get more unsociable and unsympathetic.

Mr Hoffman said of you, Frances, 'She's a lovely woman — she is a blamed straight shooter!' Well! You certainly shot straight enough to bring down bad Jack with his seven mortal sins! . . . . .

1923

JACK TO FRANCES (in England)
(this letter was forwarded by Louis Wilkinson[1])

[Printed:] The Belvedere at Baltimore, Maryland, USA
[1923]

I shall be glad when I hear from your mother again, Frances. You know I have not even yet heard where you are living. Is it Suffolk I wonder – or not?

I suppose you will be having Livio back again anyhow for Xmas – eh? I had the nicest letter I have ever had from my son the other day . . . . .

And little Betty? Eh! I remember how she used to like being swung in the air by Signore Jack – will she recognise me again, I wonder? I am working hard at a novel [*Ducdame*] which I hope will be better – quite a lot better – than the one where the young lady 'tripped demurely' down the aisle! [*After My Fashion*] *That* never saw the light! Lulu condemned it even worse than you.

It will be strange – when actually and really our voices are lifted up, to the dismay of all present, in one of our ancient fierce disputes – but it may occur before very long; because I hope to arrive in England by April this 1924 – 1924! Aye how the years pass. I now have to go and lecture at Notre Dame Convent, where Arnold Shaw's daughter, Edith, is a pupil now. I remember how I came to Baltimore years and years ago . . . . .

The gods be with you –

144

131

FRANCES TO JACK

Brightlingsea Cottage, Parham, Wickham Market, Suffolk
[November 1923]

I don't write, my dear Jack, because my days are both busy and troubled – but not at all because I 'curse you'. Well, good luck to all you Powyses. In my day I loved three of you – you and Llewelyn and Bertie.[1] You most, of course, then Llewelyn and then Bertie because life seemed to have hurt him in the way I understood.

But all that is past and I would not go back.

I walk a narrower ledge now than that one where Lulu teased us, but this time I am not afraid for Death begins to wear a kindlier face. My thoughts of you always begin *'dear* Jack'.

Write to me more often and never give up writing to my mother.

Oh what a world, my Jack!

132

FRANCES TO JACK (in Patchin Place, New York)

[Parham, Wickham Market, Suffolk]
[31st December 1923]

[typed]
My dear Jack,

I wish you would stop bothering yourself and me, as to whether you are good, or better, or worse, and who is responsible for it. The only possible evidence of your being 'good' would be in your writing a really fine book that proved a pure and selfless interest in beauty, or, if you like, in truth. As far as the conduct of life goes you are neither better nor worse than the rest of us. Naturally I don't take any credit for the change that you fancy you see in yourself, since the most frequent and lasting emotions that I have stirred in you have been malice and venom.

I did not include Theodore [Powys] in the list of the Powyses whom I have loved because I never loved him. I respected him, and respect is a thing of the reason and not of the heart. However I shall love no Powys again.

I blame you very much for your first ugly blustering letter.[1] Your vanity could well be quiet for a time before such a broken spirit as mine.

I don't know where we shall be in April. Wandering probably in search of a home, or wandering among the shades.

I am glad you speak as you do about Louis. Of course I love him too, and very tenderly. He is not changed in any way from the Louis you have always known. He was always a bit blind in his social relations, but if I could tolerate that when others were the victims, naturally I don't flare up and hate him when I happen to be the victim. You will enjoy seeing him, and the girl [Anne Reid], too, for she is like all your dreams come true.

Your second letter had an amusing drawing. But you know these fits of remorse of yours, there's a good deal too little of affection for me, and a good deal too much of settling your halo straight, for them to be much comfort.

I really shall not write to you again. I got exactly what I deserved for that weak pleading gesture towards you, and I shall not forget this time.
[*added in ink*]

This letter is not meant to hurt you —and I shall be sorry if it does. It is only that I am taking a stand against being hurt by you any more. You see, my dear Jack, I need all my strength for my immediate problems.

1924

133

FRANCES TO JACK (in Patchin Place)

[Parham, Wickham Market, Suffolk]
[8th February 1924]

Dear Jack,

Don't pay too much attention in my wild letters. I get absolutely swamped in misery and I always get fearfully homesick for you. But don't worry about us nor think about us.

Louis has sworn that he will bring a countersuit naming you as correspondent if I bring any pressure to bear upon him in the way of providing for us. He wants us to take 112 pounds a year.[1] I want the 250 pounds continued, I can't support us on less — and if I get a job I want to put away what I earn for Oliver's future. Louis' idea is to put him in a bank or office when he is fourteen. So I am bringing pressure to bear on Louis at the risk of your reputation.

I don't really think Louis will bring you into it — it would take a deal of proving and he would have some rather odd little explanations to make.

My dear it's time you chucked us all.

134

FRANCES TO JACK (in Patchin Place)

[Parham, Suffolk]
[April 1924]

Dear Jack,

Only a mean pride has kept me from writing before. Each night I have

147

planned the letter that I meant to write the next day. Sometimes they were as short as 'forgive Frances', but really I believe that my pride is broken at last.

I have thought of so many things. I remember what I had said in that letter – and it seemed unfair, because I had not said, as well, a deep deep gratitude of all sorts of things that I have to you. It hurts my pride to say – don't hurt me – and yet I do say it.

And do you know I went back to that old fantastic dream of lying dead beside you. If only I had that to hold to as the end of all things. I do believe then that in the reforming of the worlds we would rise again one flesh. And only that would really quiet me. Oh why do I deny it? What an unguarded cry this is . . . . .

I suppose my mother has written to you. Here are the *facts* you always want to know, if she hasn't. We go to London in a small apartment next week, or rather about the 18th.

Primroses are just in bloom and I should like to stay. Louis insisted upon divorce[1] and I have begun proceedings. I have gotten work to do at a pound a week,[2] but probably more later on.

135

JACK TO FRANCES (in Westbourne Grove, London[1])

East Chaldon[2]
[September 1924]

It's extraordinary how nervous I am about writing to Frances . . . . .

. . . . . Mrs Powys at any rate does not find partisanship unphilosophical! She has always consistently been a champion of women against men. It's one of her best characteristics and comes from her having a good deal of a sort of fierce Diana of the forest under her traditions . . . . .

I have been reading Theodore's old MSS[3] and especially *our* favorite – 'Georgina a Lady' – and I find in this MSS your corrections just as you made them such years ago. I noted that. You have always recognised Theodore – before anyone – just as you recognised before anyone that the Bolsheviks would turn into a new order of successful middle-class! Aye! you do hit the mark sometimes with your ice-blue searchlight! I left your address with Bertie and Dorothy.[4] I rather fancy Bertie will be very glad to be treated nicely by you for he is not very often treated nicely by anyone and abominably by Dorothy. *Really* it is awful what he has to put up with, but of course he's very fond of Isabel[5] who *is* a beautiful being!

You think I daresay that it wasn't anything to me to have that final time with you after those honest people [the Macphersons] had gone upstairs and you sat on the table!

That's all you know!

Aye Frances! Aye Frances! Aye Frances! . . . . . It is queer how you have scooped out with your long silver crook the very sea-silt at the bottom of the sand on the floor of my soul. It shows that pride is my dominant characteristic — let my enemies call it conceit — I know it isn't vanity! Well enough to chatter about Jack's character. What I want to think of now is that you are happier than you have sometimes been[6] — oh what you have suffered! Aye, I know it — and that you should ultimately get into your own in writing & I have a certainty that you will. I shall never forget those hours with you. I remember every moment of them. I'll write again. Send my love to Madonna and the children and please give my greeting to the Mcphersons; and please tell that little boy[7] that he must go on drawing land-battles and sea-battles. This is a letter intended as a holding of Frances' hand even though it is shut like a fist as it was on that tram.

136

JACK TO FRANCES (in London)

[September 1924]

I just add this note in case my other one goes astray by any accident.

I'll be waiting for you in the centre of Oxford Circus at 6.30 p.m. in this Monday night. And if there is *no* centre to Oxford Circus where a person can wait, I'll wait for you by the ticket office in the Oxford Circus Tube Station.

I'll wait at one or other of those two places until you turn up.

6.30 Monday evening — and then when we've had our meal we can spend our evening in Oxford Gardens, eh? But we shan't have to have our friends [the Macphersons] with us, so we shall be able to talk and scold to our queer hearts' content.

6.30 — in the middle of Oxford Circus *or* in the Tube Station.

1925

137[1]

JACK TO FRANCES (in London)

4 Patchin Place
Feb 6th [1925]

. . . . I have no conception of exactly how far or deep your friendship with this boy[2] – I keep forgetting how his name (a medieval over-chaste name I think it was!) – actually goes, but I am indescribably glad you've got someone's love to turn to, however bending a branch it may be when you swing in the wind. And I know – who knows if not I? – you deserve to sublimate viciousness & frailties & perversities into some kind of beautiful power of force or sensitiveness.

I wish I could recall your friend's personality more vividly than I can. I hope for the best . . . . . Youth in itself (as Oscar Wilde[3] said when he met Richard le Gallienne[4]) is a kind of genius. I fear I may exploit Phyllis'[5] gentleness to me very often by my bad nature. *You* know what I am. It's something to find anyone who can put up with my fads and fancies and peculiarities . . . . .

I am so constantly thankful that we had those talks together on the bus, in that ABC and by the table in your room. I can see your face so clearly Frances. And there isn't one little incident or gesture of yours that I have forgotten, any more than I have forgotten Ashtead Heath[6] where you lost your coat and where the dry pond was, or that walk through the wood when you noticed some greenish sheafed tall umbelliferous flower in the hedge at Three Bridges,[7] and you read a page of the much abused 'Complex Vision' in the carriage which we had to ourselves!

. . . . . I can think few can have a child more winning and tactful than your little Livio. I trust all goes well with his future. I do like him so

150

well! I so often think of him. I never felt so much affection for him in these days when he was so very *practically* my rival,[8] as I seem to do now when he is more grown up.

. . . . . Well! I must make you an old sign over the distance between us and thank you from my heart for this letter —

J. [*a large cross*]

138

FRANCES TO JACK (in Patchin Place)

[Postmarked:] London W1 May 6 [1925]

Darling Jack,

I need no sign — [*a large cross*] — to arrest my attention and make me think of you. I never stop thinking of you. There is no single day without my turning to you for something. But you will never understand I think. No, you will *never* understand.

But first, thank you so much for getting 'The Hunchback' taken. I have no illusions about its being taken on its merits, but at the same time I get a peculiar pleasure from having that particular one taken, — and something in me is appeased by *you* having done it for me.

Oliver is not well. It seems that there is some thickening of the glands at the base of the lungs. I have always been a little fearful for him. There is something in his nature so like Llewelyn[1] used to be — something too light and sweet and caressing — that I have often wondered whether he too was not strong.

But I have no fear now of Death for anyone.

However Oliver shall be strong.

My soul has gone mad, Jack — not my brain but my soul. There can be a deeper madness than any fantasies of the brain.

Thank you for that letter. It drew me back towards you . . . . . and until this boy [Kenneth Macpherson] gathered me in I was very much adrift. Our drama, yours and mine, goes steadily on. If this boy loves me, then the light will pour backward and flame through my love for you. But if he does not love me then I shall draw away from everybody —

from you most of all—and go on to the end alone.

I can't justify my feeling for him by anything that he is—and I know that all that my mother says of him is true—but at the same time he sweetens everything in life for me—no struggle and no privation matters. He takes all the hurt out of all the past—no wound throbs and I forget.

I wish that I could have this for the end of my life—but there seems no possible chance.

———————

Jack—couldn't you put everything out of your mind about me for a little while except what you used to feel when I was frightened at night? I do so long for you—and yet we will never be together again.

139

JACK TO FRANCES (in London)

May 19th [1925]

. . . . . Here is one of those tight hugs for Frances that hold her safe from all alarms and soothe away all wild fears and stop her from throwing the water-jug, poor driven darling, out of the window on to the leads in a great smash![1] Thank all the gods my dear that you have been able to care for this boy of yours. What does anything else matter? Nothing, I say *nothing* except that he shall care, even more, for you . . . . . Think how easily it might have happened that the fierce wild ebbing & flowing of our feeling for each other—for so long, and not over and never quite quietly calm, ebbing & flowing back & forth in so many whirling tides and with so many echoes — should have embittered us to a point of preventing us from ever caring gently or deeply for anyone again . . . . . Instead of that it has come to pass — by some kind of intermission of some tutelary spirit or other—that your young man & my young woman accept without question, as certainly mine does, and with a queer kind of silent respect, all that we remain to each other and our queer funny hold on each other's mind. After all it is something . . . . . to have three women only, Mrs Powys, Frances and Phyllis, in the space of forty years, from ten years old . . . . . to fifty years old—as really important . . . . . And now I can see that it will be like that until I am dead—three women and three men! Do you want to know who the three men are? Old Littleton, Lulu, and young Littleton![2] Well, there is a person's life—the life of John—from ten years old to—we don't know, and I shall never

know, unless it happens that my head is awfully clear when I lie a-dying!
. . . . . Six human beings who have made dints never to be obliterated
out of thought and memory till all thought and memory is over. You
have already got your three males – Livio, this boy, and Signore Jack. If
by some manner of large thinking and feeling, everything considered, you
added Louis to this list you'll have beaten me! For I certainly haven't
any intention of adding any fourth on either side. Of course I've left out
the one human being who in an odd way, is with me always, more than
Lulu or Frances, or the two Littletons or Phyllis, and I've left out
my father too, to whose ways ere now I have returned with such a sense
of obstinate escape from everyone! But we needn't go back to the
origin of our existence, or you would be put to it to analyse the unspeakable good and bad bond that binds you to that dear harassed and
obstinate figure at your side, whose queer 'corner' with me is so largely
the wild unhappy one we both can't 'handle' (as James [Henderson]
would say) or forget! ha! Well – isn't that a chronicle of events and
people? And yet I daresay when next we are all in a London Subway it
will be Betty and Jack who flirt so abominably!

You need never think it would be possible to get the Frances dint out
of my skull. That isn't so easy to forget as was that writing in the sand
at Dunwich which Frances – was it Dunwich we went to in that crazy
carriage driven by Frances? – obliterated in a savage mood with her foot!
Be at rest, wild heart of Frances! Be at peace. Love your boy. He will not
fail you . . . . .

I can hold you safe over miles and miles and miles of land and water.

140

FRANCES TO JACK (in Patchin Place)

[Postmarked:] London W1 June 17 [1925]

Darling Jack,

We are moving into a single room this week. The flat is sublet, which is
a good thing for it was too expensive. I liked the address, though.

I will send you the new one when we find a place.

The boy[1] did 'fail' me after all. One cannot blame him – he was very
young. I grieved over it in my queer blind way, and all the old griefs
came back. But I am so preoccupied with the intent to earn for the
children and to achieve my purpose that I have not time to grieve really.

But oh Jack I wish I could hide my eyes against you. I have wanted you really dreadfully these last weeks.

I wish that there was no one else at your side sometimes so that I could be near you alone. I am glad of course that you are happy!

They are all well. My mother, I think, enjoys the moving on.[2] I heard from James [Henderson] today. We none of us change very much I find.

Write to me more often for a while. Don't say anything about me but tell me what you are doing and thinking. And at night sometimes put out your hand — the *other* side — and quiet my restlessness.

141

JACK TO FRANCES (in London)

See enclosed £1.

4 Patchin Place
Sept. 6th [1925]

Your letter, Frances dear, about those things you *had* 'taken'[1] did hearten me up so, and I wish I could find the right words . . . balanced exquisitely between the most shameless confessions of wounded vanity and the most free and nice analysis of where I feel your estimate of my peculiar *kind* of egotism goes astray . . . to satisfy your mind — that old mysterious mind that has so often challenged and challenged only to come up against that irritating quality in my nature that made [Theodore] Dreiser once call out, 'It's like shooting at a mountain of feathers', or something of that kind!

But, leaving all that, it gives me, let me tell you, a most wonderful sense of how unchanged you are in all essentials that you should still be reading your Novum Testamentum, your η $\kappa\epsilon\iota\nu\eta$ $\delta\iota\alpha\theta\eta\kappa\eta$ — if I have not altogether forgotten that Greek original of it. But oh my dear I have no 'style' — that's just the thing I haven't got . . . and in some way I still think that just that very lack proves that my egotism is a negligible superficial drawback — for having no rooted banked-up engrained style gives me the freedom of all the world of ideas — something protean and fluid that really in its way is an important asset. A 'poseur' is the thing they call me over here you know and nothing — nothing I say! — could be more absurdly off the mark. I am on the contrary naively simple, with all my serpentine convolutions . . . What a quaint difference between us — you think you're hard on the track of the secret of the

Universe *sans* style to express it when you've got it —*I* think I've got such a line on the secret of the Universe that it saves me the trouble of bothering about style at all[2] . . . And meanwhile . . . the Universe. . . . . .!

Well I suppose it'll be there and not much more explained – when two mounds, somewhere or other, nod to each other over the rim of earth! . . . . .

. . . . . I've had an awfully worrying time lately over Arnold [Shaw]. He's now in a Sanatorium . . . practically a lunatic asylum – but a very good doctor has it and I think he'll cure him and that he'll come out of that cured 'pro tem' – but no money at all and his wife and son and Edith[3] – no money – and his wife likely to have another child soon – and no money – and the bill of the sanatorium unpaid – and no one will *ever* pay it – no one!

I spent a night with him at this sanatorium – such an experience with people very mad, rather mad, and almost well – several practically all right like Arnold himself who was radiantly – too radiantly – happy. He had confidence in the doctor with whom I had a long talk about him – but not on the subject of how on earth he was ever to be paid! Do great psychiatrists ever cure patients for love or for science? He has not yet seen Arnold in his depressed mood, only in his hyper-excited mood . . . . . I confessed to the doctor that I thought by my peculiarities I had been an unlucky influence for Arnold but the doctor seemed to think that this collapse had been coming on for a long time and had its origin in his whole character . . . . .

Well, the gods guard you Frances!

142

FRANCES TO JACK (in Patchin Place)

Post Office Cottage, Charmouth, Dorset
[September 1925]

Dearest Jack,

I have given up my office, or rather it has given me up, because they got two younger women who could do stenography at 30/- a week. I was getting Three pounds. They offered to keep me on at Two pounds, but my lunches and fares cost 10/- a week, and the extra 30/- would not have paid the high rents of London and Betty's schooling. I am going to live in the country now, at Badingham, Suffolk,[1] near the Lings. Marjory

Ling[2] found a house for me at twenty five pounds a year. The Lings, you remember, are the Solicitor people of the Wilkinsons,[3] but their daughter who is a few years younger than I am is a very nice creature who has taken a fancy to me, and whom I like very much. She is a quaint bird as you may imagine. You must meet her the next time you come over. Goodness! how long will that be? I shall love to see you. My feeling to you has undergone the queerest change. I am no longer in love with you a bit. That is the smashing of a state of mind that has stood the wear and tear of twenty years. Longer, for I was considerably less than twenty when I first fell in love with you.[4] My love for that boy, — over and done with, — seems to have purged my heart and soul as a bad illness will sometimes do, and I feel extraordinarily refreshed and invigorated and ready to begin a new life – but I am through with love forever and forever and forever.

We have had some funny times lately, for my mother had forgotten that she had asked you to write to her at the American Express, and her pension cheques were lost in the post as well – they have not turned up yet either. So that I had to finance her down to my last penny. Then when things were looking black I insisted upon her writing to the Express offices on the chance. You know how she is, she swore that she had never given you or anyone that address, but anyhow your four letters turned up just in time to save us from disaster. We camped out a good deal, but we had not warm enough night coverings and no tent, only a sheet that we tied to bushes. It was amusing, but not always comfortable. Which reminds me, please send that motoring article[5] of mine back, please at once.

The money that we have taken from you, and are still taking, is a nightmare to me, but please keep it up for this one winter. After that it must stop altogether and I will try to get it paid back. And will you please give me a present that I can't pay for now. It is this year's edition of '1001 Places to Sell Manuscript'. I think it costs a dollar. I think James would send it to me if you can't afford it. You could ask him anyway. Llewelyn of course never sent me his books and never will. But that was wrong of him.

Do you know I *loved* Bertie[6] last year, and wished very much that I could have had him for a friend.

There were moments when I resented your having refused to let me see Bertie unless I was friends with his wife[7] as well. I don't know that you were always so careful to be friends with people's husbands! I don't mind Dorothy, but honestly she has a very cheap and tawdry mind. I mean she is superficially original, but there is no real depth of any kind in her, and she bored me — though I liked her funny littleness, and her quaint vanity.

Please write me more often, though I quite see that it is beginning to be a great effort to you to write to me. I am like an almost forgotten wooden headed doll pushed back in the corner of the toy cupboard. Jack has new toys these days.

1926

143[1]

JACK TO FRANCES (at Oaken Hill Hall)

[*One or two pages missing*]

. . . . . O dear such sad things have been happening. I had a mad letter from Arnold [Shaw] and when I was at Baltimore I went to his house there. Do you know what I found? — He had that very day just before I came been taken to the State Lunatic Asylum. His wife was in the hospital having had a child[2] a week ago! His father-in-law died a few weeks ago and his mother-in-law (without any money) is on their hands, nervous and collapsed, saying she will take the place of a servant! In his flat there was Edith, Lizzie's[3] daughter (who has a small job in an office) — Arnold had turned against her in his madness — also his little boy about 4, also a certain 'Miss K', an old stenographer of his (now married), the one who used to persecute Louis so, when you were *out there* by the sea — He had telegraphed for her as well as me and she had been much more help than I could be . . . . . I went to the British Consul & to the Episcopal Clergyman (this latter a brute). But I think the old Rector, Arnold's father,[4] will send them some money. Meanwhile there is a kind society woman who has paid something to help — she is trying, this person, to get Arnold moved to a nicer Asylum — without having to pay too much. But that clergyman was a brute. Arnold had annoyed him — He was glad he was in an Asylum . . . . . The mother-in-law said that Arnold had borrowed on the furniture and she feared the bailiffs would take it away . . . . .

I really think, Frances, that the older you get the more calamities you encounter — How little one used to believe one's parents as to what existence held of worries & troubles! I am at this time alone, for Phyllis has had to go to Missouri to help her mother with the old man, her father (aged 86), who is now in the hospital . . . . .

158

1. Louis Wilkinson, c. 1920

2. Frances with her son, Oliver (aged six weeks), 1915

3. Powys family group, showing, *back row left to right*: Dorothy and Bertie, Jack, the Rev. Charles Francis Powys (father), Louis Wilkinson, Willy Powys; *middle row*: Marian Powys, Margaret (Jack's wife), Mary Cowper Powys (mother), Frances Gregg, Gertrude Powys, Katie Powys; *front row*: Young Littleton (Jack's son), Isobel Powys-Marks

. Frances, Louis Wilkinson,
ulia Vanness Gregg, Jack and
Teddy'. *c*. 1912.

5. Julia and Frances, Philadelphia, 1912.

6. John Cowper Powys's wife, Margaret, with their son Littleton Alfred. *Courtesy Francis Powys*

7. Hilda Doolittle — 'H.D.' — with Julia Vanness Gregg, on the voyage to England, 1912

8. Jack with Frances, dressed in boy's clothes, in the Colosseum 1912

144

JACK TO FRANCES (at Oaken Hill Hall)

4 Patchin Place
Feb 5 [1926]

Just a line, Frances, dear dear Frances, to say I've got your letter. You are right, 'Faithfulness is more than money' and it's being unfair to you to assume that the childish disappointment of a letter *without* a package will be so great that it spoils the pleasure of the letter! Once let me get lodged in my foolish skull or pate or head, which sometimes really I think is doting or dotty, that it *is* a comfort to you to hear from me even without any 'enclosed', and I'll write you more often.

. . . . . My affairs should not, will not and must not (or your tragically hard affairs, as I think of them, must not either) interfere with my writing naturally and easily to you and you to me! . . . . .

Think of you having had a poem in The Spectator! I am glad it was a poem once again. How well I recall that one[1] in The Forum, which you gave me at that Germanstown lecture. I don't know what to say of this business of your getting another job – and when you say 'taking Betty with you' I am non-plussed and puzzled.

. . . . . It's awful to think of you actually selling the Crooked Cross.[2]

145

JACK TO FRANCES (at Oaken Hill Hall[1])

Hotel Charlton, Wellsburg, W. Virginia
March 22 [1926]

. . . . . I have a concern now on the horizon of my days because Phyllis' father, a very wise old man of whom I am extremely fond – fonder than any old man I've known since *Mr de Kantzow*[2] of whom I used to tell you – has been for the last two months afflicted by a more trying kind of suffering. I'm sure I don't know whether he'll get well or not, this time. He may, for he's got astonishing resilience, but he's as old as Thomas Hardy[3] himself! And I'm teased so often by a suppressed fury with my manager, Mr K,[4] but I daresay it's not his fault – tho' lecturers (like musicians) always curse their managers! But poor Arnold, now in a

lunatic asylum because of financial worry, used himself to say sometimes, 'John's a fizzle!' . . . . .

But now I shall just go on and finish this huge new novel of two
volumes[5] (about four hundred pages each). It won't be finished till the
middle of the summer or till the end of the summer . . . . . and then it's
only too likely that no publisher will take it . . . only too likely —but I
pray won't be long! —in *MSS*!

. . . . . Have you always perhaps demanded of me, not what I'm capable of doing, but what *you* yourself, if you had the gifts I *have* got,
would be driven to do? . . . . . What wickedness it was in you, old friend,
when you used to say, 'Get a definite philosophy of life and art!', for
deep in your nature you must have perceived that what is most saving
and hopeful in me is that very fluidity w[h] you so curse, for it's that that
has kept me from stiffening into a groove, before the hour arrived when I
could 'move altogether if I moved at all' —kept me chaotic in fact while I
was chaotic in my slow deferred long-delaying mental growth! But on the
other hand (I confess it!) you were wise when you spoke, as you often
did, of the necessity of absorbing all the elements of my nature (and
'sublimating' them somehow) in place of letting 'em sway back and forth
(the 'divine' and 'devilish moods'!) like a tiger and a great horned ram
locked in one cage! . . . . .

Bless you —

146[1]

JACK TO FRANCES (in London)

See 10s   4 Patchin Place
                                                                 Sep 22 [1926]

I keep feeling so anxious about you and your existence, Frances, old
friend. I do pray that the Herne Bay House[2] won't swallow up all your
bitterly earned money. But I still feel so happy about Livio, as your son,
and about his having been able to spend his holidays with you.

. . . . . It is so awful for you to do this work and live so beggarly without a margin for leisure, I beg and implore you to note the blundering
sagacity of Signore Jack when he says that it's better to be spiritually sad
than perforce made bad & you know well how the navel string tugs at
you — left and right — between mother and daughter! Haven't I heard you
discourse again and again on that very thing — on the mysterious link

made of honeyed nettle-stalks joining mothers and the daughters of mothers!

On the other hand to come 'home' to that hall-bedroom[3] — God! I do know how awful it is. Maybe even to feel fretted and chafed and angry while you snugly lie back upon 'your own' is better than to *try* to lie back upon the callous tortoise-shell slipperiness and hardness of 'alone-in-London'! I don't know, Frances, old friend, I don't know. But anyhow, we know, you and I, how your peculiar nature wd. 'kick against the pricks', wherever you were. And yet — on my faith — I *have* seen you with your face lit up in sheer simple happiness.

Well, the good powers protect you . . . . .

1927

147[1]

JACK TO FRANCES (at Oaken Hill Hall)

4 Patchin Place
Feb 1st [1927]

. . . . . You are not like Theodore[2] who used to send me such lovely letters when I put (enclosed £1) on the top of *his* each week but now, though I wrote to him one of the longest letters I have ever written, I have heard nothing. I hope his inspiration for writing his books has returned to him, for that had failed him when I stayed there in June – but it is so necessary to him to get that little extra money, it will be serious if it goes on – this inability to write . . . . .

I keep wondering how everyone got on during that terrific storm[3] we read about over here . . . . .

I have had a hard winter financially, but of course the absence of lectures has meant that I have just been living on here and writing my huge book [*Wolf Solent*] which has now reached 1250 MSS pages . . . . . I have written in a very eccentric and very rambling way; just enjoying myself in writing it . . . . . Day has followed day in New York writing and writing on and on – a completely isolated life – but except for our money anxieties all has gone well . . . . . What trials you and the Madonna have weathered side by side – and you sometimes scolding her so – and she sometimes teasing you so! . . . . . I do wish that some fairy, as lovely but more powerful than your little daughter, could steer your tossing boat into a safe harbour! O I do hope Livio is stronger these days! . . . . .

I hope your daughter's struggles with that tedium of book-learning – so different from the magic country of her self-told stories – have got easier and smoother to her.

How one scene and another returns to me! How I can recall that walk

162

to . . . . . that boat at that place in the woods where there was a frog among the rushes, one of those days when I didn't wheel you in that chair[4] . . . . .

. . . . . Do you remember how Lulu and I quarrelled at the Miramara?[5] How far off it all seems—like a play . . . . .

And how we shouted for 'Teddy' late at night—what a dog! Curse his blood and rest his ghost! —what a dog! all down the avenues by Pulaski.[6] How, I wonder, is that *little* dog you've got now and Barbara the goat? . . . . .

I wonder so much how your turbulent and mysterious heart is now responding to these new lovers of yours . . . . . Let us remain friends, my old companion, calm and detached and free from these hate-loves and love-hates . . . . . You will anyhow, anyway, for so it *must* be, think hard thoughts of Signore Jack. Didn't even the good James cry Poor Jack! with a deep authentic sigh when he read 'The two Brothers'?[7] Maybe he opined that peradventure his own turn was coming soon – the poor old bugger!

I wonder what people inhabit that little house on Derby Rd where you used to live in West Philadelphia now?[8] Do they ever see queer wraiths of former scenes enacted to their disturbance?

Ezra [Pound] courting H & F [Hilda Doolittle and Frances] at the same time. Jack bringing his chapter on the Ode to the Nightingale[9] and stretching his arm along the edge of the horsehair sofa!

. . . . . Our existence here is really happy —on the whole. But are you like Theodore [Powys] and are now sympathetic – indeed *only* sympathetic—when people are *not* happy? . . . .

148

JACK TO FRANCES (at Oaken Hill Hall)

June 24th [1927]

O there is such a quaint little old-fashioned Dickens character here in Patchin Place that Phyllis and I met at a regular Mad Hatter's Tea Party in the rooms of a Romanian Gypsy lady[1] who lives opposite us. Her name – I mean that fantastic little Dickens character—is Miss Julia Wells of Philadelphia. She must have quarrelled with her grand relations, and be in extreme poverty. She says she lived in Patchin Place with Ezra Pound and with Hilda—and she *thinks*—but is not quite certain—that she remembers you in those old days . . . . . She is, I fear, terribly poor; like many others in Patchin Place at this time . . . . . I shall go with Phyllis to her parents . . . . . It's lucky for me that they are such nice people or they might be annoyed at my sending everything I make to Mrs Powys . . . . . Saturn must be afflicting Sagittarius just at present.

I've had . . . . . to give up *even tea* these last days which is one of the chief pleasures of my life. Do you recall how you used to scold me for living on tea and bread with much wicked relish? . . . . .

149

JACK TO FRANCES (at Oaken Hill Hall)

See 10ˢ   914 8th Street, East Las Vegas
New Mexico
[August 1927]

. . . . . I *am* so glad that your boy and your girl are like what they are. How many trials it does redeem — I cannot believe that it is only my laziness timidity and inhumanity that makes me so reluctant to worry my son[1] with any attempt to pull him across the No man's Land wʰ divides his mother's place from mine in his regard . . . . . I think he & I are sufficiently like each other to find a queer remote romantic pleasure and even piquancy in our quaintly aloof and detached relations . . . . . I think he's got well into his head that I'm someone to fall back upon at any pinch . . . . .

As for me, O Frances, I never cease from my obstinate and rooted manner of living — a mingling of what I daresay you'd call a bastard stoicism with a bastard epicureanism! I've had one good piece of news — an article taken by *The Century* ['The American Scene and Character'] — a funny rambling article on this country — but to confess the honest truth more of it is Phyllis's than mine!

. . . . . However *The Century* article is taken — and as you I daresay have felt it with your *Criterion* article[2] — there's no lotion or potion for a wounded frame like the acceptance of our Writings!

Oh dear but the great T.S. Eliot[3] is beyond my mark — for his *Waste Land* is one of my great admirations & has been for a couple of years . . . . .

I'm *now* going to return to my book about the Blackmore Vale [*Wolf Solent*] — a romance but not a silly one — I tell you! . . . . .

150

JACK TO FRANCES (at Oaken Hill Hall)

4 Patchin Place
Aug 30th [1927]

. . . . . Arnold – with his wife and two children (one 18 months) – has landed himself on Staten Island . . . . . He was turned out for not paying the rent and I had to give him every penny I could rake up to pay for their moving to another place – but now he's got a job (book-keeper in an Italian Coal Yard) 10 hours a day . . . . . But as his mind is all nervous of going crazy again heaven knows if he'll be able to do it . . . . . I shall have to postpone Mrs Powys' remittance till my lectures begin again . . . P. [Phyllis Playter] has been very good about it . . . but of course Arnold is a remote personage to anyone who didn't know me when I was so mixed up with him. His really gallant effort to . . . . . start on this job which is not an easy one, does make my helping out, just a little less like throwing money into the sea than it often is with him!

Then a few days ago came an SOS from the Sacco-Vanzetti[1] Defence people in Boston for a speech at their Memorial Service or Meeting. God! Frances – your old master-pupil in the casuistry of ill-used children and meowing cats had some heart-beatings over this little jaunt . . . for the Boston Authorities are in the most touchy frame of mind. I feebly tried to get out of it (for really I was in what Livio would call a funk) on the grounds of not being able to afford the journey; but when they wired they'd pay it there was no way out. However! It wasn't I but a certain Professor Horace Kallen[2] – such a charming man too he was! – who was arrested and for what do you suppose? – for *blasphemy*, because he said that your queer god Christ – le bon Sansculotte – was an Anarchist – like Signor Vanzetti! But now I read in the paper & they confirm it round here that the Judge who issued the warrant for Kallen's arrest has himself withdrawn it – probably craftier ones in that wicked Commonwealth told him he'd make them all look fools over such a ridiculous trial. So my absurd dread of your American Police has now quieted down . . . and really I got through my confession of this surreptitious trip – so contrary to all managerial contracts – pretty well at '*The* Office' though they'd seen a notice of it . . . so it was a good thing I didn't try to hide it up! . . . . .

Well, and now to your Kenneth's caricature of you![3] I kept dipping into it – at once interested because it *was* you – and violently repelled by that peculiar 'obscure-aesthetic' style which is always so alien to my rustic Powysian mind! . . . . . I couldn't —hard tho' I tried —read it right straight through. I *couldn't* even for your sake — for the style and turns of expression were so unpleasing to my disposition. But I got enough of it to see that you must have made an indelible and deeply branded impression on this youth's sensibility. He is like a young steer with a great 'F' branded on his forehead between his horns — just as I am an old OX, with another 'F' in neater Greekish letters branded —nearer the brain —behind the left ear!

I suppose *really* the pointed-bearded Ezra influenced you yourself most of all your devotees, for the very reason that by reason of a certain butterfly-like speed of movement *he* wouldn't wait till those branding irons were got into position!

. . . . . I shall understand better, when I see you, what strange new dimension your 'horse of fire' gallops over and against what adversaries! . . . . .

151

JACK TO FRANCES (in London)

See one pound!

4 Patchin Place
Sept 14th [1927]

. . . . . James came in last night and tells me that he has begun very seriously — old James par le Bon Dieu! — contemplating a novel himself! . . . . .

. . . . . I have agreed (to get my huge book [*Wolf Solent*] taken) to cut out 320, no! 350 *pages* — practically the whole of the 3rd volume — the work of half a year . . . . .

Have you got with your other scruples this ferocious aesthetic morale that your old Maître dans les Arts Ezra held up as his high gonfalon? and under which his yellow-grey Van Dyke beard doubtless wags still! . . . . .

152[1]

JACK TO FRANCES (in London)

See 1£ 4 Patchin Place, New York City

Sept 28 [1927]

Very pleased & relieved was I, O my old friend & prophetic one, when I got your typed letter telling about your holiday and about Monsieur Scarboro'[2] (beautiful according to the great creative Nature – but ugly according to mortal man's garb 'when 'a owes the worm no silk, the sheep no wool, the cat no perfume') and about your tall son (beautiful always, *as I well believe*) . . . . .

Why does the *anger of women* –especially of Frances – tyrannize over me to such an absurd extent? I seem always prepared to risk the anger of men so lightly by comparison! I must have been a slave of Hippolyta, queen of the Amazons, in my last incarnation . . . . .

I recall being once staggered by what seemed to be the monstrous Jesuitry of your casuistical defence of getting angry with your mother! – You've probably quite forgotten the incident . . . but you said that your anger distracted her attention from things that would worry her or (as James wd say) wd 'bother' her *much more*.

Tell me this. Why is it that in my long and unpardonable acquaintance with feminine butterflies – I have never known one, or barely one, who confessed to being *in the wrong* . . . . . . Are they *always* right?

The only thing in this your letter . . . and that of course was half a jest . . . that did make me wish that *you* yourself wouldn't be 'airy' over so very serious a thing – (now here is the table turning and the worm turning, ha!) and *that* is when you speak of selecting a future partner for your fairy daughter. I have just been reading the Life of Goethe[3] by that Jew Ludwig[4] – and it was Goethe choosing Ottelie as the wife of his son August that ruined the luckless youth. Didn't we visit his grave in Rome in the Shelley and Keats cemetery?

However – probably it is my extraordinary purity of conduct (not half enough praised by Frances) over this little daughter of yours that has made me into a very old-fashioned Moralist where she is concerned! . . . . .

But I *am* glad about Scarborough for after all it is to youth –especially to young men – that we all turn – we Prophets of the Lord – for theirs is the kingdom, the power & the glory. I too have, *this very minute*, said goodbye to a young man for whom I suddenly felt an extraordinary and tender wave of affection – surprising to myself & I daresay incredible

to anyone who knows me!
Well – the lord be with you old friend.

153

JACK TO FRANCES (in London)

see 10s.

4 Patchin Place
Oct 13 [1927]

Frances old friend –

I had a perfectly lovely letter from old James [Henderson] yesterday which I find I owe entirely to you, for you told him I had missed his appearances lately here. He writes that he has been engrossed in a regular embroglio of philosophy – Croce[1] – and *Whitehead*[2] – a very difficult mathematical genius, seems so to me! And that he has got thrilling delight from both these arduous and complicated tasks, as he got nearer and nearer to these precise and nicely adjusted ideas – whatever they are! Some of the summer he says he suffered in – other portions were happy – and he wrote happily. Hit me, confound me, as hard as you like, my fierce one, I still obstinately hold that *happiness* is the sole purpose, justification, cause, end, meaning, ideal, consolation, secret object, aim, raison d'etre etc. etc. etc. of this troublesome world.

. . . . . A sweet boy has just knocked at this door to ask if we are Catholics and belong to the Parish. I rather liked that question. It had a pleasant mellow reassuring sound – I liked the word *Parish*! O Frances – I *have* got to speak for Isadora Duncan's[3] Memorial Service in St Marks. I cannot tell you how I hate Mr Guthrie and St Mark's. It's only that I *know* the lady would not give a fig for those prejudices of mine and would only think of dancing anywhere, and being loved and praised anywhere – and after all that *is* 'a strange brooch in this all-hating world' – and to make all your feelings into dances and not with any affectation and often *very badly* – is uncommon! . . . . .

154

JACK TO FRANCES (in London)

See 10 shillings.   4 Patchin Place
                                            Thursday [October 1927]

Not very nice to have a letter in this mail box to say that Frances has
decided to have an operation for cancer.

Oh my dear my dear! What you are — writing of this ghastly thing so
calmly just as you did of that nail in your flesh[1] —more calmly . . . . .

. . . . . Just understand, old friend, that I am now over the air and sea
with you — now when you are at this instant reading this — and lodging
like a sea-hawk or a finny-footed foolish Guillemot in your brain, like a
sentinel to share a fragment of your cup, your bitter thoughts; to bear
some of them anyway . . . . . How much braver Frances is than S.J.! I
mean Signore Jack—not Sanctus Johannis!

. . . . . How I do congratulate you about Oliver's publication in *The
Bermondsey*[2] —I should think he has beaten us all!

. . . . . I am lucky to have any sort of tour—so old a veteran lecturer as
I am; and they all so fickle, as they are! . . . . .

As you read this I am standing, foolishly faithfully inside one lobe of
your forehead like as if I were a good small William Blake's black angel to
soothe your thoughts!

155

JACK TO FRANCES (in Whitechapel Hospital, London)

                                            The Dinkler Hotels
                                        Piedmont Hotel, Georgia
                                            [November 1927]

. . . . . To me forwarded — yes! even to me forwarded to Georgia—far
off in the swamps too, in such a queer backwater place (for here I am
only changing trains i' the dark) came the news in that letter-card—and
ah, what memories of England — righteous and the reverse, pardie! — do
letter-cards recall! That even now you are *in the hospital* . . . . . The day
that postcard came — behold! I wrestled with your spirit, like Jacob with
the angel. All the morning with the spirit of Frances I wrestled;

remembering so many many things! O I prayed for you — you may believe, old friend — to the powerfullest of all, as far as my poor prayers go up! . . . . .

I *did* speak for Isadora — yes I did! but aye, Frances, Guthrie's church was all I anticipated. What a wicked masquerade! . . . . . Well, Lulu and Alyse must be settled, D.V. in Patchin Place by this very time[1] . . . . .

156

JACK TO FRANCES (in Whitechapel Hospital)

see 10[s]

Mountain Inn
Fayetteville, Arkansas
[mid-November 1927]

Frances, Frances, this is in great haste for I am rushed from Pillar to Post and it's not easy to catch a moment.

Not a word since your letter-card. Oh Frances, for heaven's sake write a line & let me hear what has happened to you . . . . .

Do write if you are not in Paradise, like the good Thief! . . . . .

157

JACK TO FRANCES (in Whitechapel Hospital)

see 10[s]

Chicago
Nov 28th [1927]

Well, Frances — not a word yet from you as to what happened in that Hospital. For all I know I may be writing to an immensely relieved and let off Frances who never had that terrifying thing the matter with her at all . . . or I may be — the gods forbid! — writing to Frances already walking in peace in a land more suited to her wild injured soul than this world of selfish Englishmen and awful jobs and difficult decisions and all the rest of it . . . . .

But I am sure it isn't so — I should surely have known it.

158

JACK TO FRANCES (in Whitechapel Hospital)

See 10ˢ.

4 Patchin Place
Dec 9th [1927]

Well – you are out of the wood, Frances, Frances, and now I pray I'll learn by all authority and indubitable verdict that this awful experience has removed peril from now on . . . . .

Comfort yourself, therefore, O my troubled and injured heart of Frances, for this really and in good truth may turn out to be the crisis, the reef, the crest of the storm – and once thro' this, why should not quiet waters for the rest of your outward life await you? . . . . .

. . . . . Those last notes were not such as I could construe otherwise than as meaning that the moment was a pretty dark and terrifying one . . . . . You've braved it. You've gone thro' it. It's past and over now, Frances, old friend, so don't think of it. Don't let your mind go back over those awful moments. You were brave – braver in this terrific crisis than when Lulu made you cry in the Stoke Road about the Apple-tree when you were scared of Rider Haggard's leap as we called it on Ham Hill¹ that easy carefree time. O well-a-way! how far have your feet travelled since you made for Lulu that embroidery of Glastonbury – no! since he made it for *you*.² But how easy for Jack to tell you not to go back in your thoughts over what you have gone through – how easy for him to advise this or that of crafty mental adjustments – as though Sisera should dictate the stanzas of the Song of Deborah!³ Walking along the edge of the railings of Sheridan Square, where Seventh Avenue drives its lorries thro' these sham-artists' shanties, I can shoot my consciousness over the sea over Essex over Whitechapel into your ward in the hospital, but *you* are the one in the hospital now, as I was when I said a snatched goodbye at the platform of Rockaway, but I can know some of your miseries . . . . .

I am sure I congratulate *you* of what you spoke of in that published paper⁴ of the great shop to be managed by you – as long as it doesn't quite dissipate your power; but leaves your untouched inspiration free for your real 'work'.

But I think of you as I walk along; and of all the waves between – [*see JCP's drawing on the following page*]

. . . . .

See letter number 158

1928

159

JACK TO FRANCES (in Westbourne Street, London W2)

4 Patchin Place
Feb 20 [1928]

I *was* so glad to have, my old friend, that photo of the Rectory where you live & the two children[1] —not to speak of your *very* nice letter.

How astonishingly *tall* Oliver looks and indeed so does Betty & what a dignified and stately little house & in such a spacious purlieu full of air and winds & clouds. You get such a lovely feeling from its looks in this picture and a sense of the fields and orchards out of sight & the freedom from intrusive neighbours—and what a big house! And it looks neither so old as to be ramshackle or sinister —nor so new as to be pretentious or like a villa . . . . . Oh dear! but this return to your job & your rooms and your loneliness and all the hardships of editing that paper —I fear it will be hard in your semi-convalescent state[2] . . . . .

Well — may the blessed fairies work it out for the best, by the aid of *chance*!

Y^r J & the Lord be with 'ee!

160

JACK TO FRANCES (in Westbourne Street, London)

See *1£*

4 Patchin Place
March 9th [1928]

. . . . . My days are so broken into that now that I am off I don't know where & it is all hard. Too many people, Frances, for a hermit — an immoral patient hermit — like me! It is hard to keep up heart & steer right onward, as Milton says, though I am happy at bedrock, as you might say!

But raked & harrowed combed-out & grooved into furrows on the surface of my life.

But in main issues all is well . . . . .

I do so want to finish my book.[1]

161

JACK TO FRANCES (in Westbourne Street, London)

See 1£   4 Patchin Place
                                                     March 22 [1928]

You poor lonely wild being, sitting there with your left arm half numb still at that awful desk — getting thro' all your work I warrant with skill & speed astonishing to them all — but with this stark feeling of weariness, known to none, in your secret heart. Don't you ever think that your faithful Signore Jack doesn't realise all you go through, my dear — well! probably not *all*, for who knoweth the bitterness of another's heart & *such* another's? But a good deal of it, old friend! . . . . .

Peace & quiet is what I crave. I am old, Frances, yes, I am getting old [*he was 56*] . . . . .

Aye! what memories came rushing back when the other day by chance I saw the words 'Baron Corvo'![1] It is I daresay just the simple universal 'struggle for existence' that I grow aware of now, so much further on than *half* of my really protected life! 'Well, we'll see now the resources of your spirit,' was what Keats used to say to the hard-pressed of his acquaintances — and that is what Jack must say to Jack! What Jack must say to Frances is quite different — just a sign of imperfect & clumsy but none the less undeviating recognition! . . . . .

162

JACK TO FRANCES (in Badingham, Suffolk)

See enclosed 1£   May 18 [1928]

While I am writing this an Irish tramp is fussing round my room drinking the water carrying off a quarter and if I had a daughter! He's a a bequest from Lulu and Alyse – and oh, my dear, such a trial! for I'm not able to deal with him – I corrupt him & he infuriates me, below my 'kindness'! He comes twice a day now that *pro tem* I am unprotected – for P. [Phyllis Playter] has gone to her parents – & times his visits to a nicety when the tea-pot is on the table. Well I shall be off my self in a fortnight . . . . . to New Mexico where I have, as last year, some lectures & where I shall see again that 5*th* Cousin of mine [Warwick Powys] who is out there as a sort of gentleman-janitor of some Easterner's Ranch, guarding it from robbers in its owner's absence & living as solitary as Robinson Crusoe – with a cat & a cow.

Old James [Henderson] came in the night before last. Time does not wither nor age stale his rooted benevolence & affectionateness – and once more, but as ever in vain, he tried to make me understand the philosophy of Croce. I *cannot* get even the rudiments of this philosophy and yet James does his best each time to make me see it. It's some twists given to Hegel's[1] 'Spirit', turning it into I *can't* make out just what 'experience' – 'history' – but how can it be *history*? How can 'history' have anything to do with the secret of the universe? & *whose* history? *whose* experience – James'? – Frances'? – Signore Jack's – or God's? It is the most extraordinary philosophy I've ever heard about.

I am struggling on revising this huge book in the carbon copy – it took 3 hands to type it & pay as it went! chapter by chapter.

Not a word from Schuster,[2] my first string – But I give him till next Thursday & then try my 'second string', namely Longman's Green . . . . .

163

JACK TO FRANCES (in Badingham, Suffolk)

See 1£   *New Mexico*
June 23rd [1928]

Frances must have begun to fancy her aged friend was dead & buried – and so in a sense I *was* as far as the world was concerned . . . with my Cousin Warwick Powys . . . . . We had no milk on this forlorn domain – but lovely *scenery* –& the butter had a tendency to get a bit queer owing to the lack of ice. But Cousin Warwick cooked oatmeal & made macaroni & cheese very well & there were eggs, so we got on.

Since then . . . . . I've had the poor chap here in my lodgings to give him a bit of a change. His loneliness is awful & none of his relations (I am only his 5th cousin) do a thing for him. He was robbed of every penny & of his books & even his clothes by an insidious pair of Irish rogues (a Mr & Mrs) who got him, in his abysmal *simplicity*, completely in their hands, then cleared off to Colorado leaving him with nothing but his father's medals & his mother's watch . . . . . And now, since he's lost his cat, not a living person does he see, except for two hours on Sundays when he walks over — for he can't even ride now — to have a meal with the Foreman of a neighbouring ranch & get what letters may be there, w^h are few enough! He's got that feeling of being a failure, useless & helpless but not brave enough for suicide, w^h lonely people get sometimes, but he amuses himself by composing queer little ditties, humorous & sad enough, to w^h he invents tunes and he has a few books out there & makes the days pass by cutting wood & keeping his house spotlessly clean. He looks like Don Quixote sometimes & sometimes like a very aged March Hare standing on its hind legs. It's an incredible chance I ever found him — but directly I got here I heard rumours of 'poor old Mr Powys'[1] . . . . . I can't afford to get him away but I can write to him & keep up his spirits a bit—& who knows? some day some book of mine may make a bit! At the present moment every one of my works is out of print. No more news of my 'philosophical novel' — but at least it hasn't been rejected yet.

I can't help being so glad & relieved that you are thinking of that old Westminster School[2] for your son . . . . . It is wonderful what you've done & are doing. . . Have you really got a little girl[3] to be a companion for Betty?

164

JACK TO FRANCES (in Westbourne Street, London)

See 10^s!

c/o Mrs Steinmetz
914 8th Street, Las Vegas
New Mexico, U.S.A.
July 10—Sunday [1928]

. . . . . So far the only one of my essays taken is one of the Hebrew Moscow Players on a weird play called 'The Dybbuk',[1] and that has not been yet paid for —but maybe I shall yet have some luck with the rest. It was very tiresome to have to stop writing my book for these confounded essays & now if they're not taken — well! I'll then know that I *can't* write for the magazines! . . . . .

165

JACK TO FRANCES (in London)

See 1£   [Printed:] Hotel Statler, St Louis
                                                        650 Rooms, 650 Baths
                                                        Nov 19th [1928]

Frances, I am vexed to find that a letter w^h *must be from you* along
with another which must be *from* Theodore [Powys], has gone astray
without reaching me . . . . . Frances and Theodore travelling together
(honest strange queer companions!) – & I can imagine the low oracular
dialogue that takes place –

Frances' letter –	Jack is too fond of comfort.
Theodore's letter –	I've got a smear on my cheek.
Frances' letter –	He is too self-indulgent –
Theodore's letter –	It's these rich postmen's fingers. Rub against me & see what you can do –
Frances' letter –	He has chosen the path of ease –
Theodore's letter –	to get this dirt off –
Frances' letter –	I was talking about Jack –
Theodore's letter –	Eh?
Frances' letter –	I said Jack –
Theodore's letter –	Hee! Hee! Hee!
Frances' letter –	I *won't* be laughed at!
Theodore's letter –	If you young ladies would do what you're asked and not be loving –
Frances' letter –	W – h – at?
Theodore's letter –	What is *inside* you?
Frances' letter –	W – h – at?
Theodore's letter –	I can read it –
Frances' letter –	You can't!
Theodore's letter –	It's your fault we're lost.
Frances' letter –	*I* can read what's *not* inside *you*; but what *ought* to be!
Theodore's letter –	What are you talking about? Did you hear what I said just now? I said *it's your* fault we're lost!

. . . . . It *is* vexing and it is odd that these two particular letters should have eloped together like this! You'll say – 'Jack's only entirely honest correspondents!' What a story I could write of a group of letters going like the Musicians[1] thro' the world! – each a gesture of the person – a sort of half-person made up of the mood of an hour! Who knows what letters can't do & *where* they can't go?

But I think they'll turn up . . . . .

O dear O dear I hear that Lulu, indeed both Lulu & Alyse,[2] have got a fever in Palestine and are at the German hospice on *Mt Carmel* . . . . . Ah! that temperature of Lulu's – How its ups and downs have played their part in the life of Signore Jack! He came thro' Venice . . . . . He visited the Lido – He visited the Principessa Giovanni Hotel – He said it looked faded but the white roses were still in the garden – He saw the place where he bought red currants – He saw the pigeons – He saw the shop where I bought him a ring w^h was destroyed in Africa . . . . . That night on the water when you fooled us so about the noble Ezra [Pound] ; of whom I have nowadays felt, in my lectures, I can say nothing but good!

I haven't yet on these travels got hold of that *2nd American Caravan*[2] but when I do you can believe I'll read every word.

I have just finished Sir Walter Scott's *Fortunes of Nigel*[4] . . . . .

Well – as it says in the *Paradiso* – 'in la sua voluntade e la nostra pace'[5] – my one line of Italian – only to whom does that 'sua voluntade' refer; & to what? But *peace* is what we want – that at least is certain.

Well – the Powers be with you, Frances –

166

JACK TO FRANCES (in London)

See 1£   [Printed:] Book-Cadillac Hotel, Detroit
Dec 6 [1928]

Frances I have so well liked your letters of late! It seems to me that I detect a note of quite simple & natural happiness in them (like Frances at 28) & I keep wondering if this is due to your son having got safe into Westminster & going to live with you or to the magical virtue of that nice youthful friend of yours [Charles Scarborough] whose name and retiring appearance & all you tell of him does interest me so much and pleases me so well! Maybe it's a bit of those things & also a bit of some fragment of new psychic philosophy that you have discovered for yourself – If so –

hide it not from your old stumbling blundering & blustering crony . . . . .
. . . . . Frances, Lulu has been sick — the old blood-spitting again — in
Jerusalem. I only pray by *this* time he's safe on his way home. But it is
so far — so far — & poor Alyse's last letter was so agitated — as *well* it might
be — We know — none better — *I* know — none so well as I — what it's like
to be with Lulu when he's ill in a foreign land. O I pray he is on his way
home by now — perhaps in Naples.[1]

Well, I am slowly heading east-ward after this interminable tour.

167

JACK TO FRANCES (in London)

See 1£   4 Patchin Place
                                                             Dec 14 [1928]

Aye! Frances, I am back here at last & it is such a relief! I have not
seen James yet — but he'll 'see the light' no doubt ere long & turn up. I
hope this catches the Berengaria & doesn't get wrecked on the rocks like
the Celtic did. A young Collegian of the University of Pennsylvania told
me yesterday at Wilmington that his Professor had made him study the
works of — Theodore[1] . . . especially *Mr Tasker's Gods* . . . a strange
thing, after all these years, to think of, eh?

How well I recall that little room on the Derby Road & how I gave
you to read my book on Keats & how you lost the chapter on the Ode to
the Nightingale!

And travelling to Wilmington from West Philadelphia along the
Delaware I thought of that other little house you were in that day I first
met James, and so gravely he handed you over to me. Not less gravely
than I handed you over (what a 'package'!) to Louis![2] . . . . .

And do give a really nice signal from me to Mr Scarboro'![3]

168

JACK TO FRANCES (in Badingham, Suffolk)

See 1£   4 Patchin Place
                                                             Dec 28th [1928]

. . . . . Our James has not been quite fit — 'poor old James' (*who* really
has, when you think, *quite* so good & sweet & faithful a nature?) must be

exactly what he is called in heaven among the livelier seraphs with such celestial mockery on their illuminated phyzonomies as they gossip . . . . . His book I fear has not advanced. But someone has given him a thrilling present – namely *both* volumes of *Spengler.*[1] I am now struggling with the second volume & I say unto you, Frances my old friend . . . . . that these two volumes of Spengler are 'The greatest book of our time' . . . . .

. . . . . Dreiser is engaged in some literary row (over some question connected with his articles on Russia) with the new wife[2] of Sinclair Lewis.[3] I hope this latter red-haired sabreur won't attack our old acquaintance (when driven on by love & drink) in any *violent* manner. But no doubt Dreiser is a match for most. But I fancy you never know what funny nervous imaginations vex the heart of the bravest now & again! . . . . .

I am now being stirred up . . . . . by the publishers to *get on* with my proof-reading – but when my acquaintances are so merciless in their visits – what can I do? Nor can I (as we like to do) put the blame on P. for these incursions; for the worst of them are men (& my own dear friends) going back before her regime. The truth is the kind of feminine electricity of understanding w^h makes me (as I once announced so boastfully, to your amazement, but still maintain the same!) the best critic i' the world, is exactly in this tough city, what extra-virile demi-semi-philosophers don't seem able to get from any bobbed head of their acquaintance – don't in fact seem able to get anywhere except in the upper room top floor of Patchin Place. I could easily do little else but listen – listen – listen – and P. do little else but hand round scarcely noticed cups of tea! This room grows daily more like one of those rooms in some tall house on the edge of a muddy plain where some group of mystic-headed-doddipole-supernumaries, 'of our town', discuss works they've never written and causes they've never defended and ladies they've never kissed while Stephan Trophimovitch[4] upholds the very cloudy trophies of the Good the True & the Beautiful & the Samovar bubbles & bubbles its aged old-maid contempt for such a lot of fuss about nothing.

. . . . . I am as you know, for all my airy flights, a very simple and very sleepy son of the Rev. C.F.P. and have 'to go to bed' *come what may.* How many hours do you *have to have* for sleep, Frances? I get dyspepsia & get cross & crusty if I don't have *nine!* In fact I think (if Nietzsche says fresh air and honey and very strong tea are necessary to good thoughts) *sleep* – long hours of sleep – are the only thing for any thoughts of any kind. Aye! but New York is not arranged for a son of Charles Francis to get long hours of sleep in! It was nice of 'Hilda' [Doolittle] – your 'Hilda' who I can't believe I ever scolded – with Bobbie [Perceval Roberts], now dead, in Victoria Station – to send James a Christmas card . . . . .

1929

169

JACK TO FRANCES (in London)

See
£1

4 Patchin Place
Feb 7th [1929]

My head, bad Frances, good Frances, not ever one of the *stablest*, has been completely turned today by reason of my having met the grandson of one of my childish heroes & yours too, I dare warrant it, my dear! None other than that General – Listen! *now before* you turn the page – guess who it was – his grand dad's name – the most Celebrated name in Europe – but curiously in disgrace today – particularly now that the Pope has got back his temporal power & Canon Law & papal decretals etc etc & the Papal State in microcosmo – A sad day, a woeful day, a wicked day, a reactionary day, for General – the grandson of General – Have 'ee guessed yet, old friend? eh? I met him at a performance before a crowd of Jewesses who hired us both to make sport for them & I believe if I'd had my wits a bit more about me & been a trifle bolder than I am I could have cajoled *him* down here to tea in this very room. How P. w^d have opened her eyes if I had said – 'I've brought General – to tea.' Both Oliver and Betty w^d jump with interest to hear his name. The most famous name in Europe after Bonarparte. Probably he's working as a cook in New York making spaghetti for he's out of favour *very much* with his nation's government at the moment . . . Have you guessed yet? – Although his father – no! his grandfather – stands up with his sword half drawn out of the sheath in that statue in the middle of Washington Square! Now you know who I mean?
    It was
        General

181

GARIBALDI[1]

Well, he was exactly like Captain Blunt in Conrad's[2] *Arrow of Gold* that you read for the 1st time after you returned from Lakewood & that you typed for me to send to Reedy's Mirror . . . . .

170

JACK TO FRANCES (in London)

See 1£

4 Patchin Place
April 5th [1929]

Well Frances old friend can you believe that I've had a hurried visit from none other than *Maurice Browne*[1] who says that he has seen you *several times* . . . & is I really cannot quite tell *what* kind of terribly grand Pasha of theatricals.

I cannot help wishing he had hurriedly (as I w[d] have done being a Miser) clapped a good iron key to a box in the floor & put all his money into it for certain safety. I should be so very nervous of 'companies' etc etc —. In these things *my* point of view would be that of Père Goriot, or Mr Scrooge or that old fellow in George Eliot's tale [*Silas Marner*] — in other words the sly cunning of an old hedger or ditcher of Broadmayne or Sturminster-Newton, or Western Zoyland, or Little Puddletown, who has lit upon a smuggler's bag of doubloons in a smuggler's lane (at the back of Wash Lane). But I suppose Maurice Browne knows what he's about — I *hope* he does. But it certainly did my heart good to see him; like a Fairy Prince; or like Little Claus turned into the Marquis of Carrabas, his head full of incredible Plans & an Ebony Cane in his hand!

I have just read Ralph Straus's book about Dickens,[2] which interested me profoundly as I've never read *through any* life, tho' I used to possess Forster's[3] (the mere thought of w[h] book in its red cover carries my mind far away from here). I don't think it's badly done at all. It isn't cheeky and shallow and silly like this awful *This Side of Idolatry*,[4] w[h] I have just skimmed too. No wonder the family was up in arms — I'd be furious myself if this book had been about — well — my Grandfather even! But it's so dull and stupid and shallow that they might just as well have ignored it. How *could* it have sold so? . . . . .

. . . . . Will you be, do you suppose, in London about *June 14th or 15th*? For it is I think about that date that I hope to temerariously shuffle into that Metropolis . . . . .

171

JACK TO FRANCES (in London)

c/o Llewelyn
The White Nose Cottages, Warmwell
Dorchester, Dorset
Wednesday [early August 1929]

. . . . . Aye! but I did so like seeing you[1] – and, if you will allow me to say so, I did so deeply get that sense that Frances was a much nicer human being than ever before – I mean mellower, wiser, gentler, more tolerant of the weakness of her fellow-creatures. I didn't like to see, my old friend, that lamentably sad and wounded look w^h now & then was in your blue eyes – *behind* them rather – but as you say, & let's hope (I suppose) that so it was, that look was more due to *physical* than mental suffering . . . . .

. . . . . I do want to make this book [*The Meaning of Culture*] a sort of hand-book of self-culture for the young boys & girls of my adopted land who, as you know, need such a thing and who are so touchingly humble mentally – so different from our own young generation over here! But aye! how I do appreciate the politeness of English people w^h I am sure comes from their being so touchy that it's a sort of self-denying Ordinance not to risk offending each other's egoism.

Over there, it must be allowed, they are a tiny bit wooden by contrast! What Gertrude Stein[2] calls Stupid Being occupies too large a part of their identity.

How nicely that Policeman stopped the traffic for Frances and Jack lost in argument![3]

Lulu[4] is thin & very highly strung, but you are right he is a lovely being to be with, in this hard world, & Alyse[5] is incredibly considerate.

It was pathetic to see Faith[6] being led like a gentle heifer to the encounter in Gertrude's[7] room with Aunt Etta.[8] I begged Bertie[9] not to subject her to the ordeal of visiting Theodore,[10] but I daresay he w^d have behaved all right . . . . .

Terrific arguments still go on about D.H. Lawrence.[11]

O Frances I *am* so glad that menace over your job[12] sank down so quickly. I would like seeing exactly where you work. I did like that nice gentle sad lady.[13]

I saw a look on your face, Frances, that touched me not a little, this was a look of pleasure & most sensitive happiness, when we went down Bertie's garden to that wall over-looking the river — who knows not *that* look, if not I.

The Notes

NOTE TO LETTER 1, ?JANUARY 1912 (page 1)
1. Julia had been born in New Orleans. Her mother was a northerner, though, who had married a southerner, and had travelled to New Orleans with him. On his death, during the Civil War, she had travelled back, 'through the lines', with the infant Julia and Julia's brothers. See also Biographical Note.

NOTES TO LETTER 2, ?FEBRUARY 1912 (page 2)
1. The Alleghany Mountains, that Jack mentions, are between Rochester, in Michigan, and Philadelphia.
2. The reference to Plato — the Greek philosopher (c. 427-347 B.C.) — indicates 'platonic love': that love between opposite sexes that does not prove itself in erotic action.

NOTE TO LETTER 3, [FEBRUARY 1912] (pages 3-4)
1. This seems a steep descent from 'platonic love', and is one of the few references in Jack's letters to sadistic practice.

NOTES TO LETTER 4, 21 MARCH 1912 (pages 4-5)
1. As Jack was already married, he had praised Frances to his fellow lecturer, Louis Wilkinson, and Louis Wilkinson to Frances, in such a magical rhapsodising that, when he introduced them in March 1912, they admired each other so much that a marriage was arranged.

James Henderson, who had been Frances's suitor, tried to be philosophical about this. He became, however, puzzled and sad. See also Biographical Note.
2. Louis Wilkinson, who became 'Louis Marlow', the writer. See also Biographical Note.

3. Tiberius (42 BC - AD 14), soldier and Emperor of Rome, till he retired to Capri where, with a strange retinue, he practised every possible perversion.

4. Arnold Shaw, Jack's 'Manager'. See also Biographical Note.

NOTES TO LETTER 5, 10 APRIL [1912] (pages 5-12)

1. The wedding day. Frances and Louis Wilkinson boarded the Cunard ship R.M.S. Caronia, immediately after the wedding, with Jack and his sister Marian and Perceval Roberts (see Note 3, below): all bound for Britain, and leaving Frances's tearful mother and the puzzled James Henderson behind.

2. Marian Powys, Jack's sister, the third in age of five sisters and the only Powys — says Louis Wilkinson — to have any business sense. See also Biographical Note.

3. Perceval Roberts, or Bobbie, as he is called in some of the letters: a dandy with suicidal fixations. See also Biographical Note.

4. Because of the suddenness of the marriage it had been arranged between all concerned — to the special approval of Frances's mother — that it would not be consummated for a year.

5. Louis Wilkinson, brought up in the Suffolk town of Aldeburgh, had met the novelist, George Meredith (1812-1909) there.

6. Virgilian lots because the writings of Virgil (70 BC - 19 BC) became, after his death, sacred books, and were used for divination.

7. 'ALL AS YOU WOULD TWO THINK OF YOU ALWAYS FRANCES JACK — 9.28 pm'
The 'official' so pared down the first version that it became almost meaningless.

8. Louis Wilkinson thought Swinburne shamefully underrated and fought always for his reputation.

9. Edward Fitzgerald (1809-1883) — Louis Wilkinson very much liked his version of the *Rubaiyat* of Omar Khayyam.

10. 'Here as I point my sword, the sun arises.....' (*Julius Caesar*, Shakespeare, Act II, sc. i). The conspirators are planning the assassination of Caesar.

11. Walter Pater (1839-1894) of exquisite writing —*Marius the Epicurean*, etc. He was more appreciated in the early years of this century.

12. The *Titanic* had sunk, to the north of the 'Caronia', two days before, on Sunday, 14 April. The table-turning took place on 16 April. The name 'Laroche' is unusual, to English minds. When they were able to check with a casualty list, the name 'Laroche' was on it. The event was well authenticated and the 'message' was reported to the Society for

Psychical Research. 'The Occult Review' published an account of it. This led to a meeting between Frances and W.B. Yeats, described in Frances's *The Mystic Leeway*.

In 'The Times' for 16 April 1912, three 'Laroches' are in the list of survivors: Miss Louisa Laroche, Mrs Joseph Laroche and Simonne Laroche, but one, a Mr G. Laroche, was drowned.

13. John William Williams, Jack's Welsh friend who had converted him, for a time, to Roman Catholicism.

NOTES TO LETTER 6, 29 APRIL [1912] (pages 12-13)

1. Frances's husband was lecturing in Dresden.

2. The Powys family vicarage.

3. Jack had identified Frances and himself with 'Cathy' and 'Heathcliffe' in *Wuthering Heights* (Frances admired most of all women writers Emily Brontë) and turned this into the sign: ✒︎ . When Louis Wilkinson saw this – for there was no secrecy between any of them and they all saw each other's letters – he said it must stand for 'hellish copulation'.

4. 'I love, I hate – why do I do that, you may well ask. / I do not know. But I feel this is happening – and it tears me apart!'

5. 'Lulu' – Llewelyn Powys, Jack's younger brother: suffering from tuberculosis. See also Biographical Note.

6. Perceval Roberts was a gambler.

7. The Hotel Daniele still exists, near the Doge's Palace. It is now called the Hotel Daniele Royal Excelsior.

8. There is no Grand Hotel on the Grand Canal now. It has probably changed its name.

9. Because of Llewelyn Powys's tuberculosis.

NOTES TO LETTER 7, [2 May 1912] (page 13)

1. This letter, and Frances's other letters to Jack, during 1912, Jack ceremonially destroyed.

2. Lear: 'He that parts us shall bring a brand from heaven, / And fire us hence like foxes.' (Shakespeare's *King Lear*, Act V, sc. iii).

NOTES TO LETTER 8, [8 May 1912] (pages 13-14)

1. The Hyperboreans were believed to have lived beyond the North Wind in a sunny land.

2. In comparing Frances to the Egyptian goddess of the Earth and the Moon, Jack is reassuring her, for Frances had thought that Llewelyn, deeply concerned about his brother Jack's welfare, might attack her in a barbaric, English way.

3. Llewelyn Powys had been at Cambridge with Louis Wilkinson, his closest friend.

4. Gabriele D'Annunzio (1863-1938), the Italian writer and airman.

5. His son, Littleton Alfred Powys, then ten years old: a boarder at Sherborne Preparatory School, where Jack's brother Littleton was Headmaster. See also Biographical Note.

NOTES TO LETTER 9, 14 MAY [1912] (pages 14-15)

1. Jack — as a born writer who is only writing letters — is teasing Frances about her being a Christian — commenting on the dove, symbol of the Holy Ghost, or, in other words, that devil in celestial feathers, that doubtful Holy Ghost with whom sometimes you feel in touch.

2. Let the bird of loudest lay,

   On the sole Arabian tree,

   Herald sad and trumpet be,

   To whose sound chaste wings obey.

   — 'The Phoenix and the Turtle'

3. Walt Whitman (1819-1892), the great American poet and author of *Leaves of Grass*, etc. Jack was giving Whitman's work to his sister, Katie Powys, to read.

4. Associations of his early lecturing in girls' schools there; of young prostitutes who told him of their trade; of roaming the beach for female forms; and of Brighton as the place of some of his most intense sadistic visions.

5. *Apologia Pro Vita Sua*, Cardinal Newman's autobiography.

6. Aldebaran, the red star in the constellation of the Bull.

NOTES TO LETTER 10, [19 MAY 1912] (pages 16-17)

1. Harry Lyon was Jack's brother-in-law. He did not approve of Jack.

2. Henri Bergson (1859-1941), the French philosopher; Nobel Prize winner in 1927 and author of *Time and Freewill*, etc. '. . . . . change is the material of reality.'

3. Friedrich Wilhelm Nietzsche (1844-1900), the German philosopher. Frances read his works with great critical interest. I remember her giving me in my adolescence his *Thus Spake Zarathustra*, with its 'poetry in prose' and his ideas of the 'superman'.

4. Jack is remembering that Peter the Great worked for some time as a shipwright, and that, in 1698, he collected information, including knowledge of shipbuilding at Deptford and London, and he took back English artificers, engineers and others with him to Russia.

5. '. . . Well I know, now, this dark tarn of Auber, this ghoul-haunted

woodland of Weir.' 'Ulalume' by Edgar Allan Poe. Thomas Hardy had introduced this poem to Jack.

NOTES TO LETTER 11, JUNE 1912 (page 18)

1. Jack and Llewelyn Powys had joined Frances and Louis Wilkinson in Venice. Llewelyn had fallen in love with Frances. Jack was already in love with her. Louis Wilkinson had remained urbane but watchful. There is an account of this time in Jack's *Autobiography* and in Frances's *The Mystic Leeway*. During the Venetian adventure Llewelyn had had a recurrence of tuberculosis and Jack was now getting him back to England as soon as possible.

2. Llewelyn, in spite of being ill, had given Frances a book on Mantegna (1431-1506), the Italian painter.

3. 'Down with the eternal gallows and long live the bastard truth!'

4. Castle of the Sforzas, the famous Italian family, 'the stormers'.

NOTES TO LETTER 12, [LATE JUNE 1912] (pages 18-20)

1. The Wilkinson home: the Wilkinson Prep. School was also in Aldeburgh.

Louis Wilkinson's father, the Reverend Walter George Wilkinson, had started the Wilkinson school at Aldeburgh, Suffolk. He was a Classics scholar but, as a Fellow of Worcester College, Oxford, he could not marry, so he resigned. He also resigned from his parish, for he could not have a living without subscribing to the Thirty-Nine Articles, and he felt some of these were nonsense, and refused to sign. He then married. To earn his living he started the Aldeburgh school, that continues to this day —in an expanded form—at Orwell Park, Ipswich. He had died in 1906.

2. Jack's brother-in-law, who disapproved of Jack.

3. His brother, Littleton Powys — Headmaster of Sherborne Prep. School. *Old* Littleton as opposed to *young* Littleton, his son.

4. Jack is throwing together an impression of the last months, including talk.

5. Dr G.R. Rickett M.A., B.Sc., Cambridge, 1903, was the School Doctor; also Assistant Surgeon at Yeatman Hospital, Sherborne, and Surgeon Lieutenant of Dorset.

6. Young Littleton, a boarder at Sherborne Prep. School.

7. They all, except Llewelyn, had gone ashore at Tangiers, when the ship docked there.

8. *Odes and Other Poems* and *Poems* by John Cowper Powys, published over ten years earlier.

9. The Don's bony horse in *Don Quixote* by S. Cervantes (1547-1610).

NOTES TO LETTER 13, 6 JULY 1912 (pages 20-21)

1. The remaining Wilkinsons, especially Louis' mother, Charlotte Elizabeth, seemed formidable to the lone American. Frances, however, fought back against what she considered English hypocrisy (see *The Mystic Leeway*).

2. Jack compares, once or twice in the letters, Frances with Circe, the enchantress, who could change men into animals. Odysseus, the king of Ithaca, figure of all man's ingenuity, stayed over a year on Aeaea, Circe's island, on his great journey back from the Trojan wars; and he loved Circe; though he fought against some of her magical tendencies.

3. Frances's mother, Julia, was literally on her way to Britain. Jack frequently refers to Greek, and sometimes Roman, mythology, because he knew that Frances, partly because of the influence of Hilda Doolittle ('H.D.') and Ezra Pound (see Biographical Note), was familiar with both. But Jack sometimes calls Julia, 'St Anne', the mother of the Virgin Mary.

4. Louis Wilkinson's mother had known Jack's mother, as Mary Cowper Johnson, in earlier days; that was the first link between the Wilkinsons and the Powyses.

5. Willy Powys, the youngest of the Powys sons, and the most handsome, worked Manor farm, at Witcombe on the banks of the Yeo. See also Biographical Note.

6. Emily Clare, their old nurse, had returned from America to help Willy Powys at his farm.

7. Louis Wilkinson always expected the best in everything and usually got it.

8. Catherine Edith Philippa ('Katie'), the youngest but one of the Powys sisters. See Biographical Note.

9. Mary Shirley was 'Aunt Mary' to most of the Powys brothers and sisters, but she was in fact, a cousin. Her brothers were the Hon. Ralph Shirley, who appears quite often in the letters, and Walter, who in 1912 succeeded as the 11th Earl Ferrers. They were the children of Walter Waddington Shirley, D.D., Regius Professor of Ecclesiastical History at Oxford, and Philippa (*née* Powys).

NOTES TO LETTER 14, 16 JULY [1912] (pages 22-24)

1. The visit to the Powys family went well, though Frances at times felt herself to be surrounded by inspired lunatics. She returned with Louis to the composed but disturbing sanity of Aldeburgh.

2. 'Yea they sacrificed their sons and their daughters unto devils.' — Psalms 106, verse 37.

3. Frances's other name was Josefa: or sometimes she spelt it 'Josepha'.

4. Frances had, momentarily, been driven into fury and deep melancholy by the calm, so 'nice', rebukes of her mother-in-law, and by what Frances considered her entrenched lack of compassion (see *The Mystic Leeway*). At one point Frances walks by the sea to get away from the Wilkinsons, and so misses a special lecture Louis was giving in Aldeburgh; and the Wilkinsons are so 'good' about Frances's further fall from grace, that it makes her feel suicidal.

5. The thought that was seriously in Jack's mind was that Frances should leave Louis and all the Wilkinsons and elope with him.

6. Because of Shelley's belief in 'free love', including incest: Jack himself strongly defended incest, urging that it should be made legal.

7. Saxmundham is a fairly long walk from Aldeburgh; but Frances had regained her American poise, and was taking part in the Wilkinson and Aldeburgh activities, such as polite readings of Shakespeare (see *The Mystic Leeway*) and formal tea parties; though sometimes with an *élan* that disturbed her mother-in-law.

NOTES TO LETTER 15, 18 JULY [1912] (pages 24-27)

1. As the 'Snake' accused the 'Tiger' of cowardice.

2. Jack would not have hurt a fly, in spite of his mental sadism; and both Frances and her mother rescued not only human beings, especially children, but animals; and were horrified at the way *pâté de foie gras* is made by the forcible feeding of geese.

3. Dr Bernie O'Neill, the great influence on the Powyses, in literary and in many ways: see the *Autobiography* of John Cowper Powys and *Swan's Milk* by Louis Marlow (Louis Wilkinson). See also Biographical Note.

4. Tom Jones, of the Liverpool Cotton Market, had encouraged Jack's cerebral affair with a quaint prostitute. *The Buffoon* by Louis Wilkinson has an account of this. Tom Jones also introduced Louis to young Liverpool women who were accommodating, pretty and pleasant; and he supplied a Liverpool house in which they could all meet. See also Biographical Note.

5. When Frances had been arrested in Venice for wearing boy's clothes she had faced her police accusers in silence, giving a stiff dignified 'Gregg bow' that greatly impressed Jack.

6. At Aldeburgh, Jack formulated a plan by which Frances would elope with him on a horse that he would hire at Ipswich. In the event, he was unable to find a horse.

NOTE TO LETTER 16, [3 AUGUST 1912] (page 27)

1. His two published works.

NOTES TO LETTER 17 [7 AUGUST 1912] (pages 27-29)

1. Early in August, Frances's mother, Julia, landed in England. She went to Aldeburgh, stayed at 'Deepdene', and within the first day or so of her visit was thrown from a pony-trap, breaking her leg.

2. Julia was lame for the rest of her life, though she did not limp badly.

3. This was published as *Lucifer* in 1956 by Macdonald, London, with woodcuts by Agnes Miller Parker.

4. The Hon. Ralph Shirley, his cousin. See Biographical Note.

5. Ralph Shirley's wife.

6. Dr Bernie O'Neill, 'pitied' because he was married to Belle (See Biographical Note), large in body and broadly dominating.

7. As a 'magic man', Ralph Shirley cast horoscopes. Louis Wilkinson writes, 'He cast my horoscope wrong in every detail'.

8. Ralph Shirley's daughter.

9. Willy Powys, the youngest brother, and the most practical and adventurous of them; with a very realistic Powys humour, too, that was giving Jack considerable pain in its uncompromising comments on Jack's situation and behaviour.

10. His wife, not his mother.

11. This seems inexplicable, but we leave it in, in case anyone can give a solution. The reference to Pythagoras, the Greek philosopher (6th Century B.C.) is only because he was a mathematician. The clue may be in writing by Frances which she did not submit for publication. In this, a Frances-like character takes a Jack-like character to a hotel in an earnest if ignorant attempt to become pregnant by him. There seems to be no result at all from this, and the Frances-character is more bewildered than ever. This does not ring true of the actual Jack/Frances relationship, and was probably written as a might-have-been fantasy, some time after Frances was married to Louis, and could look back on her ignorance with some irony. Even if there is a clue in the story, it would not explain Jack's sums.

NOTES TO LETTER 18, 10 AUGUST [1912] (page 29)

1. The parson at Burpham. Frances's mother, Julia, was religious in an orthodox way, and probably wanted spiritual sustenance in her pain, which was considerable, from her injured hip and broken leg.

2. Jack was drawn back, over and over again, to Brighton. Now he

planned to meet Frances and Louis in Glastonbury.

NOTE TO LETTER 19, 22 AUGUST [1912] (pages 29-30)

1. His sister Philippa, known as Katie, had had a mental breakdown at Willie Powys's farm, and had been taken to Montacute Vicarage. See John Cowper Powys's *Letters to Llewelyn Powys* which supplement Jack's letters to Frances at this period.

NOTE TO LETTER 20, 24 AUGUST [1912] (pages 30-31)

1. Gertrude Powys, the eldest sister who looked after them all. See also Biographical Note.

NOTES TO LETTER 21, 25 AUGUST [1912] (pages 31-32)

1. Stephen Reynolds had been helping the fishermen of Sidmouth, with Union matters; and he published work about his life with them. Katie had joined him in Sidmouth, and they had been in love. See also Biographical Note.

2. Perhaps 'Stephen Reynolds'; or 'seagulls and ravens'.

3. Dr Bernie O'Neill worked, for £200 a year, in the office of 'The Occult Review', the periodical of Jack's cousin, the Hon. Ralph Shirley, who had a controlling interest in the publishing house of William Rider and Son, which published Jack's books of poems.

NOTES TO LETTER 24, [18 SEPTEMBER 1912] (page 34)

1. Katie Powys had been installed in a Mental Home where patients did farm work. Katie was practised in agriculture. She soon recovered and was writing poetry.

Jack, on leaving Katie, had joined Frances and Louis Wilkinson in Paris; and had now returned to Burpham.

2. Mrs Lucy Penny, his youngest sister, married, not very happily, to a miller. See also Biographical Note.

3. Frederick Rolfe, self-styled 'Baron Corvo', author of *Hadrian the Seventh*, etc., by whom they had been entertained in Venice, early in the summer. Jack, out of fixed and nervous determination to get rid of Rolfe's too insistent hospitality, had been abominably rude to him.

4. By Venice.

5. The sentence is obscure. One can only guess that in the talk between Frances, Louis, Jack and Llewelyn, Villon (the French poet and criminal of the fifteenth century) was somehow voted out of his glory, together with Thomas Hardy and Ezra Pound; but Frances would have defended Ezra Pound, and Jack would have defended Thomas Hardy,

whom he knew; and Louis would have defended Villon; and Llewelyn would probably have defended all three (if, that is, he was as widely read as the others; which is doubtful at that time; though his range was as varied as any of them later). The sentence remains a mystery.

NOTES TO LETTER 25, [OCTOBER? 1912] (page 35)

1. Dr Bernie O'Neill and his wife, Belle, had let their house to Louis Wilkinson and Frances.

2. Queenstown, Cork Harbour.

3. Jack met Frances in London on 9 October. After that, it was time for him to return to the United States, for his lectures started before Louis Wilkinson's.

4. It is clear that Frances and Jack met in Bond Street and, at some point, took the 'trolley to Twickenham'. On reaching Ravenscourt Park, they may have made their way through it, walking and talking as they had done in America. Ravenscourt Park leads to Chiswick High Street, and off Chiswick High Street is Hadfield Road, where Frances and Louis were staying in the house of Dr Bernie O'Neill and Belle. It is probable that they were making for that; especially as Frances knew that Mrs Pegge (mentioned later in the letter), who as a regular visitor may have been a 'help' in O'Neill's surgery, or in the house – would ring (at the door, presumably, not on the telephone).

The reference to a game of chess (referred to in later letters) may possibly be in a code that the reader can feel free to decipher.

This is speculation. We know, though, that 9 October was the day after Jack's birthday, and that it was shortly before he sailed for the United States. It was a special meeting. It was also the end of a turbulent phase – and the beginning of another turbulent phase.

5. Frances and Jack later published an article on Strindberg, who wrote with a mad and keen perception about – among other sides of life – the relationship between men and women. Frances was particularly struck and horrified by his play, *The Father*, and she wrote very well about him.

NOTE TO LETTER 26, [OCTOBER 1912] (page 36)

1. Jack's second letter to Frances from R.M.S. Baltic – not included here – consists almost entirely of part of his translation of Homer's *Iliad*. This one, included, is written from the United States, with no address or date.

NOTES TO LETTER 27, 29 JANUARY 1913 (page 37)

1. Stations in Philadelphia.

2. 'But where is the brave Alexander?'

NOTES TO LETTER 30, 13 FEBRUARY 1913 (pages 40-42)

1. Jonathan Swift (1667-1745), author of *Gulliver's Travels* and *A Tale of a Tub*, etc.

2. Stella — Esther Johnson — of Swift's *Journal to Stella*.

3. Ovid (43 BC-AD 17), the Latin poet.

4. 'Where there is fierce indignation the heart cannot be torn.'

NOTES TO LETTER 31, [APRIL 1913] (page 42)

1. Back to England again, after the lecture season in the United States. Frances and Louis had already sailed on the Cunard R.M.S. Ivernia.

2. Arnold Shaw, his agent.

NOTES TO LETTER 32, [15 APRIL 1913] (pages 43-46)

1. In pencil, on pages torn from an exercise book.

2. Jack had persuaded Frances in 1912 to improvise the Borgias with him, as a new kind of lecture, telling her that the words would come naturally to her as she stepped on to the stage. They didn't. See *The Mystic Leeway*. The Borgias — the family of Renaissance Italy generally remembered now for their use of poison on one another and on others — were apt subjects for dramatisation; but Frances says that Jack's knees were too bony in tights, and rendered her speechless, for a time anyhow.

3. Lucrezia Borgia (1480-1519) was infamous for her assassinations and immorality, but died in the odour of artistic patronage. Jack took the part of her brother Cesare, a skilful soldier and subtle poisoner. Lucrezia married Sforza, Lord of Pesaro.

4. By Victor Hugo (1802-1885).

5. By Alexandre Dumas (Dumas père, 1802-70).

6. By Alexandre Dumas.

7. Patroclus, the friend, in Homer's *Iliad*, of Achilles, for whose death Achilles 'sulked in his tent', refusing to fight the Trojans.

8. For his first American lecture tour.

9. Coloured — as Uncle Remus — and 'wrong side of the blanket', Manfred, King of Sicily, was the illegitimate son of the Emperor Frederick II.

10. Honoré de Balzac (1799-1850), author of *Le Père Goriot*, etc.

11. Heinrich Heine (1797-1856), German poet and revolutionary writer.

NOTES TO LETTER 33, [APRIL 1913] (pages 46-47)
1. The Casquet Rocks, in the Channel Isles.
2. H.G. Wells (1866-1946): *The First Man in the Moon* (1901).
3. Cesare Borgia, whom he had acted to Frances's Lucrezia Borgia.

NOTES TO LETTER 34, 18 [APRIL 1913] (pages 47-48)
1. Both Jack and Frances knew Isadora Duncan, the originator of the free style of inspired dance, based on movements of figures on Greek vases. See also Biographical Note.
2. Christoph Willibald Gluck (1714-87), Austro-German composer. His *Iphigénie en Aulide* was a great success in 1774.
3. Pornography.

NOTE TO LETTER 36, 23 APRIL [1913] (page 49)
1. Lady Warwick was a friend of the Powyses, and had helped Katie Powys after Katie's breakdown.

NOTE TO LETTER 37, 28 APRIL [1913] (page 49)
1. This and other essays by John Cowper Powys are collected in one volume edited by Paul Roberts.

NOTES TO LETTER 38, 5 MAY [1913] (page 50)
1. Frances and Louis were trying to shake off Jack's constant pursuit. Frances was trying to be a good *English* wife to Louis.
2. August Strindberg (1849-1912). When Jack's article failed to find a publisher, Frances rewrote it and it was published under both their names in 'The New Age'.
3. A list of new publications.

NOTES TO LETTER 39, [17 MAY 1913] (pages 50-51)
1. In her letter of rebuke to Jack, Frances had suggested that he should try to make friends with his wife, even to love her.
2. Michelangelo (1475-1564), the Italian artist, whose works Jack and Frances had seen in Florence.

NOTE TO LETTER 40, [27 JUNE 1913] (pages 51-52)
1. This refers to Frances's violent criticism when they were in Rome. Partly this had continued the cauterizing criticism of their Philadelphia days; partly, though, Frances felt that she ought to stop Jack's continual siege of Louis and herself, while at the same time not wanting to lose Jack altogether.

NOTES TO LETTER 41, [NO DATE, 1913] (pages 52-53)

1. The 'explorer' was the father of a friend of Jack's son, Littleton, then ten years old. His wife and Jack's had a close friendship.

2. Talleyrand (1754-1838), the French statesman – one of the members of the assembly who drew up the Declaration of Right and who later worked closely with Napoleon.

NOTE TO LETTER 42, [NO DATE, 1913] (pages 53-54)

1. The Wilkinson Prep. School, where Frances was again undergoing something of an ordeal as an American among the English.

NOTES TO LETTER 43, [25 JULY 1913] (pages 54-55)

1. Jack had been invited to lecture in Oxford. Frances and Louis, Theodore, Bertie and Llewelyn Powys were planning to hear him there.

2. The Hon. Ralph Shirley, the 'magic man' and a relation of the Powyses.

3. Albert Reginald Powys ('Bertie'), 'Brother Positive', the architect. See Biographical Note.

4. Theodore (T.F.) Powys. See Biographical Note.

5. According to Frances, Jack's Oxford lecture was bad at first, then finer than usual. The whole visit seems to have turned out happily. There was more tension when Louis and Frances stayed in the Powys family home, Montacute Vicarage, in Somerset. Louis Wilkinson, when feeling the full force of the Powys assembly, with their barbaric race-pride, would recite a jingle that he had composed as an undergraduate at Cambridge:

Mirabilie Genus
Carmen Triumphale

Proud is the devil below
As he prods at the souls of the damned,
Proud is the Punch at the show
With his Judy belaboured and lammed,
But prouder than Punch or the Devil are we,
For we are *Powyses*, you and me,
Powyses! POWYSES! don't you see?
From the Lord knows when to eternity!
God! what a glorious thing to be!

Hallelujah!

NOTE TO LETTER 44, [NO DATE] (pages 55-57)

1. Paul Verlaine (1844-96), the French poet and author of *Les Fêtes Galantes*, etc., who, like Jack, travelled to escape marriage and who also, for a time, taught in English schools.

NOTES TO LETTER 46, AUGUST [1913] (pages 58-59)

1. Remy de Gourmont (1858-1915) had completed most of his work, *Promenades Philosophique*, etc.

2. François Gounod (1818-93), the French composer. His opera, *Faust* (1859) had established his greatness.

NOTES TO LETTER 47, [25 AUGUST 1913] (page 59)

1. *Jean Christophe* by Romain Rolland (1866-1944), the French writer, Nobel Prize winner; pacifist and anti-Fascist.

2. 'A woman can sometimes have pity for those to whom she has, pitilessly, given pain. Instead of the expected male friend there is another. Instead of the expected woman friend there is another. Illusion! Instead of that woman friend, there is nothing.'

NOTES TO LETTER 48, [SEPTEMBER 1913] (page 60)

1. Jack returned to the United States for his new season of lectures.

2. Teddy, the Newfoundland dog, that bit people.

3. Jack's well-to-do friends.

4. Lola Catesby-Jones, a lively, pretty girl, characterised by Marian Powys as 'very talkative'. She was much involved with Jack and Llewelyn Powys. Lola was an artist and designer.

5. James Henderson, who was still in love with Frances.

6. Vera, a Russian immigrant, was a translator and an artist.

NOTE TO LETTER 50, 1 OCTOBER [1913] (page 61)

1. Theodore Dreiser. See Biographical Note.

NOTES TO LETTER 52, 15 OCTOBER [1913] (pages 62-63)

1. By Llewelyn Powys.

2. Charles Augustin Sainte-Beuve (1804-69), the French poet and critic. He was a lecturer, too.

3. Pierre de Ronsard (1524-85), the French poet and author of *Odes, Amours*, etc. His fame suffered an eclipse after his death, but revived in the nineteenth century.

4. Paul Bourget (1852-1935), the French writer. *L'Etape* is probably his best known novel, but he was at his finest as an essayist.

5. Harry Lyon, Jack's brother-in-law, whose tongue was pointed like 'the spire of Salisbury Cathedral'.

6. Henry Bordeaux (1870-1963), the French novelist who defended family life.

7. Villiers de L'Isle-Adam (1838-89), the French writer who founded the Symbolist movement.

8. Not subject to moral laws.

9. Barbey D'Aurevilly (1808-89), the French poet, novelist and critic.

NOTE TO LETTER 53, [22 OCTOBER 1913] (pages 63-64)

1. *Faust* by Goethe (1749-1832).

NOTE TO LETTER 54, [28 OCTOBER 1913] (pages 64-65)

1. Adrasteia: the female version of Adrastus, king of Argos and leader of the expedition of the 'Seven against Thebes'.

NOTE TO LETTER 56, [13 NOVEMBER 1913] (page 66)

1. Louis Wilkinson's first novel, published in 1905, is called *The Puppets Dallying*.

NOTES TO LETTER 57, 27 NOVEMBER [1913] (page 67)

1. Hannibal, the town on the border between Missouri and Illinois, due south of Burlington – and Hannibal (247 BC - 183 BC), the Carthaginian.

2. Maurice Browne, a Cambridge friend of Louis Wilkinson, had started The Little Theatre in Chicago, and was running it, with distinction, in collaboration with his wife, Ellen Van Volkenberg, of the Chicago family. See also Biographical Note.

NOTES TO LETTER 59, [JANUARY 1914] (page 69)

1. When Frances and Louis arrived in the United States for his new batch of lectures, they stayed with Frances's mother in Pulaski Avenue.

In January 1914 Frances and Louis met Jack again.

Jack's sister, Marian, had travelled over with Frances and Louis. Marian adored Jack, and was determined to look after him, but she was also determined to make money, so that she could be independent.

Both Frances and Louis were trying to get the writings of Theodore Powys (T.F. Powys) published. Frances was typing out his stories and saw genius in them. (Frances's own short story, 'Whose Dog?', had just been published in 'The New York Forum'. It was re-published in O'Brien's *Anthology of Best American Short Stories*).

Llewelyn Powys had had a short story, 'The Stunner', published at the end of 1913. Llewelyn was thought to be the successful writer of the family. Jack loved Llewelyn too much to be jealous, but he began to feel that he himself was, in spite of his great success as a lecturer, the failure of the Powys family.

2. *Wood and Stone*.

NOTES TO LETTER 60, [MARCH 1914] (pages 69-70)

1. Jack wrote to his brother Llewelyn ('Lulu') about Frances:

No sooner is one meal prepared and the dishes washed than it is time for another – And the mother is a little trying – like a dead weight around her neck. Will she never be free of her?.....Our One-of-All is fairly trapped between the mother and Louis.....On the whole Louis is kind to her – but the cruelty of turning her – her of all the world – into a domestic drudge makes me frightfully sad. Here – for these 12 weeks – she will have written nothing and read nothing, and not enjoyed herself at all – and you know how happy she can be. Her mood to me varies between bursts of irritation which heaven knows I can easily enough forgive – for I love her – exquisite child that she is whatever her badness – and those sort of silent appeals – you know the way she does, with her hands – that are enough to make you cry.

.....But it is no use Lulu my dear – we are helpless to come to the rescue – you are caught by consumption, and I by 'Mrs Powys' and 'the little Boy'.....

2. The season of lectures in the United States was over. Jack was about to return to England, to his home in Burpham, Sussex. Frances and Louis planned to land briefly in England, then to travel to Italy.

NOTES TO LETTER 61, [12 APRIL 1914] (pages 70-71)

1. Adonais, beloved of Aphrodite, was killed by a wild boar. Her grief was so great that he was allowed to spend six months of every year with her: the revival in Spring.

2. Jack usually referred to Frances's mother as the 'Madonna'.

3. The St Vitus dog (see Letter 48).

4. Le Néant – the nothingness of things. 'Le Néant' was the nightclub which Frances, Louis and Jack had visited in Paris.

NOTES TO LETTER 62, [21 JUNE 1914] (pages 72-73)

1. Before travelling on from England to Italy, Frances and Louis had spent some time with Frances's friend, Hilda Doolittle (the poet 'H.D.' – see Biographical Note) and her husband, the writer Richard Aldington.

Hilda had thought she was engaged to Ezra Pound (see *Herself Defined* by Barbara Guest) but Ezra had married Dorothy Shakespeare. The three couples had met at The Cave of the Golden Calf, a cabaret Theatre Club run by Mrs A. Strindberg, Strindberg's second wife. Ezra Pound had sent on to Frances the invitation to the club.

From Italy, Frances wrote to tell Jack that she was pregnant.

2. Jack, in pain from his stomach ulcers, had taken his father, mother and brother, Llewelyn, for a holiday at Seaton, in Devon.

3. 'My Dear', in Spanish.

4. Louis made no secret of his visit to Tom Jones's accommodating girls in Liverpool.

NOTES TO LETTER 63, 28 JULY [1914] (pages 73-74)

1. Acreman House, where his brother, Littleton, was headmaster of Sherborne Prep. School.

2. Goethe also had a hopeless love for the fiancée of a friend.

3. Jack was writing his Keats book in 1911, but *The Death of God* – the long poem published in 1956 as *Lucifer* – he completed in 1905. However, he may have been revising it in 1910-11.

4. 'In the midway of this our mortal life, I found myself in a gloomy wood astray, gone from the path direct.....' – Dante, *Divine Comedy, Inferno*, i. I.

5. 'In the generation of generations.'

NOTES TO LETTER 64, [SEPTEMBER 1914] (pages 74-77)

1. Llewelyn Powys –in spite of having his story published –found the months at Montacute slow and depressing, except for writing in his diary, and falling in love with his cousin Marion Linton. He now fell more deeply in love with her: partly to fall out of love with Frances. His brother, Willie, had written to Llewelyn suggesting the high altitude of Gilgil, British East Africa, might cure him of his tuberculosis. See *The Life of Llewelyn Powys* by Malcolm Elwin.

2. Katie Powys, fully recovered from her mental breakdown.

3. Gertrude Powys, who looked after all the others. She painted whenever she could.

4. The *Cap Trafalgar*, a nearly new German liner fitted up as an armed merchant cruiser –and sunk after a fierce battle, on 14 September 1914.

5. Mrs Barry was looking after Willie Powys in British East Africa.

NOTES TO LETTER 65, 6 SEPTEMBER [1914] (pages 77-78)

1. His sister, Marian, in New York, and working as a typist.

2. As Jack sat with his old friend 'the Catholic', they were amused by the rumour that a huge Russian army was passing through Britain, with snow on their boots.

NOTES TO LETTER 66, 25 SEPTEMBER [1914] (pages 78-79)

1. Jack had dreaded his return to the United States for his lectures. In the previous season, his agent, Arnold Shaw, had had a love affair that had resulted in his failure to make bookings, and had acted so wildly that Jack thought him mad. He in fact found Shaw this time full of life, full of plans and determined to become a publisher. *The War and Culture* by John Cowper Powys was his first publication. This was later published in England, by Rider, as *The Menace of German Culture*. It was a reply to Professor Munsterburg (see note 5 below).

2. The word 'Chautauqua' – the most westerly county of New York State – was used to describe religious and educational meetings held, since 1871, in summer at Lake Chautauqua. In a more general sense this word came to mean any similar group of educators and entertainers sent out on circuit to hold meetings.

3. Jack had moved in with his sister Marian again.

4. Professor Munsterburg, in 1892, had become head of the Psychology Department, Harvard, at the invitation of William James. Professor Munsterburg was a forerunner of modern behaviourism. His method – in his pro-German propaganda – was to raise the reports of German vandalism into the sphere of large political ideas, adding, 'War is war'.

NOTES TO LETTER 67, 26 OCTOBER [1914] (pages 79-81)

1. *King Lear*, by Shakespeare, v. iii. 8.

2. Nevertheless, Jack has said that of all families the Powyses should champion incest, make incest again as natural as in ancient Egypt.

3. Theodore Dreiser had by this time published *Sister Carrie*, which was attacked as obscene, and *Jennie Gerhart*. Later he published *An American Tragedy*. He was about the same age as Jack, and, as he was arrested for taking part in a Civil Liberties demonstration, shared the same general view as Jack.

4. Louis disliked the emphatic intellectual John Bullishness of Dr Samuel Johnson (1709-84), as he disliked the so-correct selfishness and hauteur of *Letters to His Son* – his illegitimate son – by Lord Chesterfield (1694-1773).

NOTES TO LETTER 68, 3 FEBRUARY [1915] (pages 82-83)

1. Frances and Louis's son, Oliver Marlow, was born on 28 January.

To Frances, having a child was the greatest achievement in life. To Frances's friend, Hilda Doolittle, having a child was an interesting development. Hilda had been told on the morning of the declaration of war with Germany, that she was pregnant; but this first baby, by Richard Aldington, was stillborn.

2. Louis Wilkinson had developed a habit of pinching Frances in public, when he disapproved of her.

NOTES TO LETTER 69, 28 DECEMBER [1915] (pages 83-84)

1. *Humiliated and Offended* by Fyodor Dostoevsky.

2. Louis Wilkinson, with Frances and their son, and a fifteen-year-old Italian nurse, Amelia Genai, 'Lala' (see Biographical Note), had sailed for the United States in July. Louis, with Frances's help, completed *The Buffoon*, in which there are lampoons of Ezra Pound, 'H.D.', John Cowper Powys and others; though Louis makes himself the 'buffoon'. Jack was helping them to submit it to Alfred A. Knopf, without realising that he himself appeared in the novel. Frances was still typing out Theodore Powys's work, and all three were trying to get Knopf to publish it.

Arnold Shaw, having had a success with his first publiaction, determined to publish more. Jack was writing for him at breakneck speed. Arnold published *Wood and Stone* by John Cowper Powys.

Bertie Powys, 'Brother Positive', joined up and was about to go to the Front.

Theodore Powys wrote to Louis Wilkinson:

I was going to run off to Dorchester and serve my country, only I happened to see a corporal by the sea-shore who arrested us for bathing with my family. Such a corporal! God! I would like to see him prod a little stick into your belly. Anyhow I have kept home since and leave the Country to serve itself.

Francis, Theodore's youngest son, has described how, as a child, he saw his father marched off, stark naked, to the lock-up.

NOTES TO LETTER 70, [NO DATE, 1916] (page 85)

1. There are very few letters from Jack to Frances in 1916, 1917, 1918, and none surviving from Frances to Jack, because Jack was often with Frances and Louis.

It was in 1916 that Arnold Shaw published Theodore Powys's *The Soliloquy of a Hermit*.

A pamphlet by Louis Wilkinson called *Blasphemy and Religion* (a dialogue about John Cowper Powys's *Wood and Stone* and Theodore Powys's *The Soliloquy of a Hermit*) was published. In it, Louis, in the character of a Marquis arguing with his son, says that Jack's *Wood and Stone* is a blasphemy '.....as sounding brass and tinkling cymbal.....' while '.....they'll be reading *The Soliloquy of a Hermit* in a hundred years.....'

2. Frances and Louis' infant son, Oliver.

3. Marian Powys, having started a lace shop, became in time the leading authority on lace in the United States. She would never insure her stock, but kept a revolver under her pillow.

NOTES TO LETTER 71, [NOVEMBER 1916] (page 86)

1. In April, *The Buffoon* by Louis Wilkinson was published by Alfred A. Knopf. For the first time, Jack read of himself as 'Jack Welsh'. He sat under a tree to earth his hatred.   Llewelyn Powys loathed the book, and wrote to Louis from Africa to tell him so. Theodore Powys loved it. Ezra Pound, who appears in the book as 'Raoul Root', wrote with due praise, and accute irritation, to Frances. Marian Powys wrote to Louis about *The Buffoon* with anger and affection. *The Buffoon* was republished by the Village Press, London, in 1975, because of its special interest as a portrait of the years 1912-14.

In June, Jack's article on Auguste Strindberg, rewritten by Frances, was published in 'The New York Forum'.

There were occasional violent quarrels between Frances and Louis (made worse by Frances's mother, Julia, though she managed to put a stop to Louis' physical violence). Aleister Crowley, the Black Magician, became one of Louis' friends. He called frequently. Frances realised what he was, and tried to protect Louis.

On 17 June, Jack's *One Hundred Best Books* was published. It was immensely popular, running into several editions.

On 5 December, Arnold Shaw published what Jack called his 'book of literary devotions *Suspended Judgements* — essays on books and sensations.

2. *Rodmoor* by John Cowper Powys was published in October 1916. by Arnold Shaw.

3. 'The Going-Wrong of Sylvia-Ann' by Frances Gregg. Frances also had a story published in 'The New York Forum', and re-published by O'Brian in *The Anthology of Best American Short Stories*.

NOTES TO LETTER 72, [24 JANUARY 1917] (page 87)

1. Jack was now known as a writer as well as a lecturer. Nine books in two years and innumerable lectures had drained his energy. Exhaustion hit the pit of his stomach, giving him continual pain for days on end.

2. Frances's birthday was 28 April.

3. Maurice Browne decked out his Little Theatre, Chicago, for Jack's lectures. These were attended by the company and, often, by Theodore Dreiser, Arthur Ficke, Edgar Lee Masters and other writers.

NOTES TO LETTER 73, [MARCH 1917] (page 88)

1. On 28 March, Frances and Louis' daughter, Elizabeth Josepha, was born in Philadelphia.

2. Jack's son, Littleton, was then fifteen years old.

3. When Jack and Llewelyn Powys had joined Frances and Louis Wilkinson in Spain, during 1913.

NOTES TO LETTER 74, [OCTOBER? 1917] (page 89)

1. Jack had had – as he writes in his *Autobiography* – '.....the operation they call gasterenterostomy under the miraculous hands of Dr John Erdman.....' – with Theodore Dreiser, in a surgeon's gown, in attendance.

For his convalescence, Jack went to his sister's cottage at Northvale.

2. Helen Wylde, an actress who played at the Little Theatre, Chicago, amongst other theatres.

3. Nelly Browne, Maurice Browne's wife, who in her professional and maiden name of Ellen Van Volkenburg, supplied her parents' money and her own talent and organising ability to the Little Theatre, Chicago. See Biographical Note.

4. Frances did visit Jack, leaving the two infants with the Italian nurse, Amelia Genai, in a cinema. Frances wrote to her mother, Julia:

.....Jack sitting in a chair and walking about – looking curiously well but hollow! – really almost ethereal without loss of flesh or colour..... His girl Helen was there all the time. Lovely to look at, like a bit of pale amber and with grey gold hair. Her mouth is like, really like an animal that tears with its teeth, not gross but thin and red and flexible, the lips pointed together in the middle and you see white small teeth where they open. Jack was tender with her.....

NOTE TO LETTER 75, [EARLY IN 1918] (page 90)

1. For *The Complex Vision* by John Cowper Powys: though this book, very much more than a series of essays, is a complete philosophy.

NOTES TO LETTER 76, [APRIL 1918] (pages 90-91)

1. In April, Jack had returned to England in a fleet of eleven ships, and so to Burpham and his wife and son, Littleton Alfred, now sixteen years old.

2. 'Jack Welsh' is the John Cowper Powys character in *The Buffoon* by Louis Wilkinson.

NOTES TO LETTER 77, [JULY? 1918] (pages 91-92)

1. Where the Powys father, the Reverend Charles Powys, had retired with his daughter, Gertrude, to look after him.

2. This was Jack's second attempt to enlist. Earlier in the year, in America, and in spite of his second operation, Jack began to nag himself for not doing war work. He went to the British Propaganda Bureau in New York. A man yelled out to the British recruiting officer, 'Well, we've got a lusty recruit for you today!' Jack was rejected. See his *Autobiography*.

3. Jack's brother, the headmaster of Sherborne Prep. School. See Biographical Note.

4. His wife, Margaret (see Biographical Note), had fought the idea of his returning home from America, on the score of expense. She was determined to keep their son, Littleton, at Sherborne School, and Jack's American lecture fees were needed. But Jack insisted on doing war work and was sent by the War Office to lecture around England on 'War Aims'. He gave his own version of these which seems to have astonished some members of his audiences. See his *Autobiography*. The need for money forced him back to the United States in the autumn.

5. *Wood and Stone* by John Cowper Powys, published in 1915.

6. Thomas Hardy (1840-1928) had, two years after his first wife's death, married Emily Dugdale, in 1914.

7. In Toledo they had seen the Church of Santo Domingo el Antiguo, where El Greco had painted the decorations in 1557.

NOTES TO LETTER 78, 5 MAY [1919] (pages 93-94)

1. In the autumn of 1918 Frances and her son, Oliver, were stricken by the world-wide Spanish 'flu, and were rushed into a New York hospital, where every corner – wards and passages – was crowded with patients.

On the other side of the Atlantic, in the last German drive, Jack's brother, Bertie – 'Brother Positive' – was taken prisoner. On 11 November 1918, the armistice was signed between the Allies and Germany.

Frances, Louis and their children remained in the United States; Louis lecturing and writing; and increasingly involved with other expatriates – Frank Harris, Aleister Crowley, Maurice Browne, etc.

A Chaste Man by Louis Wilkinson – about the perils of chastity – was published in New York and London.

Frances was happy with her children; but tension increased in her home. Aleister Crowley had threatened her children. She fought and defeated Crowley's attempts to certify her as insane. Her heart, never strong, grew weaker. Jack took charge, insisting that Frances should have a complete rest from everybody — except himself. He took her to Lakewood, New Jersey. When Frances grew better, Jack had to travel to California, where his indiscretions while lecturing in the east of the United States sometimes forced him. There the famous couple — Erskine Wood, the poet and pioneer, and Sara Bard Field, the reformer who had left her husband to be with Erskine Wood, thirty years older than herself — befriended Jack.

2. Sara Bard Field, then thirty-nine. See Biographical Note.

3. *Marius the Epicurean* by Walter Pater (1839-94).

4. Dorothy Powys, the wife of Bertie Powys, the architect brother, who had been affected by his experiences in the trenches and who frequently woke screaming. Bertie recovered sufficiently to take on his job as Secretary of the Society for the Protection of Ancient Buildings.

NOTES TO LETTER 80, 9 MAY [1919] (pages 96-97)

1. Erskine Wood, the adventurer, war poet, pacifist and crusader. See Biographical Note.

2. Aristophanes (*c.* 448 BC - 388 BC), the Athenian poet and satirist, whose plays fearlessly attacked the corrupt and the foolish.

3. Haephaistus, or Vulcanus, the god of fire — and, with fire, a worker in metals.

4. Socrates (469 BC - 399 BC), the great teacher who was condemned to death for 'corrupting youth'.

NOTES TO LETTER 81, [MAY 1919] (pages 97-98)

1. Teddy, the Newfoundland dog — that bit.

2. Littleton Alfred was then seventeen.

NOTES TO LETTER 82, [MAY 1919] (pages 98-99)

1. Amelia Genai, 'Lala', the young Italian nurse.

2. Jack then gives a detailed account of how to travel via Omaha and Ogden, three nights in the train: '.....I will meet your train on the ferry *on the Berkeley side......*'

NOTE TO LETTER 83, 20 MAY [1919] (pages 99-100)

1. Gertrude Josepha Heartt, who lectured on temperance, venereal disease and women's rights.

NOTE TO LETTER 84, 20 MAY [1919] (page 100)

1. The plan had changed. Instead of Frances, her children, her mother

and the dog, Teddy, living permanently with Jack, it was now to be a visit, more for Frances's health than anything else. The change was partly caused by Louis Wilkinson's letter to Jack. This letter is not available, but one can infer the contents from Jack's reply, in which he writes:

> As far as I can make out, your idea is that I am to 'have' you and Madonna and Amelia, play tigers with Livio, hunt for silver pins with Betty and retain fraternal relations – in the English not the Italian way – with Frances – while my attitude to Teddy will be regulated according to local customs in Suffolk.....

NOTES TO LETTER 85, 23 MAY [1919] (page 101)

1. *The Complex Vision* by John Cowper Powys.
2. Jack rented a wooden house near Sausalito. By it were fields in which cattle grazed. There were a few other houses around them. Their neighbours included a family of German extraction who were ostracized by most people but befriended by Frances and Jack. Frances found that a small boy was being beaten by his parents. With Jack's help, she stopped this and took steps to see that the boy was protected by the authorities. His parents had thought him to be mentally deficient but, according to a later letter of Jack's, he turned out to be brilliant.

The sun shone but Jack wore heavy suits, and heavy, on the heavy cloth of his waistcoat, rested his gold watch-chain with gold pieces, seals and talismans. Jack often crossed the Golden Gate by ferry to lecture in San Francisco.

Soon, Frances's mother, Julia, with the Italian nurse, 'Lala', in charge of Betty, then two years old, arrived with the Newfoundland dog, Teddy, who continued to bite nearly everyone he met.

Jack took Frances to a sanatorium, where she was told that her lungs would probably recover, but that her heart would remain erratic.

Frances typed out Jack's *The Complex Vision*, but left out the 'not' when Jack wrote that he did not believe that a God existed. Jack restored the 'not'. Frances had by now typed the works of Jack, Theodore and Llewelyn Powys.

For a fuller account of Frances's stay with Jack in California, see 'A Rival to Jack', by Oliver Marlow Wilkinson, in Belinda Humfrey's anthology *Recollections of the Powys Brothers* (London, Peter Owen).

Frances decided to return to Louis.

Llewelyn returned to England from Africa; was advised by Louis to put his money into German marks, and lost his entire savings.

Theodore Powys was so poor that he accepted help from his brother,

Littleton, headmaster of Sherborne Prep. School. Jack, too, had to ask Littleton for money 'to keep Margaret going for a bit'.

NOTES TO LETTER 89, [7 NOVEMBER 1919] (pages 102-103)

1. Jack asks Frances, at three different points in the letter, in three different ways, to be sure to write the time that her train arrives.

2. Gilbert Cannan, the novelist, dramatist and critic from Manchester, England, was then thirty-five. He had a reputation as a 'daring young writer' and his book *Round the Corner* was banned for being too outspoken. In this very year, 1919, he was certified insane.

3. Rollo Peters, an actor.

4. Edward Dunsany, 18th Baron, the writer (1878-1957).

5. Hugh Walpole (1884-1941), the novelist, had been at Cambridge with Louis Wilkinson and Llewelyn Powys. Llewelyn, in *The Verdict of Bridlegoose*, writes a vignette of Walpole in New York.

6. Dorothy de Poillier, who was madly in love with Jack.

NOTES TO LETTER 90, 1 DECEMBER [1919] (page 103)

1. Frances sailed for England, with her two children, her mother, Amelia, the Italian nurse, and Teddy.

2. Because their nurse was Italian, the children used Italian slang: 'Licite' for lavatory, etc.

3. Liveright of Boni & Liveright, the New York publishers.

4. Sigmund Freud (1856-1939), the founder of psycho-analysis, who was later to have Frances's friend, Hilda Doolittle, 'H.D.', as a patient. See *Tribute to Freud* by H.D.

NOTES TO LETTER 92, 24 DECEMBER [1919] (page 105)

1. Leonard Andreyev, the Russian dramatist and novelist (1871-1919).

2. Woodrow Wilson (1856-1924), twenty-eighth President of the United States.

3. Maxim Gorky (1868-1936). Fania, Jack's friend, had translated the play *A Night's Lodging*.

4. Helen and Conroy were both on the stage. They married, divorced, then remarried each other.

5. Charlotte Wilkinson — Louis Wilkinson's mother, at Aldeburgh.

6. Dr Thomas looked after Jack and May. He had referred Jack to a surgeon for the stomach operation in 1917; after that he had rescued Jack from near-madness. 'The best of all family doctors', Jack calls him in his *Autobiography*, 'our unequalled Dr Thomas'.

NOTE TO LETTER 93, 30 DECEMBER [1919] (page 106)
1. *The Moon and Sixpence*.

NOTES TO LETTER 94, [13 JANUARY 1920] (pages 107-108)
1. Louis and Frances's house in Hampstead was peaceful. Frances's mother, Julia, was some safe miles away in Southampton. Jack was in America. Frances and Louis seemed happy again. Lala – Amelia Genai, the pretty Italian nurse – returned to Italy, to her love and to her mother. Louis employed the homeliest of bony English nurses, who wheeled the children round London like a starched automaton.

It is evident from their letters of the time that Frances and Louis Wilkinson were still in love with one another, in spite of all the turbulence. Frances exclaimed to me once, 'If only I'd *known*, Louis was a good specimen of an Englishman!' Increasing impingement of Frances's mother, Julia, on the household, and Louis' strictness with the bony nursemaid, began to disturb the marriage.

2. Frances was shocked when she saw Louis ring the bell for the maid to hand him a book not six feet away; but she understood this to be something that Louis had been brought up with, like a family disease.

3. Dorothy Richardson (1873-1957), the English writer, pioneer of the 'stream of consciousness' writing. She collected her novels under the title, *Pilgrimage*.

NOTES TO LETTER 95, 26 JANUARY [1920] (page 108)
1. The painting by Raymond Johnson is a striking full-length one of Jack. It was in Marian Powys's keeping, and later with her son, Peter Powys-Grey, in his New York apartment.

2. Judas Maccaboeus, who directed the Jewish War of Independence in 166 BC.

3. 'Assumption of the Virgin', that had been the centre-piece of El Greco's decorations for the Church of Santo Domingo el Antigua, in Toledo, Spain.

4. Mr Spring was a hunchback dwarf, and he came near to answering Jack's cry, 'If only we had a Manager to manage our Manager!' for Mr Spring, as secretary to Arnold Shaw, greatly improved the workings of the Lecture Agency.

NOTES TO LETTER 96, 27 JANUARY [1920] (pages 108-110)
1. Frances found that her friend, Hilda Doolittle, was becoming well-known as the poet, 'H.D.'. Hilda had had a miscarriage; but her second child, Perdita, by Cecil Gray, a musicologist, had been born on 31 March

1919. Bryher – as she called herself – had fallen in love with Hilda's poetry, and then with Hilda (see also Biographical Note). She now financed Hilda, her work, her daughter – and, even, later, Hilda's lovers. Bryher hated Frances. This added more tension to Frances's life, but she and Hilda continued to meet.

Hilda was divorced from Richard Aldington. He had threatened to take her to Court if Hilda claimed that the child, Perdita, was his. See *Richard Aldington* by Charles Doyle.

2. In 1912, when Ezra Pound had stopped Hilda Doolittle travelling with Frances and Louis to Germany – 'to give', as Ezra had said, 'some chance of happiness to Frances in her marriage.' See *Herself Defined* by Barbara Guest.

3. Louis had accepted a post at Benson's, the advertising agency. It was the only office work he ever did. He grew restive. One day his friend, Oswald Green, and others at Benson's, chatted to Louis about beer, for Louis wrote their 'copy' about alcohol, especially wine, of which he had considerable knowledge. 'What do you associate with beer, Louis?' 'Beer? .....' repeated Louis, vaguely, '...beer ... well ... beer ... is ... *good* for you!' So, 'Guinness is good For You' was born. Louis, in spite of the good salary, the lavish luncheons, and their treatment of him as a distinguished guest rather than an employee, could not stand the regular hours of work. He resigned after a few months, to continue lecturing and writing.

Brute Gods by Louis Wilkinson was published by Alfred A. Knopf in New York.

NOTES TO LETTER 97, [*c*. 17 February 1920] (page 110)

1. Jack lived and wrote on the move in the United States, in trains and hotels. This was expensive and, in spite of 'things beginning to pick up splendidly' – Jack's first book of philosophy, *The Complex Vision*, that Frances had typed out, had been accepted by Dodd, Mead & Co., of New York – Jack's money was running out fast.

2. His son, Littleton, then eighteen, was now at Sherborne School.

NOTES TO LETTER 98, [*c*. MARCH 1920] (pages 110-111)

1. François de Marsillac, Duc de La Rochefoucauld, the French writer, chiefly famous for his *Réflexions, Sentences, et Maximes Morales*.

2. It was Frances's birthday.

NOTES TO LETTER 99, 6 SEPTEMBER [1920] (page 111)

1. At the end of April, Jack had arrived in England with James Henderson. Jack and Llewelyn Powys (Lulu), and Frances and Louis,

met in London. James went on, with Frances and Louis, to Louis' mother's house, 'Deepdene', in Aldeburgh, Suffolk.

James Henderson, heart-broken in an amiable way, returned to the United States.

Jack saw Frances and Louis and the children in London. Then, on 14 August, Jack and Llewelyn set sail for America on the 'Aquitania'.

Frances moved her mother into a hotel in London, and joined her there with the two children, and the Italian nurse, Amelia Genai, whom she had recalled from Italy.

Louis, though, took a house in Church Walk, Kensington, where he and Frances had lived before, opposite Ezra Pound, and moved Frances and the children to it, separating Frances from her mother.

2. Helen Wylde, the actress, who had been with Jack after his operation.

3. Dorothy de Poillier, now a secretary on the magazine, 'The Dial', and still deeply in love with Jack.

NOTES TO LETTER 102, [OCTOBER 1920] (pages 112-113)

1. There was another crisis in Frances's marriage, as she tried to reconcile care for her husband and children with concern for her mother.

2. Stewart Ellis, the writer, and editor of *The Unpublished Letters of Lady Bulwer Lytton*, lived in Southwold, a few miles along the coast from the Wilkinson home and School. He was also a friend of Bernie and Belle O'Neill, who provided a liberal haven for homosexuals.

3. George Meredith (1828-1909), the writer.

4. *After My Fashion* by John Cowper Powys, was finally published by Picador, in 1980, with an introduction by Francis Powys, his nephew.

5. Mrs Edward Wilkins, Secretary of a society for bringing 'distinguished scholars' to Joplin, Missouri, invited Jack to lecture there.

In Joplin, Jack met Phyllis Playter. She was at that time, she told me, a waitress in a local restaurant. Phyllis was the daughter of a miner of precious stones who had been drummed out of three towns that he himself had founded. Phyllis indicated that her father had a tendency to become over-dictatorial. See also Biographical Note.

NOTES TO LETTER 104, 22 NOVEMBER [1920] (pages 113-114)

1. Frances went to Paris with the two children and her mother, Julia, and her mother's dog, Teddy. She planned to go to a wine-making part of France, so that Louis, with his love and great knowledge of wine, would be tempted to follow – at least for a time – and be reconciled to her having to look after her mother. Louis hated Julia, partly because she

threatened to go to the police when Louis had, in an argument, knocked Frances down, shortly before Frances was to give birth to her daughter, Betty. Julia had thrown Louis into a panic. She had made him sign a confession. She also made him cancel a sum of money that she had borrowed from him. Louis had come to hate her more and more.

Louis was left suddenly in England. He was now a successful writer. His novel, *Brute Gods*, which had been published in the United States by Alfred P. Knopf in 1919, was published in London by William Heinemann. Louis still wrote under his own name of Louis Wilkinson.

In the United States, Llewelyn Powys was becoming well-known for his articles in 'The Saturday Evening Post'. When he was signing the register in a hotel, the clerk asked, 'Are you *the* Llewelyn Powys?'

Theodore Powys had as yet published only his early work. His manuscripts were piled in a cupboard.

2. Frances was too busy regaining her authority, and developing her ideas — some of which can be seen in her letters — to be home-sick. Her mother, Julia, though, remained a patriotic American citizen: reciting American poetry to the children, singing American songs, reciting all the States of the union in order, and the American Constitution together with Lincoln's Gettysburg address. She also had her American dog, Teddy, but he was getting old. Julia was just a little contemptuous of the English; and now a little suspicious of the French. Sometimes she would shut herself in her room, when she longed for home, and play rather discordantly; but she played well enough to join local orchestras. She received a teacher's pension from the United States; but generally she saved the payments, in case of a disaster.

3. Marcel Proust (1871-1922), the French author of *A La Recherche du Temps Perdu* in thirteen volumes, and other works of introspection.

4. Yet read Jack's brilliant account of Marcel Proust in his book, *The Pleasures of Literature*.

5. Jack is presumably referring to the compilation called *L'Enfer de la Bibliothèque Nationale* by Apollinaire and others. This was named after the special section of the Bibliothèque Nationale reserved for books that for reasons of obscenity, etc., are 'enfermés' and shelf-marked 'enfer'.

6. Immanuel Kant (1724-1804), the German philosopher.

NOTES TO LETTER 105, 29 NOVEMBER [1920] (pages 114-115)
1. Frances had moved her children, her mother and her mother's dog to Burgundy, to the village of Bligny, near Beaune. She rented a large, pleasant house with a spacious garden and she barricaded her mother off

in half of the house. Over a very large window in her bedroom that she kept open, Frances nailed chicken wire, and hung it with little bells. She wanted fresh air but not intruders. She was slightly on edge, because she had heard that Aleister Crowley was returning to Europe. Her friend Hilda Doolittle, 'H.D.', was being threatened because of an association she had had with Aleister Crowley in the past. Frances never told me how Hilda had become involved with Crowley's Order.

2. 'I can do nothing else.'

3. Rembrandt (1606-69), the Dutch painter.

NOTES TO LETTER 106, 13 DECEMBER [1920] (pages 115-116)

1. See *Porius* by John Cowper Powys.

2. She was the second wife of W.L. George, the author of the successful *A Bed of Roses*.

NOTES TO LETTER 107, 23 DECEMBER [1920] (page 116)

1. Marion Linton, a cousin of the Powyses, was the daughter of the Hon. Ralph Shirley's sister, Alice, who was married to Mr Linton of Shirley Rectory in Derbyshire.

Llewelyn had been in love with Marion Linton, but she had entered a convent, while he had been in Africa during the war.

2. Edna St Vincent Millay (1892-1950), the American poet. She had already published *Renascence* as one poem, and as the title of a collection of her poetry, and, in 1920, she published *Figs from a Thistle*. See also Biographical Note.

3. Maurice Browne, the Cambridge friend of Louis Wilkinson, had been directing the Chicago Little Theatre with his wife, Ellen van Valkenburg.

4. Rollo Peters, actor.

5. Duncan — Isadora's brother — was also an exemplar of a new kind of dancing.

6. Dorothy Cheston was an actress who lived with Arnold Bennett, the writer, '....but,' says Louis Wilkinson, a friend of Arnold Bennett, 'she nearly drove him to distraction, and killed him by her careless ways when she gave him contaminated water. She was a pleasant girl, though, when very young.' Louis remembers her as '....not really a very good actress.....though she had some distinction.....'

Dorothy Cheston was a colleague of Mrs Patrick Campbell and of Viola Tree.

NOTE TO LETTER 108, 31 JANUARY [1921] (page 117)

1. J.B. – Josephine Brewer – a well-connected eccentric in New York, who suffered from delusions. Jack explains in a letter written at this time to Frances's mother, Julia, that Josephine Brewer had had envelopes printed with her name under Jack's, and had been writing to Nell Brinkley – a 'Lonely Hearts' columnist – demanding money, in the grossest terms. Arthur Brisbane – a well-known journalist of sensational claptrap – had rushed to the defence of his friend, Nell Brinkley, and had told the police to arrest Josephine Brewer.

She had persecuted Mrs John Barrymore in the same way.

Jack, in fact, did not want the eccentric 'shut away', so when she interrupted a lecture of his with a speech to the audience about a 'mystical marriage' between herself and Jack, he submitted himself to her harangues. After a police warning, and the intervention of her brother, she finally ceased her persecution.

NOTES TO LETTER 109, 15 FEBRUARY [1921] (pages 118-119)

1. *Ulysses* by James Joyce (1882-1941) was banned in Britain and America. Ezra Pound had persuaded Margaret Anderson and Jane Heap to publish it in their 'Little Review'. He himself had serialised Joyce's *Portrait of the Artist as a Young Man*, in 'The Egoist' in 1914. *Ulysses* was published in Paris in 1922, but remained banned in Britain and America for much longer.

2. John Sumner was the head of the Society for the Prevention of Vice.

3. Margaret Anderson was a figure on the American literary scene. She had founded 'The Little Review' in 1912. The magazine had distinction, but led a hand-to-mouth existence and would have collapsed but for Margaret Anderson's grand manner in collecting subscriptions from bewildered stockbrokers. The prosecution that put Margaret Anderson and Jane Heap in the dock was against the Washington Square Bookshop.

The two women were found guilty of publishing obscene material, namely Episode XIII of *Ulysses*. They were fined a hundred pounds and had their fingerprints taken. Jack, giving evidence for the Defence, was the only 'expert' witness called: a measure of his literary standing at the time.

4. This may well have been the Managing Editor, Alyse Gregory (see Biographical Note), with whom Llewelyn Powys was to fall in love, after making love to every girl his brother Jack had known in the United States.

NOTES TO LETTER 110, 10 MARCH [1921] (pages 119-120)

1. Katharine – Sara Bard Field's daughter.

2. Genefride had long been one of Jack's loves, but, as Jack said, Llewelyn's only real fault was making love to his friend's girls.

NOTES TO LETTER 112, 6 MAY [1921] (page 121)

1. Jessica Colbert, the Lecture Manager, in San Francisco.

2. *The Complex Vision* by John Cowper Powys had been typed out by Frances in 1919, and published in the United States in 1920.

NOTE TO LETTER 113, 12 MAY [1921] (page 122)

1. Noel Sullivan was a rich young man of aristocratic manner who was helping to back Jessica Colbert's plans. Part of his house was a convent in which, as Llewelyn Powys wrote, 'he kept his pet nuns'.

NOTES TO LETTER 114, [JUNE 1921] (page 123)

1. Jack is, of course, writing about 1922.

2. Mlle Jaflin was the local schoolmistress. She had beautiful eyes and the slightly cat-like look of certain beautiful old maids. She let Frances's son sit at the back of her class. She loved Frances very much.

3. Amelia Genai, 'Lala', had returned from Italy, at Frances's summons, and had told Frances that she was pregnant.

NOTES TO LETTER 115, 10 JULY [1921] (pages 123-125)

1. On his return from New York, Jack moved to the Hotel Holly Oaks, with Llewelyn, because he could no longer stand the Philipine servants at Hotel Alta Mira who sometimes served him uncooked meals, under the impression that he preferred these. The Hotel Holly Oaks was in Sausalito where Jack, in 1919, had taken a house for himself and Frances and her family.

2. James Anthony Froude (1818-94); Suetonius (75-160 A.D.); Julius Caesar (*c.* 100 BC - 44 BC) – because Jack could have 'mugged up' his subjects from the writings of these three.

3. Earlier in the year, Llewelyn had walked too far, and had discoloration -- blood spitting – on his return. He was persuaded to go to a Dr Abrams, the Faustus of the Twentieth Century, who painted Llewelyn's right shoulder blade a brilliant marsh-marigold colour, and attached him to his electrical machine. In ten minutes he pronounced Llewelyn cured. He refused to take money. Many people said that Dr Abrams was a quack, but Llewelyn had no further trouble with tuberculosis for three years.

NOTE TO LETTER 117, 11 AUGUST [1921] (pages 126-127)

1. 'Mr Welsh' – 'Jack Welsh' – the character based on John Cowper Powys in *The Buffoon* by Louis Wilkinson.

NOTES TO LETTER 118, [AUGUST 1921] (page 127)

1. Oedipus, who killed his father and married his mother: *Oedipus the King* and *Oedipus at Colonus* by Sophocles (*c.* 496 - *c.* 405 BC) – the Athenian playwright.

2. Louis Wilkinson's mother, Charlotte Elizabeth.

NOTES TO LETTER 119, 19 AUGUST [1921] (pages 127-129)

1. Reading about St Francis (1180-1226) in San Francisco, to 'mug up' a lecture.

2. Rather than pay insurance. Her stock of lace, though, had been burgled.

3. 'The Two Brothers' by Frances: the story in which a famous lecturer, like Jack, lies dying, remembering the woman whom he had sadistically married off to a vicious friend. The story had been published in 1915. Frances had written it in a rage of indignation.

NOTES TO LETTER 120, 14 SEPTEMBER [1921] (pages 129-130)

1. When Frances had dressed as a boy in Venice.

2. 'Mr Welsh' – Jack in Louis Wilkinson's novel *The Buffoon*.

3. Andrew Lang (1844-1912), the Scottish writer who translated Homer's *Iliad* and *Odyssey*. Lang wrote much else, including those fairy-story books in different colours.

4. 'Evangeline', the most popular poem by Henry Longfellow (1807-82), the American poet.

'This is the forest primeval. The murmuring pines and the hemlocks.....'

5. Mrs Klang was their landlady in California, 1919.

6. Robert Minor was an American who, on his return from Russia, was imprisoned for his Communist associations.

NOTES TO LETTER 121, 11 OCTOBER [1921] (pages 130-132)

1. Margaret Mower, the pretty actress who had worked at Maurice Browne's Chicago Little Theatre.

2. Rob Parker: Marian Powys told me that he was a good writer, critic and companion at 12, West 12th Street, New York, where Jack and Marian lived.

3. Marian Powys said that he was the English actor who put on Jack's dramatisation of Dostoevsky's *The Idiot*.

4. Kirah had been a mistress of Theodore Dreiser.

5. On their return from California Jack and Llewelyn had stayed for one night in a hotel. Their sister, Marian, was pregnant and was at her house at Sneedon's Landing, where Llewelyn – in spite of Marian having so resented his coming to live with Jack and herself in New York – often called on her.

6. In 1909, when Jack had tried, unsuccessfully, to teach Llewelyn to lecture.

7. Because of the burglary.

8. Marian Powys thought that John Fanshawe may have been an out-of-work actor; but she could not remember him.

NOTES TO LETTER 122, [MID-OCTOBER 1921] (page 133)

1. Siva, Hindu god of destruction.

2. Llewelyn found the room so uncomfortable; it had only a coal bag, a heap of splintered wood and a few sticks of furniture. As a result, he had to go and write in the open air of Washington Square (see *Honey and Gall* by Llewelyn Powys). He found that his articles that had been rejected were now accepted by the critic Van Wyck Brooks, for 'The Freeman'. Llewelyn also received books for review. See *The Life of Llewelyn Powys* by Malcolm Elwin.

NOTES TO LETTER 123, 30 OCTOBER [1921] (pages 133-134)

1. Edith Wharton (1862-1937), the American writer. Her husband had become insane in 1912, and she was now divorced. *The Age of Innocence* had been awarded the Pulitzer Prize in 1920, though *Ethan Frome*, published in 1911, is generally regarded as her best work.

2. Frances's daughter, then four years old.

NOTES TO LETTER 124, 1 NOVEMBER [1921] (pages 134-136)

1. The marriage with Louis Wilkinson was finally breaking up. Louis had come to stay with Frances in Beaune. Vast efforts were made by Frances and the Italian nurse, 'Lala', to make him happy and comfortable. A tin bath had been put on the lawn for his morning cold bath, and Frances's mother was kept firmly in her side of the house. Louis gravely enjoyed the pleasures; took his son walking, and gave him grenadine. Louis had then returned to England.

2. Jack uses, in his own writing, this 'lodged belief' of Frances.

NOTE TO LETTER 125, 23 DECEMBER [1921] (pages 136-137)

1. The little boy whom they had rescued from frequent thrashings,

in California, 1919.

NOTES TO LETTER 126, [MAY 1922] (pages 138-139)

1. In his letters to Frances's mother, Julia.

2. Jack's book of poetry, *Samphire*, which Llewelyn had cajoled, criticised, edited, had — largely through Llewelyn's efforts — been published by Thomas Seltzer.

3. Where Louis, who had now fallen deeply in love with Nan Reid (see Biographical Note) — who was as small as Louis was tall — often stayed with Bernie and Belle O'Neill.

4. *Ebony and Ivory* by Llewelyn Powys, with an introduction by Theodore Dreiser. Llewelyn was beginning to think that he would have to do far more than write these stories about Africa, to right even the smallest part of the wrongs he had seen suffered by the black man at the hands of the white man. *Ebony and Ivory* had been rejected by four New York publishers before being accepted by the American Library Service controlled by Symon Gould.

5. Fyodor Dostoevsky (1821-81), the Russian novelist. Both Frances and Jack read and re-read his works, *Crime and Punishment*, *The Brothers Karamazov*, etc.

6. Michelangelo (1475-1564), the Italian artist, whose works Frances and Jack had seen together in Italy in 1912.

7. Sandro Botticelli (1444-1510), the Florentine whose work Frances loved almost more than that of any other Italian painters.

8. Edna St Vincent Millay was thirty-two then.

NOTES TO LETTER 127, 8 JUNE [1922] (pages 139-140)

1. The house in which Alyse Gregory lived. Llewelyn Powys had first met Alyse late in 1921. She was then the Managing Editor of the famous American periodical 'The Dial' (see Nicholas Joost's book on 'The Dial'), which had accepted some of Llewelyn's work. Alyse had invited Llewelyn to her home in Patchin Place. They fell in love.

Jack saw less and less of Llewelyn, but in June 1922, he moved to an upstairs room in 4, Patchin Place — where Llewelyn now shared the ground floor with Alyse, who did the cooking for the three of them.

Frances knew the house. Ezra Pound had once lived there. Frances and her mother had sometimes called there, with Hilda Doolittle, 'H.D.', long before Frances had met Jack.

2. Constance, who married Ted Pearce of Corpus Christi, Cambridge.

NOTES TO LETTER 128, 8 OCTOBER [1922] (pages 140-142)

1. Jack had visited his family in England, but had returned to the United States for his lecture season.

Frances had taken the Italian nurse, Amelia Genai, 'Lala', to Beaune, to the Hostel-Dieu, built in 1443, to have her baby. Amelia had then taken her baby back to show her parents in Siena. All this took money. Louis sent no money. Jack saved the day. From Burpham – where his wife had had the house enlarged and renamed 'Warren House' – Jack sent Frances's mother something like 1,600 francs, in three instalments – adding, in the last batch, '.....Will you acknowledge if you please the receipt of all three?....don't bother to write till you get this. Well! You've got it now, so please answer.....'

2. Julia's dog, Teddy, had died the previous year in Beaune, after days of lying prostrate in a corner of Julia's side of the house, and of being watched night and day by her and by Frances. The large corpse, with its curious rancid-sweet smell of disease, was buried with some difficulty in the orchard.

3. Frances had two lessons, knocked down a wall, then drove her family westward – sometimes on the edge of cliffs, then in thick fog, once nearly into a canal. The car, an old Brazier, was loaded with chickens in crates. The crates were smashed in a crowded market, and the chickens retrieved only with difficulty. To save up for the car, Frances and Julia had had to learn how to use dandelion leaves as lettuce, and how to cook nettles; and how to keep chickens.

At Arcachon, Frances took her family by the little steamer to Cap Ferret, which is, on one side, bordered by a bay that seemed almost tropical and, on the other side, by the Bay of Biscay. They moved into a villa. Frances's family had a wonderful time there. The Italian nurse, 'Lala', rejoined them with her thriving baby. Mlle Jaflin visited them there. Frances had changed Mlle Jaflin's life; and they kept in touch for a long time after this.

4. Peter Powys-Grey, Marian Powys's son.

Jack wrote to Frances's mother, Julia, that his sister, Marian, had 'the ring of the right finger'. This was a stratagem to give the impression that Marian had married the father of her baby. Jack added that the father had since died. Marian's attitude was different. She did not think of her child as 'illegitimate' but as *her* child, all the more hers because there was no official father. When she discussed the matter with her brother, Jack said that the matter was not really either black or white: so they called her son Peter Powys-Grey. See also Biographical Note.

5. Nan (see note below) had had a daughter by Louis, but neither Nan

nor Louis knew how to look after a baby.

6. Jack's birthday was on 8 October.

7. Anne Reid — or 'Nan'. Nan and Louis brought their weak baby, Deirdre, to Cap Ferret, for Frances and 'Lala' to nurse back to health. The household seemed so unusual to the neighbours that they asked Frances's seven-year-old son, Oliver — 'Livio' — where his father slept. Not knowing, he answered, as he thought proper, 'With my grandmother'.

As the baby recovered, Nan began to resent Frances's care of Deirdre. After a while the baby was moved to Dr and Mrs O'Neill's house at Chiswick in London. It was in this household that Deirdre grew up, seeing her parents at intervals. They still did not know how to bring up a child and were busy with their writings.

NOTES TO LETTER 129, 17 DECEMBER [1922] (pages 142-143)

1. Mrs Klang, their landlady in California.

2. The piece of the 'Myrten' bush is still in the envelope.

3. The little boy in California who had been saved from constant thrashing by Frances and Jack, and who had been thought by the authorities to be partly imbecile.

4. The Hoffmans were one of the several well-to-do families Jack knew in the United States.

NOTE TO LETTER 130, [1923] (page 144)

1. This is the only letter surviving from Jack to Frances during 1923; and there are only two from Frances to Jack. The correspondence seems to have been between Jack and Frances's mother. This ended, too, when Julia wrote that they might be returning to the United States. Jack wrote back that for him to try to look after them in a land 'without the benefit of the Exchange' would be as if he were seeing Frances and her family 'like half-drowned moths in a pond, while I can do nothing but feebly poke with my stick in the muddy water'. 'You will have no doubt correctly anticipated,' he continues, 'that you would find me with some sort of new entangelmt or tie, let us put it, or "responsibility".....' The new 'responsibility' was Phyllis Playter. This letter of Jack's ended Frances's letters to him, for a long time: and so ended Jack's letters to Frances, for a time — except for this one in 1923.

At the end of 1922, in spite of all the turmoil — and though she had agreed to take less than £2 a week from Louis — Frances and her family had a happy Christmas at Cap Ferret, with each person playing an instrument in the family orchestra.

In 1923, Amelia Genai, 'Lala', took her beautiful baby, Vilda, back to her home in Siena, to Frances's great regret.

Frances put her family in the big car again, and zig-zagged across France, ending up east of Cherbourg – from which, one night of calm moonlit water, they sailed for England.

Frances's son, Oliver, was sent as a boarder to the Wilkinson Prep. School at Aldeburgh.

Jack was in financial difficulty because of the mismanagement of his lectures by Jessica Colbert. Llewelyn Powys thought so ill of Jack's *After My Fashion*, that he told Jack to forget the novel.

Arnold Shaw, with whom Jack also had a contract, forbade him to debate with Frank Harris – Louis Wilkinson's friend – saying it would finally end what reputation Jack had left to be on the same platform as such a notorious man. (This information is contained in a letter of 1923 from Jack to Louis.)

Jack's *The Art of Happiness* was published by the Haldeman-Julius Company, Girard, Kansas – the first of Jack's 'Little Blue Books', that thousands read. Oddly enough, Phyllis Playter had taken a job with Haldeman-Julius, and one of her first jobs was to proof-read John Cowper Powys's work.

Jessica Colbert published *Psycho-Analysis and Morality* by John Cowper Powys in a limited edition of five hundred copies; but two hundred were destroyed by fire.

Thirteen Worthies by Llewelyn Powys was published by Simon Gould in the United States, and by Grant Richards in London, with a preface by Van Wyck Brooks.

Suddenly, Theodore Powys's manuscripts – including those typed by Frances – began to be published, through the efforts of Sylvia Townsend Warner, the writer, and Steven Tomlin, the sculptor, who put Theodore in touch with David Garnett, author of *Lady into Fox*, etc., adviser to the Nonesuch Press. *The Left Leg* and *Black Bryony* by Theodore Powys, were published by Chatto & Windus and, in the United States, by Knopf.

Willy, the youngest Powys son, in Kenya, was awarded the Croix de Guerre de Leopold II for his war service; and was given a grant of land, on which he founded his farm.

In August, the Powys father, the Reverend Charles Francis Powys, died. Jack, at such a low ebb, with one single lecture a week, at a school in Greenwich, New York, could not return to England. Gertrude Powys, who had long looked after her father, went, after the funeral, to Paris to study art. Katie Powys – who never suffered from mental illness again – used her share of the inheritance to visit Jack and Llewelyn in the United States.

Frances and Louis continued to discuss a divorce.

Perceval Roberts – the suicidal dandy, of that journey to England in 1912 – shot himself, leaving a note, 'Eventually – why not now?'

NOTE TO LETTER 131, [NOVEMBER 1923] (page 145)

1. Bertie Powys, the architect brother, still suffered from the effects of his war service; but he was an indefatigable worker as Secretary for the Society for the Preservation of Ancient Buildings.

NOTE TO LETTER 132, [31 DECEMBER 1923] (pages 145-146)

1. This probably refers to Jack's answer to Frances's mother, after Julia had told him they might all be returning to the United States. The other letter from Jack that Frances refers to is missing.

NOTE TO LETTER 133, [8 FEBRUARY 1924] (page 147)

1. Frances had to pay almost every penny towards the clothes, trunk, play-box and so on, for her son, Oliver, as a boy at an English prep. school. The saving grace was that Louis Wilkinson's brother, Maurice, headmaster of Aldeburgh Lodge, took no fees from Frances for himself, but he had to charge half-fees for his partner, Fred Spurgeon.

NOTES TO LETTER 134, [APRIL 1924] (pages 147-148)

1. Frances had, however, written to Louis asking for a divorce.
2. The work was at an Employment Bureau run by a French lady.

NOTES TO LETTER 135, [SEPTEMBER 1924] (pages 148-149)

1. In April, Frances moved her family to a ground-floor flat in a slowly decaying London mansion in a genteely crumbling street. In the flat above were the Macpherson family. The eldest son of the family, Kenneth (see Biographical Note) – a handsome young man, with the grave, lean look of a Knight Errant – fell in love with Frances. See 'The Apartment House' by Frances Gregg.

2. Jack had returned to his wife and son at Burpham. He visited Frances in London. He then went on to his brother, Theodore, in Dorset.

3. Theodore and Llewelyn's reputations now stood higher than Jack's, but Jack always wrote generously about his brothers.

Llewelyn had at this time become ill again with tuberculosis and Alyse Gregory had taken him to the Catskill Mountains to recover.

4. Bertie Powys had married his distant cousin, Dorothy, in 1904. She seems to have bullied him.

5. Isobel, then eighteen, daughter of Bertie and Dorothy Powys.

6. Frances was happier being again in charge of her own destiny. She had earned enough money at the Employment Agency to take her family to a village near Cherbourg, in France, for a holiday.

7. The youngest son of the Macphersons, a scrawny little boy, nine years old. Frances was fond of him.

NOTES TO LETTER 137, 6 FEBRUARY [1925] (pages 150-151)

1. There had been no letter from Jack at Christmas. On New Year's Eve Frances had had a party with her family and the Macphersons. Then, alone, she had finished typing. Old clothes, given to her by her friend Hilda Doolittle, 'H.D.', had then been laid out on a chair, ready for the morning.

2. Kenneth Macpherson was in love with Frances, and planning to illustrate works of hers.

3. Oscar Wilde (1854-1900), the Irish writer, whose followers always honoured Louis Wilkinson for writing to him, when Louis was a boy at Radley, and for championing the homosexual cause.

4. Richard le Gallienne (1866-1947), the English writer; author of *The Quest of the Golden Girl*, etc. Le Gallienne lived in New York and was known to Alyse Gregory and 'The Dial' circle. Llewelyn Powys and Alyse had been staying with him at this time.

5. Phyllis Playter was now living with Jack.

6. Ashtead Heath is in Surrey, near Leatherhead and Epsom.

7. Three Bridges is a railway station near Crawley, Sussex.

8. In California, 1919. Frances, by buying little food and spending nothing on clothing, was still keeping her son, Oliver — 'Livio' — at the Wilkinson School. She was also sending her daughter, Betty, to a boarding school.

NOTE TO LETTER 138, 6 MAY [1925] (pages 151-152)

1. Llewelyn was still ill with tuberculosis. He had married Alyse Gregory. His book *Skin for Skin*, that he described as '.....a bawdy libellous bloody book.....' was published by Harcourt Brace & Co., New York. It was published in a limited edition of nine hundred copies by Jonathan Cape, in London; and re-issued with his *The Verdict of Bridlegoose* by the Bodley Head in 1927, and again in 1948. Llewelyn and Alyse were now returning to England.

NOTES TO LETTER 139, 19 MAY [1925] (pages 152-153)

1. Frances, at one point, while recovering from a heart attack that had nearly killed her, had gone to Lakewood, near Philadelphia, with Jack. She had walked in her sleep and, in the middle of the night, had piled up all the contents of a washstand onto a tray, and had thrown the whole lot out of the window onto the glass roofed verandah below, rousing the hotel with the crash. Frances had walked in her sleep quite often. Once she rose from her bed and, while still asleep, had taken up the revolver with which they always travelled, and had fired a bullet quite close to Louis' head.

2. His brothers Littleton and Llewelyn and his son Littleton.

NOTES TO LETTER 140, 17 JUNE [1925] (pages 153-154)

1. Frances had introduced Kenneth Macpherson to Hilda Doolittle (Hilda Aldington) – 'H.D.'. Frances was arguing fiercely with Hilda whom she accused of neglecting her daughter, Perdita, and of corrupting herself by her relationship with 'Bryher', daughter of Lord Ellerman, the shipping magnate.

Now Kenneth Macpherson told Frances that he was in love with Hilda.

2. Julia had now bought an old Rover car.

NOTES TO LETTER 141, 6 SEPTEMBER [1925] (pages 154-155)

1. 'The Apartment House' and 'The Unknown Face' by Frances had both been published in *The Second American Caravan*.

2. *Ducdame* by John Cowper Powys had been published. Written under Llewelyn Powys's influence, it is leaner, more concise, than much of Jack's other work.

3. Arnold Shaw's second wife, Hattie, and his son, Armin, by his second wife, and Edith, Arnold's daughter by his first wife.

NOTES TO LETTER 142, [SEPTEMBER 1925] (pages 155-157)

1. In Oakenhill Hall, an Elizabethan manor with no electricity or running water, but with a secret room and a secret passage.

2. Marjory Ling wrote plays, one or two of which were performed as 'try-outs' in small theatres in London. She kept house for her brother, who was a solicitor.

3. Ling & Co., solicitors, had arranged for the divorce between Frances and Louis Wilkinson. The decree had been made absolute on 25 May. Louis was now an established novelist, with another novel, *Mr Amberthwaite*, this time under the name of Louis Marlow, published. It

was considerably praised.

4. In an audience, listening to Jack lecturing in Philadelphia.

5. 'Pannes in France' by Frances Gregg, was published in 'The Bermondsey Book'.

6. Bertie Powys's architectural notes were being published by J.C. Squire in 'The London Mercury'. He had lectured in the United States. Jack had bound himself with the Keedick Agency – one of the main Lecture Agencies in the United States; he had not returned with Bertie.

7. Dorothy, who treated her husband, Bertie Powys, badly.

NOTES TO LETTER 143, [NO DATE, 1926] (page 158)

1. Frances's letters to Jack, in 1926, are missing. His sister, Marian, had saved some of the previous ones, from Patchin Place, finding them in a drawer after Jack had left; but she could not, evidently, save Frances's 1926 letters.

Frances and her mother, Julia, were busy in the vast Oakenhill Hall, building huge armchairs and padding them, and building great tables, with wood from packing-cases, and with tools sent by James Henderson from America.

2. A daughter, Patricia.

3. Lizzie was Arnold's first wife.

4. The Reverend Hudson Shaw, who had been a fellow lecturer of Jack and of Louis.

NOTES TO LETTER 144, 5 FEBRUARY [1926] (page 159)

1. 'Perché' by Frances Gregg.

2. This Crooked Cross – made of dark tortoiseshell, and hung from a chain made of tortoiseshell, had been given to Frances by Jack. She had not sold it, but she had pawned it.

NOTES TO LETTER 145, 22 MARCH [1926] (pages 159-160)

1. Frances and her family were happy in Oakenhill Hall, except for money worries. Then her son fell ill, and nearly died; and her daughter broke her arm and was attended by a doctor who proved to be a sadist (he was later tried and convicted for causing unnecessary pain), who hurt Betty unmercifully until Frances turned him out of the house. Frances nursed both children back to health. A young, handsome schoolmaster, while on a paperchase from a local school came across Oakenhill Hall. He entered it to ask for a glass of water and fell in love with Frances. He called there often after that. For the rest of his life, he sent Frances small exquisite presents. He was called Andrew Gibson.

2. Mr de Kantzow was an old man, over seventy, an impoverished Polish nobleman who lived in Portslade when Jack, as a young man, in 1906, had taught in Brighton girls' schools.

3. Thomas Hardy was then eighty-six.

4. Mr Keedick, of Keedick's Lecture Agency.

5. *Wolf Solent* by John Cowper Powys. Jack had already published another of his 'little blue books' of philosophy, *The Secret of Self-Development.*

NOTES TO LETTER 146, 22 SEPTEMBER [1926] (pages 160-161)

1. Jack came to England with James Henderson. They all met at Oakenhill Hall, and talked and walked and talked again, as they had done in America. James was still in love with Frances. In the end, though, he returned to the United States alone. Jack, too, returned to America. Frances moved to London to get a job; and obtained the post of shop assistant in Peter Jones, in Sloane Square. She was quickly promoted, to editing their 'Gazette'.

Kenneth Macpherson had become 'H.D.'s' lover, but was marrying 'H.D.'s' lesbian protector and lover, the rich Bryher, in a marriage that was 'of convenience' for all three; especially for Kenneth Macpherson, who was now able to develop his film magazine, the first 'cinema as art' magazine in Britain, 'Close-Up'.

2. Frances had taken her family to Herne Bay for a summer holiday.

3. Frances had taken a small room, near Victoria Station, in London.

NOTES TO LETTER 147, 1 FEBRUARY [1927] (pages 162-163)

1. Frances's letters are missing till 1935. Phyllis Playter found her later letters in a drawer at Blaenau Ffestiniog, Wales, and kept them safely.

In 1927, Jack, on a circuit of fewer lectures, wrote — mostly on *Wolf Solent* — in trains, in hotels, then again in Patchin Place, New York.

2. Theodore Powys was now enjoying a great success as a writer. *Mockery Gap* and *Mr Tasker's Gods* (one of the stories on which Frances's help had been sought) had been published in 1925; *Innocent Birds, A Stubborn Tree, Feed My Swine*, and *A Strong Girl* were published in 1926; and in 1927 *The Rival Pastors, Mr Weston's Good Wine* and *What Lack Ye Yet?* were published in limited editions. *The House With the Echo* was also published in Britain and the United States.

3. On 28 January the wind reached 109 mph.

4. In California, when Frances was recovering from severe heart attacks in 1919.

5. In 1912.

6. Frances's mother's house in Philadelphia.

7. 'The Two Brothers' by Frances Gregg, in which Frances makes the 'Jack' character completely horrible, in revenge for Jack marrying her off to Louis Wilkinson.

8. Where Frances had lived, with her mother and grandmother, in poverty, for some time.

9. From his book on John Keats. *Powys on Keats*, edited by Cedric Hentschel, volume one of which was published by Cecil Woolf in 1993.

NOTE TO LETTER 148, 24 JUNE [1927] (pages 163-164)

1. The 'Romanian Gypsy Lady' was Miss Rowe, of Jack's story 'The Owl, the Duck and Miss Rowe, Miss Rowe!'

NOTES TO LETTER 149, [AUGUST 1927] (page 164)

1. His son, Littleton, was working for his uncle, Harry Lyon, as an architect, in Cambridge.

2. 'Locust Street' by Frances Gregg. Frances had also had a story, 'Immigrant', published in 'The Bermondsey Book', with a note by the editor saying that a collection of Frances Gregg's stories should be published.

3. T.S. Eliot (1888-1965), the poet whom Ezra Pound had advised to good effect.

NOTES TO LETTER 150, 30 AUGUST [1927] (pages 165-166)

1. Nicola Sacca and Bartolomea Vanzetti had been arrested in 1920, accused of a pay-roll robbery, with murder. They had been found guilty in spite of weak and conflicting evidence against them. In 1927 they were executed, despite the fact that another man had confessed to the crime. There was world-wide suspicion that they had been victimised because of their left-wing activities.

2. Professor Horace Meyer Kallen (1882-1974), worked with William James (1842-1910), the psychologist brother of Henry James. Kellen worked with George Santayana (1863-1952), the Spanish philosopher who had moved to the United States.

3. Kenneth Macpherson had published a novel, *Gaunt Island*, in which the principal character is based on Frances.

NOTES TO LETTER 152, 28 SEPTEMBER [1927] (pages 167-168)

1. Frances moved her family to a house that was the opposite of Oakenhill Hall: a neat box facing onto a Suffolk village street. Frances

herself had to live in London most of the time, because of her work as Editor of the 'Gazette', at Peter Jones.

2. Charles Scarborough was the son of a tobacconist. He had broken away from his roots and had used his considerable brain to study Mathematics and Psychology at London University. He had a room in the same house as Frances. When he met her, he fell in love with her.

3. Goethe (1749-1832), the German poet, playwright and scientist. His work was Jack's special study.

4. Emil Ludwig (1861-1948), the German author.

NOTES TO LETTER 153, 13 OCTOBER [1927] (page 168)

1. Benedetto Croce (1866-1952), the Italian philosopher and anti-Fascist, was only restored to his professorship on the fall of Mussolini in 1943.

2. Alfred North Whitehead (1861-1947), the English mathematician. He collaborated with his former pupil, Bertrand Russell, on *Principa Mathematica*.

3. Isadora Duncan, pioneer of modern dance, had been killed when her scarf caught in the engine of her car and strangled her, as she leant over it. Her children had been killed when the cab they were in plunged into a harbour. Frances believed that the deaths were not accidents, but manipulated by some occult society that had been plaguing Hilda Doolittle, 'H.D.'. Frances had had her own conflict with Aleister Crowley. See Letter 78, note 1.

Isadora Duncan had loved Jack. When he was ill she had filled his flat in New York with red roses. She had danced for him alone.

NOTES TO LETTER 154, [OCTOBER 1927] (page 169)

1. A nail had pierced Frances's foot eighteen years before, and the point of it had recently reappeared. Frances had retrieved the whole of it, after its long journey round her leg.

2. Frances's son, Oliver, then twelve years old, had written a short story to show the split mind of a boy returning to boarding school. It had been published in 'The Bermondsey Book'.

NOTES TO LETTER 155, [NOVEMBER 1927] (pages 169-170)

1. Llewelyn Powys and his wife, Alyse, had settled in England in a coastguard's cottage at the White Nose, near East Chaldon, Dorset, where his brother Theodore lived with his family; and where his sisters, Gertrude and Katie Powys, lived nearby at Chydyok. Llewelyn Powys had, however, received a handsome offer from 'The New York Herald

Tribune' to be visiting critic for their Books Supplement, and he and Alyse had sailed to New York on 1 November. They did not return to England till April of the following year.

Henry Hudson by Llewelyn Powys was published by the Bodley Head.

NOTES TO LETTER 158, 9 DECEMBER [1927] (page 171)

1. Near the Powys home, Montacute Vicarage, in Somerset.

2. A woven case with the Lion of St Mark.

3. 'Then said Deborah.....Praise ye the Lord for the avenging of Israel.....Blessed above women shall Jael.....be.....He asked for water, and she gave him milk; she brought forth butter in a lordly dish.....with the hammer she smote Sisera, she smote off his head.....' –*Judges*, Chapter V.

4. The Gazette of the John Lewis Partnership.

NOTES TO LETTER 159, 20 FEBRUARY [1928] (page 173)

1. Frances had moved her children and her mother to an old rectory at Badingham, Suffolk. It was a more conventional home; it had a bath, it had spacious grounds, a pond and a barn.

2. Frances still worked in London, but she returned to work soon after having one breast removed, weak and in considerable pain from the scar. Money was needed for the two children, so she was obliged to continue working. She came near to collapse, but stayed in her job. Charles Scarborough helped her. Frances studied Christian Science to overcome the pain.

NOTE TO LETTER 160, 9 MARCH [1928] (pages 173-174)

1. *Wolf Solent* by John Cowper Powys was published in America in May 1929, in two volumes by Simon & Schuster; and in London by Jonathan Cape. Louis Wilkinson wrote, 'Darling Jack, I can't bear Wolf Solent.' This book, though, was Jack's first novel to attract wide acclaim and large sales. He was now fifty-six.

NOTE TO LETTER 161, 22 MARCH [1928] (page 174)

1. Frederick Rolfe, Baron Corvo, whom they had met in Venice, in 1912, and whom Jack had sent packing, partly out of nerves.

NOTES TO LETTER 162, 18 MAY [1928] (pages 174-175)

1. Georg Hegel (1770-1831), the German philosopher.

2. Max Lincoln Schuster, of Simon & Schuster, the New York publishers.

NOTES TO LETTER 163, 23 JUNE [1928] (pages 175-176)

1. Warwick Powys was, nevertheless, as proud as any of the Powyses about being descended from ancient Welsh princes. According to Richard Graves (*The Brothers Powys*), he had memorised long passages from Llewelyn Powys's writings.

2. Frances had arranged for her son, Oliver, to enter Westminster School. She had managed to get some reduction in the fees, but the top hat, morning suit and the rest of the uniform required were expensive.

3. The little girl was Nellie Johns. Frightened one night of the dark street Nellie had tried to keep pace for pace with Frances in Pimlico. She was then seven years old. Frances had arranged with the mother and father, ill with tuberculosis, to take the little girl to the Rectory, Badingham, for a time.

NOTE TO LETTER 164, 10 JULY [1928] (pages 176-177)

1. *The Dybbuk* by S. Ansky, the pseudonym of Solomon Rappaport.

NOTES TO LETTER 165, 19 NOVEMBER [1928] (pages 177-178)

1. *The Mastersingers of Nuremberg* by Richard Wagner.

2. Llewelyn and Alyse had returned from the United States, and had settled again in Dorset, but had set out again travelling to the Holy Land so that Llewelyn, who was a sceptic, could find Christ at first hand: for his book, *The Cradle of God*.

3. In which Frances's work, 'The Apartment House' and 'The Unknown Face' were published. There was also work in it by her friend, 'H.D.'

4. Sir Walter Scott (1771-1832), the Scottish novelist and poet, author of the Waverley novels.

5. 'In His Will is our peace.'

NOTE TO LETTER 166, 6 DECEMBER [1928] (pages 178-179)

1. As Llewelyn had been, when returning ill from Italy in 1912.

NOTES TO LETTER 167, 14 DECEMBER [1928] (page 179)

1. Theodore Powys had recently had *The Dew Pond* published in a limited edition of five hundred copies. *Mr Tasker's Gods* was his story on which Frances had worked.

2. Louis Wilkinson was becoming more established as 'Louis Marlow'. *Two Made Their Bed* was published by Gollancz. He and his new wife, Anne Reid, were becoming so well-known in London circles that Ethel Mannin published a portrait of them in her *Confessions and Impressions*. Anne Reid had a novel, *We Are the Dead*, published.

3. The young mathematician who had coached Frances's son for his entry into Westminster School.

NOTES TO LETTER 168, 28 DECEMBER [1928] (pages 179-180)

1. *The Decline of the West* by Oswald Spengler (1890-1936).

2. This was Dorothy Thompson, described by some as 'an intellectual Valkyrie'. She had just published *The New Russia*. She had been foreign correspondent for 'The New York Herald Tribune' from about 1920 to 1928.

3. Sinclair Lewis (1885-1951), the American author and winner of the Nobel Prize. Widely known for such books as *Babbit, Arrowsmith* and *Dodsworth*.

4. From *The Possessed* by Dostoevsky.

NOTES TO LETTER 169, 7 FEBRUARY [1929] (pages 181-182)

1. Giuseppe Garibaldi (1807-82), the central figure in the story of Italian independence. The Italian patriot fought for freedom in South America, as well as in Italy.

2. Joseph Conrad (1857-1924), the Polish born writer who became a naturalised Englishman and wrote *Heart of Darkness, Youth* and *The Nigger of the Narcissus*, etc.

NOTES TO LETTER 170, 5 APRIL [1929] (page 182)

1. Maurice Browne, of the Chicago Little Theatre, had returned to England, and had taken an option on R.C. Sherriff's First World War play, *Journey's End*, after seeing a Sunday night performance. Maurice Browne was now making a fortune out of its production at the Savoy Theatre in London. He asked Frances to read submitted plays for him; thus she earnt a little extra to meet the expense of her children's education.

2. Ralph Straus — another Cambridge friend of Louis Wilkinson's — had become literary critic of 'The Sunday Times'. His book on Charles Dickens is entitled *Dickens: A Portrait in Pencil*.

Dickens was one of the authors Frances read when, as a girl in Philadelphia, she shut herself in a cupboard with a candle. He was the author most hated by Louis Wilkinson.

3. John Forster (1812-76), the journalist and biographer. He wrote about London and Swift, as well as a biography of Dickens.

4. *This Side of Idolatry* by 'Ephesian', the pseudonym of Carl Eric Bechhofer. The book was about Charles Dickens.

NOTES TO LETTER 171, [EARLY AUGUST 1929] (pages 183-184)

1. Jack had seen Frances and her whole family at the Rectory, Badingham, Suffolk. While there, he had taken up the dolls of Frances's daughter, Betty, and had seemed to make them come alive in a way that had transfixed Betty, then twelve, and Oliver, fourteen. See 'A Rival to Jack' by Oliver Marlow Wilkinson, in Belinda Humfrey's *The Powys Brothers*.

2. Gertrude Stein (1874-1927), the American writer who settled in Paris. She experimented in speech rhythms and new concepts in her writing. Author of *The Autobiography of Alice B. Toklas*, etc.

3. Jack had met Frances in London, and had travelled down by train and bus to Badingham.

4. *The Cradle of God* by Llewelyn Powys was published in the United States by Harcourt, Brace & Co. and in Britain by Jonathan Cape.

5. Alyse wrote under her maiden name of Alyse Gregory. Her book, *King Log and Lady Lea* had been accepted by Constable.

6. Bertie Powys had divorced Dorothy and married Faith, a most pleasant woman.

7. Gertrude, the eldest Powys sister.

8. Aunt Etta, Henrietta Johnson, a sister of Jack's mother, was then seventy-three.

9. Bertie Powys – A.R. Powys – had the first of his five works on architecture published: *The English House*, in Benn's Sixpenny Library series.

10. Another book of Theodore Powys's, *Fables*, was published.

11. D.H. Lawrence (1885-1930). His *Lady Chatterley's Lover* had been published in 1928, and had been banned. An 'author's edition' was published in 1929. As Hilda and Richard Aldington had been involved with Lawrence and his wife, Frieda, from 1914 onwards, they were concerned now with Lawrence's struggle for recognition, and for freedom of speech. So was Frances. She received a copy in beautiful binding of the privately printed *Lady Chatterley's Lover*, signed by Lawrence.

12. Though Peter Jones –the big store from which Frances edited 'The Gazette' – was part of the John Lewis Partnership, and run on profit-sharing lines, there seemed to be frequent sackings, and so a nervousness among the staff. Frances thought John Spedan Lewis an original, dynamic head of the experiment, but sometimes questioned his logic.

13. This was Frances's friend, Tegan, who was mordant rather than sad. She had been sexually abused as a child, and gave that as the reason for her cynicism. She was probably restrained with Jack, but she could have a racy tongue, and she had wit and considerable style.

Biographical Notes

RAYMOND BIRT – ('Tobit') (1911-   )
– the young man who was found by
Frances in a cold cottage after he had
run away from his father, an alcoholic
clergyman. In London he started off
by speaking on a soap-box. To earn his
living, he had to write letters to himself for the correspondence column of
a daily paper. He married Marie Jeaffreson who admired Frances even more
than he did.

In the Second World War, he rose to
Major in the 22nd Dragoons; and wrote
the history of the Regiment. He was
made Governor of Kreis Gifhorn. After
the war he changed into a publisher.
Then he entered the Church of England and became an Archdeacon.

Marie and Tobit had three children:
Gillian, Christopher and a 'blue baby',
Jennifer, to whom they gave a great
deal of their time, and who, by their
care, lived till she was over forty.

MAURICE BROWNE (1881-1955) –
man of the theatre – Louis Wilkinson's
Cambridge friend. Maurice Browne, as
a young man sold the family silver,
when he set out to find the American
girl, Ellen van Volkenberg, whom he
had met in Italy and was determined to
marry.

In the United States he was so hard
up that he had to 'ride the rails' like a
tramp.

Maurice Browne found Ellen van
Volkenberg in Chicago. Together they
founded the Little Theatre there. Later
in his life, Maurice Browne was pleased
and surprised to be honoured by
American universities as the originator
of the Little Theatre Movement in
America.

Maurice Browne had been educated
at Winchester, then at Cambridge –
Peterhouse – where Louis Wilkinson
says he had a desperate gambler's look
– even when he wasn't gambling (see
Swan's Milk by Louis Marlow). He was
a reckless traveller. Once he had to
wire Louis Wilkinson from the Hima-
layas to repay a loan so that he could
move on.

Maurice Browne, with Harold Monro,
founded the Samurai Press in 1906.
From that developed the Poetry Book-
shop. Browne collaborated with
Robert Nichols in writing *Wings Over
Europe*, a play that predicted nuclear
fission. The play was produced in
Britain and America, and was publish-
ed by Corice-Friede, New York.
Separated from Ellen van Volkenberg,
Maurice Browne married Ellen Janson.
While in England, Ellen Janson divorc-
ed him, and took their son back to the

235

United States.

One of Maurice Browne's productions in London, after *Journey's End*, was the Paul Robeson/Peggy Ashcroft, *Othello*. Frances saw the first night, thought it excellent, but was shocked by Maurice Browne as 'Iago', especially by his legs that were too thin for tights, and so ludicrous that the audience tittered at his every entrance. Maurice Browne, on reading the notices of the production, immediately gave up the part to another actor.

Having lost the fortune he made on *Journey's End*, Maurice Browne became Artist in Residence at the University of California, Los Angeles, in 1949.

Returning to Britain, he settled in a pleasant country house with a pleasant north-country woman. Becoming mystical, he produced religious plays in village halls.

Fifteen people of his personal circle committed suicide, including his father and younger brother (see *Too Late to Lament* by Maurice Browne; Gollancz, 1955). There was a streak of madness in his family. Maurice Browne was aware of this in himself, but mastered it and turned it to advantage.

BRYHER (Annie Winifred Ellerman, or 'Dolly' as her father called her)(1894-1983) was Hilda Doolittle's lover and guardian. Her father was Sir John Ellerman, who was a shipping magnate, but above all a financier, with tracts of land all over Europe, property in London, and investments in newspapers.

With her father's money Bryher was a powerful friend of Hilda Doolittle, 'H.D.' Out of jealousy, Bryher was an enemy of Frances. Perdita Schaffner, H.D.'s daughter, tells me that Bryher would not allow her even to mention Frances. She also forbade her meeting Frances's son, Oliver.

Bryher was a little mad, and she communicated some of her madness to H.D. Both women had psychiatric treatment. Together, though, they made a creative partnership. Bryher gave H.D. a haven in which to write freely and without anxiety – except the anxiety caused by Bryher herself. This was at a time when Frances was at her poorest, and had to wear H.D.'s cast-offs.

Bryher's marriages to the American, Robert McAlmon, then to Kenneth Macpherson, were never consummated; they were for literary convenience. Kenneth Macpherson was H.D.'s lover. The marriages were, however, very fruitful for the two young men. Bryher's money allowed them to write, to found magazines, to travel, to make films.

Bryher may have been a little mad, but she was no fool. She had as shrewd a sense of money as her father – she was adventurous and, on the whole, used her money in wise sponsorship. Her own published books are works of criticism, biography and historical romance.

Part of her psychosis was due to her hating herself as a girl, and wishing, from an early age, to be a boy.

See *Herself Defined* by Barbara Guest, and *H.D., The Life and Work of an American Poet* by Janice S. Robinson.

HILDA DOOLITTLE – 'H.D.' (1886-1961) – was the daughter of Charles Doolittle – Professor of Astronomy and Mathematics at Lehigh University – and Helen, his second wife. Hilda and Ezra Pound first met when she was fifteen and he was sixteen. They were in love, in a quaint way, till about 1910.

Hilda and Frances and Frances's mother travelled on their first trip to Europe in 1911, and were met and shepherded by Ezra Pound. Hilda thought that she was engaged to Ezra

Pound, but he said, 'Gawd forbid!' – and married Dorothy Shakespeare.

There is a biography of 'H.D.' being researched by Sally Bingham in the United States. Existing biographies include *Herself Defined* by Barbara Guest, and *Her: the Life and Work of an American Poet* by Janice Robinson. Hilda's daughter, Perdita Schaffner, lives on Long Island, New York, and edits her mother's works. These are stored with books by her mother and her mother's friends in a house built for the purpose. Perdita says that she had a curious childhood, looked after, one moment, with love and imagination by her mother and her mother's patroness, protector and lover, Lord Ellerman's daughter, Bryher, then neglected the next.

Hilda's intensity made her subject to illusions at one point. She had analysis with Sigmund Freud. (See *Tribute to Freud* by H.D.; O.U.P.).

H.D.'s publications include *Sea Garden*, *Hymen*, *Heliodora*, *Choruses from Iphigenia*, *The Walls do not Fall*, *Tribute to Angels*, and translations of the *Ion* by Euripides.

H.D. Collected Poems 1912-1944, edited by Louis L. Martz, was published by Carcanet Press in 1984.

There is also H.D.'s autobiographical writing, *End to Torment* etc, in which Ezra Pound, Richard Aldington and Frances appear under different names.

The television documentary, *Hilda's Book*, directed by Frank Wintle for Television South-West – about the book made and bound by Ezra Pound himself, with his first poems, and given to H.D. who gave it to Frances – is about the lives of the three: Frances, Hilda and Ezra.

'H.D.' and Richard Aldington did not get divorced till 1937. Then they kept in touch for professional and friendly reasons. Through Hilda, Richard Aldington received a pension from Bryher.

Towards the end of her life, Hilda entered the Nervenklinic Sanatorium, which she left only to receive the Gold Medal of the American Academy of Arts and Letters. She returned from the United States to find that her haven, the sanatorium had been sold. Bryher established her in a hotel in Zurich, where 'H.D.' died on 27 September 1961, just after receiving a published copy of her own *Helen in Egypt* from Bryher.

THEODORE DREISER (1871-1945) – John Cowper Powys's great friend in the United States. John Cowper Powys introduced Dreiser to Louis Wilkinson. Louis Wilkinson introduced Dreiser to Aleister Crowley. Aleister Crowley introduced Dreiser to drugs. 'The Great Beast' then told him that there was a good undertaker at the corner. (See *Seven Friends* by Louis Marlow – latest republication by the Mandrake Press).

Dreiser started in real estate; then, in 1892, he wrote for the papers; and in 1894 he became Editor of a New York music magazine. His brother had changed his name and become the popular song-writer, Paul Dresser.

Theodore Dreiser's first book, *Sister Carrie*, was banned for obscenity. It is perhaps his greatest novel. Dreiser then fought against censorship. Finally he was awarded the Merit Medal by the American Academy of Arts and Letters. His many books include *An American Tragedy*.

He was often at Maurice Browne's Little Theatre in Chicago, especially when Jack was lecturing there.

Dreiser was big, slow moving, with a shock of hair turned white, and strangely blazing eyes. He had a powerful forehead, and a lumpy lower part of his face. Jack indicates that it was a face of humility and pride. Louis Wilkinson writes (as Louis Marlow) in

Swan's Milk, ' . . . His voice has a virile whine, very unusual.'

Theodore Dreiser was one of thirteen children, the whole family living in poverty. For the rest of his life Dreiser was resolute in his left-wing beliefs.

The turning-point in Theodore Dreiser's career was his novel *Jennie Gerhart*, in 1911, which was praised by the critics.

ISADORA DUNCAN (1878-1927) – was the innovator of free movement in dance. She so admired *Visions and Revisions* by John Cowper Powys that she wired him from California: 'Feeling terribly lonely and forlorn I seek your spirit for courage send me sometimes a word I send you infinite love'. Another started, 'Your soul danced with mine today . . . . .' and begged him to come to her. Louis Wilkinson thought her an irritatingly affected woman; but Jack called her one of his ' . . . . . most thrilling sensations', and Frances and Hilda Doolittle liked her. Jack did not go West to her. She came to him.

SARA BARD FIELD (1882- ?) – the American reformer and writer, whom Frances and Jack knew in California. At eighteen, she had married a minister much older than herself and had gone with him to the Eurasian Church in Rangoon, Burma, in 1900. In 1901 she had born a son. The poverty and disease of Rangoon turned Sara and her husband into socialists; on their return to America he was asked to resign from the Cleveland Church. Clarence Darrow, the great lawyer, introduced Sara to Charles Erskine Wood for whom she left her husband, and whom she eventually married. Sara organised the College of Equal Suffrage League, and spoke all over the country under the leadership of Alice Paul. Erskine was much older than Sara, his second wife. In 1942, when he was ninety, she

had to look after him in every way. By then, though, they had settled in the foothills of the Santa Cruz Mountains, under their own vines and fig trees, trying to create a sane pattern of living. This was after a lifetime of trying to fight injustice.

Sara Bard Field's works include *The Pale Woman* and *Barabas*. After his death, she edited Erskine Wood's poetry.

AMELIA GENAI – 'Lala' (1890-1974?) – the Italian nurse, an attractive girl, had admirers wherever she travelled with Frances.

She was fifteen when Frances and Louis took her from her large family, to sail from Italy to the United States, during the second year of the First World War. Amelia – or 'Lala' as the children called her – was so unused to the ways of a world at war, outside of Siena, that she left a porthole uncovered in a lighted cabin, and was arrested by the Captain, who found her so young and attractive he let her go. Louis Wilkinson found her attractive, too. Many years later he called on her family in Siena, and found that Amelia had married, and she and her husband and baby were happily settled in the United States.

FRANCES GREGG (Frances Wilkinson) (1885-1941). Much of Frances's story is told in the letters. A list of some of her publications include:
Poetry 'Le Mendiante' (Dec. 1911)
    'Amoentis' (Dec. 1911)
    'Trees by the Water' (Dec. 1911)
    'A Reed' (Dec. 1911)
    'Dreams' (Oct. 1912)
    'Two Motifs' (Nov. 1913)
    in 'The Forum', the literary and critical magazine, published by Mitchell Kennerley.
Short stories and articles 'My Case'
    'Condemned to Die'

'A Letter' in 'The New Freewoman',
1913
'Whose Dog?' in 'The Forum & The
New American'
'Caravan'
'The Two Brothers' in 'The Forum',
1913
'White Kaffir'
'August Strindberg' in 'The Forum',
1916; written with John Cowper
Powys
'The Unknown Face'
'The Apartment House' in 'The
Second American Caravan' (Mac-
aulay, 1924)

JULIA VANNESS GREGG (1858-1941)
– Frances's mother. Her story is largely
told through the letters. She was in her
eighty-third year when she was killed
during the blitz on Plymouth in 1941.

Julia was a good teacher, with originality and imagination. She lived in
England for the last twenty years of
her life, but she did not take any
country but America seriously – and
remained patriotic to the last.

Frances had her mother living with
her, or near her, all her life, except for
a few months in 1912 and again in
1937.

Julia seemed indestructible; climbing
cliffs at seventy-four, roped to Frances
and Frances's children. She had will-
power, too, and could be as fearless
as Frances.

Julia watched over her daughter,
Frances, reproved and admired her.
Frances and Julia quarrelled fiercely,
even violently, but there was
understanding between them as well as
antagonism. It was Julia who sometimes laughed first when they were in
terrible trouble, till Frances joined in.
They were used to appalling predica-
ments, and battled through them – till
1941.

ALYSE GREGORY (1884-1967) –
Llewelyn Powys's wife, had had a
varied career – as a singer, much praised; as suffragette; reporter; social
worker for the Carnegie Foundation;
advertising copywriter; tea-shop owner;
and Managing Editor of the periodical
'The Dial'. She was beautiful, and had
had several love affairs, all of which
seem – as Richard Graves describes in
The Brothers Powys – to have ended in
the death or desertion of the lover.
Llewelyn Powys describes Alyse, at
their first meeting as '. . . . . a delicately ironic hostess . . . . . her round white
arm . . . . . as delectable as dairy junket
. . . . .' This was in 1921. They were
married in 1924, in New York. Alyse
had to nurse Llewelyn through recurring bouts of tuberculosis. Sometimes
she had the help of his sisters Gertrude
and Katie. In later life, Llewelyn fell
in love with Gamel Wolsey, the poet.
Alyse, who felt herself to be, above all,
an emancipated woman with a new
morality, did not allow herself to stand
in Llewelyn's way. She determined not
to be jealous. She suffered abominably
for that, and wrote her pain into her
book *The Cry of a Gull*.

When Gamel Wolsey found that she
was pregnant by Llewelyn, she had an
abortion; and, shortly afterwards, married Gerald Brenan, the writer.

Alyse Gregory's work includes *King
Log and Lady Lea*; *She Shall Have
Music*; *Hester Craddock*; *Wheels on
Gravel*; *The Day is Gone*; etc.

During her work for 'The Dial', she
discovered and encouraged new
writers; but she turned down Ernest
Hemingway and never regretted it.

Alyse had had a wide education, she
had excellent literary judgement – as
Schofield Thayer, past owner of 'The
Dial', and one of her lovers, discovered
– but she was modest about her work.
She says of her time in advertising,

'. . . . . I knew nothing about it . . . . . but they liked me, and I kept getting promoted. I still don't know what I was about, but I reached a position in which I could have done real harm. I then resigned.'

After Llewelyn Powys's death, one of his admirers, Rosamund Rose, who was also an admirer of Alyse Gregory, gave her a house for her life-time. From there Alyse wrote many letters. These are being collected by The Beinecke Library of Yale University.

She became impatient with life – at least with the life left to the old. Calmly and efficiently she committed suicide, in the way – a painless poison – that she thought should be allowed to any old person who wished to step out of life.

JAMES HENDERSON (1885-1957) – the philosophical American who wanted to marry Frances before John Cowper Powys and Louis Wilkinson met her. This son of a rich American undertaker continued to write to Frances, and to send American candy and maple syrup, and ingredients he knew Frances and her mother could not get in Britain, and parcels of tools, as well. It was his way of declaring his undying love but, at the same time, he kept Frances informed of his American loves, describing the varying degrees of his amorous, paternalistic, fraternal and other feelings. He once delighted Frances and Julia by describing how he had put his arm round a girl's waist – and spelling it 'waste'.

In the First World War he joined the U.S. Army, but nearly went mad when spearing straw figures with a bayonet.

He recovered, and continued to train himself in self-enlightenment and good-will. He had a particular American benevolence: but a determination to be nobody's fool, a determination in which he did not always succeed.

MARIE JEAFFRESON (1906-1990) – woman of the theatre who was very much influenced by Frances. Marie based all her life and work on her Christian belief. She was of the same blood as Charlotte Corday, who murdered Marat in his bath in 1793. Marie had the same mystic will, but not to a lethal extent.

As a producer, Marie worked with Michel St Denis; and was later offered a season at the Arts Theatre in London, by Alec Clunes, whom she had 'discovered' when he was a bank clerk. Though she was encouraged by Tyrone Guthrie, Marie gave up her career when she married Raymond Birt, 'Tobit'. She continued to produce plays in churches and abbeys.

In later years she was tormented by constant pain that nothing alleviated; and she grew weaker and weaker. Her great gifts for the professional theatre now seemed to have been thrown away . . . . . 'The one thing I could do . . . . . I am not allowed to do . . . .'

Near to death, and weak, she continued to look after their 'blue child' who had reached the age of forty; but who died shortly after her mother had died.

A Bishop, two Archdeacons and a Canon presided at Marie's Requiem Mass in 1990: which was fitting enough, as she was as much of a saint as any.

KENNETH MACPHERSON (1907-1971) – the young man in the London 'apartment house', who was in love with Frances in 1924, but who left her for Frances's greatest friend, 'H.D.'; but married Bryher. Kenneth was handsome, intelligent, imaginative and rather slippery. His father had been an artist, and Kenneth himself drew and painted with flair. He looked like a lean, pale knight from one of his own drawings. The film-as-an-art magazine

'Close Up', that he founded and edited with Bryher's money, broke new ground. Certainly it tended to praise Macpherson's own work, but the articles were, on the whole, interesting, even distinguished. He remained Editor of 'Close Up' till 1933.

Bryher, with 'H.D.', gave Kenneth Macpherson scope for his talents, as they had given the American poet, Robert McAlmon scope for his.

Macpherson's films were experimental, but not – Frances thought – to much effect, even though Paul Robeson and 'H.D.' acted in one of them.

Macpherson's description of Frances, that Jack disliked as over-elaborate, starts, 'He thought of a roebuck or a snake. . . . . Then he saw terror getting mastery in her . . . . . She was no beauty. or was she more beautiful than anything he had ever seen? He saw large distraught eyes (they might have been sightless), expressions changing. She bit her lip, and he noticed her mouth and wondered why he thought of a dead satyr. He thought, "She's exquisite. . . . . the Angel of Donnatello's Annunciation, with subliminal passions".' (*Gaunt Island* by Kenneth Macpherson; Pool, Riant Chateau, Territet, Switzerland, 1927 – one of the presses founded by Bryher, Annie Winifred Ellerman. He published two other novels, *Pool Reflections* and *Rome 12 Noon*.)

Hilda Doolittle, 'H.D.', wrote *Red Roses for Bronze* to celebrate Kenneth Macpherson's beauty. There is a description of Kenneth in 'The Apartment House' by Frances Gregg ('Second American Caravan').

After he left Bryher and H.D., Kenneth Macpherson settled for a time in Tuscany, then in a New York flat, where he spent the years of the Second World War: and where 'H.D.' and Bryher visited him, when 'H.D.' was

recalled to the United States to receive her literary honours. Kenneth Macpherson finally settled in Italy, on Capri. There he became reconciled to being homosexual. He was host to Norman Douglas, who made him his literary executor.

EDGAR LEE MASTERS (1869-1950) – the writer, and friend of Jack in the United States. He was sometimes in the audience when Jack lectured in Maurice Browne's Chicago Little Theatre. Masters never repeated the success of his *Spoon River Anthology*, which satirizes the people of the American Middle West. He continued, however, to publish poetry, novels, biographies. Margaret Anderson, in *My Thirty Years War*, writes, 'Edgar Lee Masters was the funny man of the literati. His eyes twinkled (it's the only verb) and he indulged with very obvious pleasure in the lowest slap-tickle humour. He looked like Thackeray.'

It was Edgar Lee Masters who came into a meeting of Theodore Dreiser and others of his friends with the news, 'Gentlemen, the whore-house is on fire!'

EDNA ST VINCENT MILLAY (1892-1950) – the poet, and one of the greatest loves of Llewelyn Powys's life.

She was a popular poet in her time, and is still read today.

When she was young she lived in Greenwich Village, New York, and was very poor. Her verse was regarded as the voice of flaming youth.

She joined the Provincetown Players in their early days; and she published three plays in verse; she also wrote the libretto of one of the few American Grand Operas, *The King's Henchman*. In 1923 she won the Pullitzer Prize with *The Harp Weaver*. In the same year she married Jan Boissevain, whom

Jack describes as a great pirate of a Dutchman.

Like Jack, Edna St Vincent Millay worked for the Sacco and Vanzetti Committee.

She continued to live in the isolated farmhouse near Austerlitz, New York, after the death of her husband. She herself was found dead there, of a heart attack, at the age of fifty-eight.

She published, among other works, *Figs from a Thistle* (1920), *Conversations at Midnight* (1937), *The Murder of Lidice* (1942).

BELLE O'NEILL (1876-1952) – the wife of Dr Bernie O'Neill, the great friend and instructor of the Powyses – was a handsome woman. As she grew older and older she took younger and younger lovers.

Louis Wilkinson, as 'Louis Marlow', describes Belle's '. . . . . raciness and verve, the natural salt of her expressions.' He adds that she had '. . . . . a genius for retorts; was a past-mistress of "back-chat" . . . . . She could have put an art of her own on the boards . . . . . another Marie Lloyd, but always herself. She'd have been intimate with all her audience at once . . . . . And how she's have answered them back!

'During the [First World] war many of her friends thought her pacificism unpatriotic. "And where would we be now . . . . . if everyone thought like you?" one of them asked. "And where are we?" was the reply, "Where *are* we?"'

Belle and Bernard O'Neill brought up Deirdre, the daughter of Louis Wilkinson and Nan, his second wife. Belle loved babies, and she liked bringing up Deirdre, with her own daughter, Jill, and her son. Whether the house was as suitable for the girls as they grew up is doubtful. The O'Neill house was a haven of misfits. Belle could be heavy-handed, too. She was harder on her own daughter than on Deirdre. She must have stored malice against her husband, too; for, as Bernard O'Neill lay dying, Louis Wilkinson found Belle tweaking his face. With a pretence at roguishness she hurt the hapless man, while crying, kittenishly, '. . . . . There! . . . . . You can't move, dear love, can you? . . . . . And *there*! . . . . . Sweet! . . . . . How do you like that? . . . . .'

DR PRICE BERNARD O'NEILL, M.R.C.S., L.R.P. (1865-1947) – born in 1865 – educated the Powys children in literature and much else, always informally. Jack was twenty-eight when Bernie, then thirty-one, introduced him to the works of Rabelais and Montaigne and many other writers. He also made Theodore Powys read more than the Bible and Shakespeare. All the Powys children came under his influence.

Jack in his *Autobiography* describes Bernie O'Neill as, '. . . . . This man of unique genius. . . . . He was an adept in the extremist pages of all the Cagliostros of modern literature. He knew every drawing of Beardsley, every quip of Whistler, every paradox of Wilde . . . . .'

Malcolm Elwin in *The Life of Llewelyn Powys* writes that Bernie charmed the fancies of the Powys brothers with his imagination, knowledge and taste in refinements which had played no part in the Powys country upbringing. He taught them about wine, music, the theatre, the argot of the market-place, '. . . . . casually dropping arresting scraps of curious learning and worldly wisdom.'

PHYLLIS PLAYTER (1893-1982) – who lived for many years with Jack, in New York, in Hillsdale and in Dorchester, and in Corwen, then in Blaenau Ffestiniog – had a case of gems from her father, a miner of precious stones. Sometimes, when a relation of the Powyses, or of Louis Wilkinson called on them, Phyllis would give them a gem from the golds, greens and reds of her case.

Phyllis Playter was gentle, intelligent and well-read. As she grew older she looked more and more like a Dutch doll: a Dutch doll dressed in black that accentuated the upright rigidity of her figure. She had an adventurous mind. When Jack died, she decided to go round the world in a bus that started at Trafalgar Square, London; and then to live in the City of London; and to live later in the Royal Crescent, Bath.

Friends dissuaded her from the world-circling bus; but Phyllis achieved her other plans. She settled back in Blaenau Ffestiniog after that, in the little one-up-one-down cottage where she had lived with Jack.

Towards her last days, visitors found that she was living in darkness, for she could not get the blinds up. She was also living without tea, because she could no longer reach it. The blinds were fixed, and the tea put on a lower shelf. Phyllis lived on contentedly; sometimes dozing through a night without going to bed; listening to the wireless, sipping a little whisky . . . . into the morning light.

The *Diaries* of John Cowper Powys (Greymitre Press, 1987 & 1990) tell of his life with her, his indebtedness to her literary judgement, and of his love for her.

THE POWYSES
(in order of age)

THE REV. CHARLES FRANCIS POWYS (1843-1923)

'. . . . . There seemed something preposterous and unallowable about this great strong thick wall of Powys solidarity; as though it stood there blasphemous against the solidarity of the human race.

. . . . . It was the father who bound the family together.

'. . . . He loved walking. His pleasure in his walks was marred only when he passed a pair of evident lovers. Then he would sigh deeply . . . . .

'. . . . . Any language but the simplest was to him an object of suspicion and contempt.' — *Welsh Ambassadors*, Louis Marlow.

The Reverend Charles Powys was an impressive figure. The legend was that his ancestors had been Welsh princes. We know, anyhow, that some of these ancestors were prosperous gentlemen on the Welsh borders. Some of Charles's near relatives had titles, and his own father had married a rich widow.

MARY COWPER POWYS (1849-1914)

'Mrs Powys hated success,' writes Louis Wilkinson in *Welsh Ambassadors*. '. . . . . She hated, with secret intensity, well-constituted people, or even people whose health was too good.' She had a great influence on all her children, and a lasting one, particularly on Jack.

Louis Wilkinson traces the genius of the Powys children to the repressed ferocity of the father and the romantic, morbid melancholy of the mother — who was of the same blood as John Donne and William Cowper.

Mary Cowper Powys had known Louis Wilkinson's mother, Charlotte Elizabeth, in their younger days. That led to the connection between the Wilkinsons and the Powyses.

JOHN COWPER POWYS (1872-1963)

His life and his work is described up to 1941 in the Letters.

After Frances's death, Jack placed her Crooked Cross of tortoise-shell into the River Dee. He lived another twenty-two years.

Louis Wilkinson, as a member of the

Royal Society of Literature, and on their Committee, persuaded the Society to give a grant to John Cowper Powys. This, and the offer by Mac-Donald & Co. to publish everything he wrote, eased Jack's poverty, in his old age.

He continued to write; and continued to climb the hill by 1 Waterloo, Blaenau Ffestiniog. The cottage was decorated by plaques of his fame and is so still. When he was ninety he recognised visitors, but insisted on singing old school songs to them – over and over again . . . . . 'Follow up, follow up, follow up! . . . .' He became lucid when he wanted to be. When Louis Wilkinson visited him, there was still the same love and hate between them. Jack spoke of the Crooked Cross at that meeting.

So much is written of him – and of the Powys family – every year adds to the number of books about them – that it is impossible to mention any but three: *John Cowper Powys: Novelist* (1973) by Glen Cavaliero; *The Saturnian Quest* (1969) by G. Wilson Knight; *John Cowper Powys and the Magical Quest* (1980) by Morine Krissdottir.

It was particularly fortunate that Jeffrey Kwintner, on picking at random a book by John Cowper Powys off a library shelf, decided to publish all his other books, and to put them on the shelves of his Village Bookshop, in Regent Street, London. This put the works of John Cowper and Theodore and Llewelyn into present circulation: even including the more obscure titles. Works by the Powyses are now regularly reprinted by other publishers. *After My Fashion* by John Cowper Powys was, at last, published, by Picador, Pan Books, in 1980. In one of his letters to Frances, Jack gives up that book as hopeless.

There are articles about the Powyses in 'The Powys Review', edited by Belinda Humfrey, and in the Powys Society's 'News Letter'; and in the publications of the Powys Society of North America. Colegate University in the United States also publishes a Powys magazine.

LITTLETON   CHARLES   POWYS (1874-1953)

Among brothers and sisters who were bonded together in so great a loyalty that Louis Wilkinson sometimes thought of them as one monstrous 'Powys', Littleton was the first to battle against real or fancied insult to the family. Certainly he would not have hesitated to carry out the threat he wrote to the school bully in protecting Jack at Sherborne: 'Leave Powys Major alone. From one who *can* lick you.'

Louis Wilkinson in *Welsh Ambassadors* writes, '. . . . . I won't say he was dyed in the convention of the sound and decent Public School gentleman, because no Powys was ever dyed in anything but his own Powyshood, and Littleton was and is a Powys before anything else. But he accepted those conventions, he chose to live with them.

'. . . . . Now, after retiring from his Sherborne Headmastership, he assumes, actively and conscientiously, civic responsibilities . . . . .'

Littleton's wife, Mabel, died in 1942. Littleton then married Elizabeth Myers, the novelist. She died at thirty-four.

Littleton did not approve of Louis Wilkinson's influence on the Powys brothers and sisters, but Llewelyn Powys wrote to Louis, '. . . . . After all, he is the most guileless of us all and he cannot help being one who looks at the shining outside of the great kitchen saucepan of life. . . . . It is natural for him to distrust the intellectual fury that compels a philosopher to spy down the black hollow handle of such a pot to where frogs are being boiled in funeral bake-meats — where ugly slippery truths like a mess of boiling newts skip and wriggle in their death under the stew of eternity.'

Littleton published two autobiographical books. *The Joy of It* was published in 1937 by Chapman & Hall, and *Still the Joy of It* was published in 1956 by MacDonald.

THEODORE FRANCIS POWYS (1875-1953)

Theodore Powys wrote to Louis Wilkinson in 1909, 'The babes reward all one's labour, every night time one feels the reward, the feeling of the Father that increaseth, that taketh away from the self, and give to the child. Speak I too piously? Where is beauty that liveth and fadeth not? Speak, o wise one.'

That letter, about his sons, Dicky and Francis, was in language natural to Theodore Powys.

Louis Wilkinson in *Swan's Milk* writes, 'Though in Theodore's tones there could be implications of incredible inhumanity, to babies and children he could be tender with what sometimes seemed almost a mother's love.'

Theodore himself said that one day he might reach a state where he was fit to be a mother. In his many works, love is compounded with hate; the earth is a charnel house of redemption. All his work is an expression of bitter, transforming love, couched in rural fantasy. It no sooner warms and amuses than it chills.

Theodore's eldest son, Dicky, visited Willie Powys in Africa. Dicky's body was found partly eaten by lions, in the African bush. Frances refused to believe that Dicky had been killed by lions. She was right. Dicky had been killed by native warriors who had then virtually torn him apart, ritually.

Theodore's youngest son, Francis,

survived to found a bookshop and to be Literary Executor of the Powyses.

Theodore in retirement took his family — including their adopted daughter, Susan — to live in a house in the churchyard at Mappowder in Dorset. He had decided to write nothing more. He attended Communion, partly to keep the vicar company.

When Theodore was told he had cancer, he decided not to have an operation.

GERTRUDE POWYS (1877-1952)

Louis Wilkinson in *Welsh Ambassadors* writes, 'I feel conscious of a kind of impertinence in writing of her at all. The dignity and power, *and* the gentleness, the deep kindness of her presence, all it would seem, combine to put me to silence. As a person and as an artist her power is real. . . . .'

Gertrude was the sister who looked after her father, and the others of the family. On her father's death, she took the chance to study art in London at the Slade, and in Paris. Her paintings are excellent: with sensitivity, strength and clarity. Her woodcuts illustrate two of Llewelyn Powys's books, *Earth Memories* and *Rats in the Sacristy*.

ALBERT REGINALD POWYS (1881-1936)

'Bertie' — and called 'Brother Positive' because of his strong emphasis in argument. In *Welsh Ambassadors*, Louis Wilkinson writes, '. . . . . It has always been Bertie's role to put a brake on family pride, on Powys assertion. I have known him disagree with his brothers as emphatically as Littleton does, though on very different counts. I have sometimes thought him the most emancipated of his family.'

It was typical of Bertie to add, in a letter to Louis Wilkinson's second wife, Ann Reid, after his criticism of her book *Love Lies Bleeding*, '. . . . . It comes not of thinking my opinion of much importance but of thinking that I should say what I think as nearly truly as I can.'

Bertie had first been articled to a Yeovil architect. Then he had worked for Mr Weir, an architect in London. At one time, he also worked with Sir Edward Lutyens.

Bertie married a distant cousin, Dorothy, in 1904. Their daughter, Isobel, took over her father's role, as protector of the Powys name.

On divorcing Dorothy in 1929, Bertie married Faith Oliver. They had twins, Oliver and Eleanor. Oliver trained as an architect. Eleanor is a teacher, married to an inventor.

Bertie was the only one of the brothers who moved in London artistic circles and, when Jack, Theodore and Llewelyn began to be much discussed in 1935, it was Bertie who sent news of their growing reputation.

Bertie's memorial is still in the church he restored with Thomas Hardy's grant, at Winterbourne Tomson in Dorset.

EMILY MARIAN POWYS (1882-1972) – 'May'. It was Marian who looked after Jack in the United States, and who founded the famous lace shop in New York. She was beautiful and adventurous. Lucy Penny writes, 'After being taught by a governess at home, May was for a time at Norwich High School, living with two aunts (sisters of my mother) in the Cathedral Close. She came home, and with some help from Gertrude and my mother, gave lessons to Katie and me. Then she went to Newquay for a time and became interested in lace-making.'

May also studied lace-making in Belgium, Switzerland and Germany. May's son, Peter Powys Grey, writes that, in 1916, her lace shop ·was

financed by Theodore Dreiser, and by August Hechser who had employed her. Both Dreiser and Hechser were soon repaid out of May's profits.

Peter Powys-Grey continues: '. . . . . Moving to ever more elegant quarters uptown, the shop became a kind of "*bourse de dentelles*" where valuations were established, and fashions set. It prospered (intermittently) until she retired in 1945 . . . . .' It was then that she wrote *Lace and Lacemaking* that was published in 1953, after she had become lace consultant to the Metropolitan Museum. 'She conducted a famed series of seminars on lace, and lectured widely on aspects of what she called "the finest art". Often imperious, even imperial – and reckless, she was still a devoted parent, and grandparent; a homemaker; passionate gardener and orchidist; adroit water colorist; eerily prescient medium and fortune-teller; pianist; devious tennis player; incessant reader; odd but sometimes excellent chef; dangerously suicidal mycologist; insatiable traveller; and daily fast walker through the woods of Rockland County, and the byways of Manhattan.'

In her retirement in the Palisades, she let her garden become overgrown, so that her many visitors had to tread a jungle path to reach her. sitting in the sun, surrounded by giant plants.

Peter Powys-Grey ends, 'In great old age she became a near-cult figure among the "flower children", holding forth in her ramshackle Eighteenth Century house at Sneedon's Landing, with heterodox social opinions, with devastating critiques of any form of cynicism or aloofness for life . . . . . She died with a scrap of Gros Points de Venise in her hand. . . . .'

Her coffin was followed by a crowd of young people, hippies and members of gangs, as well as her family, friends and dignitaries.

LLEWELYN POWYS (1884-1939) –
'Lulu'. As a boy, and as a young man,
Llewelyn Powys was backward. On
entering and leaving Cambridge, he had
to take almost every exam twice. In
later life, he had the naivety, the un-
worldliness shared by most of the
Powyses. Louis Wilkinson in *Swan's
Milk* has told how Llewelyn had never
heard of Emile Zola. His brother, Jack,
teased him. 'What!' he exclaimed. 'You
don't know about *her*! – Napoleon's
last mistress! . . . . .' Llewelyn had
never heard of Balmoral, either. 'God!
I wish *I* hadn't!' was Bernard O'Neill's
comment.

Louis Wilkinson, in the same book,
describes Llewelyn: 'His smile alone,
with its broad sudden light, is enough
to win the stoniest heart. So is the air
of woodland simplicity and artlessness
which he can still wear, although he is
now as full of craft as the wariest. . . . .
In his youth. . . . . he had light eyes,
eager and easily troubled, a rich
unguarded mouth, a child's soft mouth
greedy of pleasure and sometimes
sulky. . . . . a stiff woolly growth of
light gold curls. . . . . crisp as a thicket
of thorns; like a vegetable growth. . . . .
resilient to the touch as dry moss is in
summer, or a cypress hedge. . . . .'

Llewelyn Powys's best writing is
autobiographical and biographical. The
published extracts of his diary, and his
other writings as a young man facing
death, are remarkable. It is remarkable,
too, that from early manhood he faced
the threat of death for all his comparatively short life, sometimes having to
lie still for days, and yet always writing
when he possibly could. He was an
essayist of the highest quality.

He was in love with Frances for a
time, and blamed Jack bitterly for
marrying her to Louis Wilkinson.
Frances was in love with Llewelyn, but
she said to Jack, 'Tell him [Llewelyn]
that I love my husband. Isn't that

enough?'

Llewelyn's marriage to Alyse
Gregory – as she continued to call herself, publishing several books under
that name – was excellent, though he
caused her great pain by his love affair
with Gamel Wolsey, the poet. Llewelyn
writes about this in *Love and Death*.
Alyse writes about it in *Cry of a Gull*.

Louis Wilkinson was always
Llewelyn's greatest friend since their
Cambridge days.

CATHERINE EDITH PHILIPPA
POWYS (1886-1963) – 'Katie'.
In spite of Katie saying that her poems
stammered, they have interesting
quality and were published by
Constable who also published her novel
The Blackthorn Winter.

It was with Llewelyn Powys that
Katie first read Walt Whitman – the
poet blamed for Katie's madness in
1912. The real reason for her breakdown was her thwarted love for
Stephen Reynolds. . . . . 'the great
romance of her life,' writes Lucy
Penny; and adds that after farming a
little from the vicarage, Katie rented a
small farm and house in the village of
Montacute. This was after the Powys
father had retired. Lucy Penny, writes,
'Katie was very much a companion
through our childhood: an eager
character feeling pleasure and disappointment acutely: always keen on
animals: driving and riding horses:
writing, too, diaries and stories, from
girlhood. Walking and reading, garden-
ing and farming also interested her
through her whole life.'

In old age, Katie lived alone in Buck-
land Newton, Dorset, bent into a bow
by arthritis. Her legs looked very long
in a pair of flannel trousers, ugly, un-
compromisingly masculine. Her mind,
though, was still in a world of magic
into which she drew her visitors.

'How discernible, from over wide

stretches of the Dorset Downs, her figure on horseback,' writes Louis Wilkinson of the old days. 'Whether she wears the oldest and most uncared for of riding habits, jacket and workman's breeches, or gown. . . . . Katie . . . . . always gives the impression of "a great lady". . . . . all the more for lack of "air" usually associated with one. All lies within, "wrought from within"; unknown to her.'

In old age Katie continued to be visited by many friends, and by members of her own family, especially by Lucy Powys, who bicycled over from nearby Mappowder; and who was with her when she died.

Jack's letters to Katie, edited by Anthony Head, will be published under the title *Powys to Sea-Eagle: the Letters of John Cowper Powys to Philippa Powys*, in Cecil Woolf's uniform edition in 1993.

WILLIAM EARNEST POWYS (1881-1978) – 'Willie'.
Willie, the youngest son, hunted the woods, setting snares, collecting eggs, tracking foxes, and running wild. His father taught him, as he taught all his children, about plants and animals. Llewelyn carried him on his back. Littleton taught him to fly-fish. Lucy Penny writes, 'In the holidays he was completely happy alone following his own pursuits in the garden or in the fields. Not at all talkative, but interested in all animals and birds – absorbed in his own thoughts and occupations.'

As Llewelyn had been Bertie's fag at Sherborne School, so Willie became Llewelyn's. Llewelyn wrote to Bertie, 'I am very lenient to him about washing up; much more than you were, you scoundrel.' Yet Llewelyn writes in his diary, '. . . . . made Will cry. What a devil I am – Good God forgive me. I consider this (brutality) worse than all impurity and dishonesty.'

When Llewelyn was with Willie in Gilgil, Kenya, he was impressed by the way Will put down attacks by their African workers, and by the way he shot snakes and prowling animals close to the home; impressed, too, by the confident way in which Will managed the large farm. Later, in the East African Mounted Rifles, Will captured six Germans single-handed.

Lucy Penny writes, 'The Government of England allotted land after the war to soldiers who wished for it. Willie has held his tract of land ever since, and has added to it other tracts of land in different parts of Kenya.'

Willie was also given a share in the farm he managed at Gilgil.

Willie and his wife Elizabeth had three children, Rose, Charles and Gifford.

Louis Wilkinson in *Welsh Ambassadors* writes, 'He is of all of them the most attractive to women, with his lithe swift body, his virile grace, and that strange faun-like feral aspect of his that, suddenly seen, can startle the beholder with the thrill of its surprise..... Willie . . . . . had . . . . . an intense and humorous relish . . . . .'

Everywhere he went, Willie painted in water-colours, as a kind of diary. He was proud of his work as a sheep farmer. Once he showed off a glass-fronted case in which there were many tufts of wool: crude wool, blended wool, fine wool, soft wool, tough wool; evolved out of countless experiments in cross-breeding. 'That's worth a novel or two!' said Willie. . . . .

LUCY AMELIA POWYS: LUCY PENNY (1890-1986)
Lucy Penny was the youngest Powys. Louis Wilkinson might have married her. As a young man visiting Montacute Vicarage, he sat for a long time one evening with Lucy in the garden. Louis writes, 'It was the most purely

romantic experience I had known.'

Lucy was a sweet, earnest little girl, pretty enough to be the heroine of an old-fashioned story. She kept her looks as she grew up. Even in old age she was neatly pretty.

In April 1911, Lucy married R.C. Penny, a miller, working on the banks of the river Test. They had one daughter, Mary.

After the death of her husband, Lucy lived for a short time at her home in Shootash, near Romsey, Hampshire. After her daughter's marriage to Gerard Casey – a farmer in Kenya who had long corresponded with Jack – Lucy went to live in Mappowder, Dorset. Silver and delicate china were brought out for the many visits to her cottage of her brothers and sisters, and of their children, and their children's children. Tea was laid for many other visitors, because she became the last surviving member of her generation of the Powys family, the repository of their work, the source of information. Mary and Gerard Casey came to live next door to her. Gerard wrote and published his books there. Mary wrote and published her poetry.

After Mary's death, Gerard Casey looked after Lucy. Her memory was as sharp as ever. She still made an occasion of every visit. Once she presided over the tea-table out-of-doors, impervious to the fact that it had started to rain, and that the rain was watering the tea, melting the cake, drenching the cloth and their clothes.

Lucy was hardy. In the bitterest winter, in extreme old age, she sat with many shawls on by a small oil-heater; her face shining like cherry wood.

Alyse Gregory in 'The London Magazine' has described her as, '. . . . . gentle, devious, complicated. . . . .'

At Lucy's funeral the church at Mappowder was full, not only of the Powys family, but of farmers, artists, politicians, musicians, publishers and the 'County'.

She had shown impatience rarely in her life, but at ninety-six when she knew she was dying, she rapped out, 'I do *not* wish to linger!'

MARGARET ALICE POWYS (*née* Margaret Alice Lyon)(1871?-1947) According to Lucy Penny, John Cowper's wife, Margaret, 'was keen on animals and flowers'. Lucy continues, 'I think of Margaret as tall and thin, with fair hair, blue-eyed, and with a delicate complexion. She had a rather high-pitched voice, and a decided 'manner".' The Ted Pearce mentioned in the Letters – Ted Pearce of Corpus Christi, Cambridge, whom Margaret's sister, Constance, married – became Bishop of Derby.

That Margaret had to have an operation – which was quite simply a de-flowering' – was entirely due to Jack's fear of making love to a virgin. It is interesting that, with all the talk of Jack's impotence, he was able to become a father.

Margaret Powys relied more and more on their son, 'Young Littleton', and it is melancholy to read of her last days: out of the world, entirely dependent on him.

LITTLETON ALFRED POWYS (1902-1953)
Jack's son, Littleton, became an assistant priest at St John's Catholic Church, Bath, after he was converted to the Roman Catholic faith.

Littleton Alfred had a good-humoured, ironic manner with his father: not lacking in respect or affection, but ensuring an ease of relationship. His father had been a great deal absent from his boyhood, but there was love between them.

In 1945, 'Young Littleton', had an accident on his motor-bike. His body became useless, his speech became blurred. His only hope was in his devoted admirers. With a peacock's feather in his mouth, he pointed to letters on a board, and, in this way, with the help of a young Catholic girl, Dinah White, he wrote a poem, 'Ode to the West Wind'. His uncle, Littleton, had the poem privately printed; it is reprinted as Appendix 2 to *The Letters of John Cowper Powys to Ichiro Hara*, edited by Anthony Head (Cecil Woolf, 1990).

Young Littleton's death was an enormous blow to Jack, especially since Jack's brother, Theodore, had died a short time before.

VIOLET POWYS: VIOLET ROSIE DODDS (1887-1966)

Theodore Powys's wife. Her grandfather took messages from Thomas Hardy at Max Gate in Dorchester, Dorset, to his mother in Brockhampton. Lucy Penny writes: 'Violet's grandmother lived in Dorset, and when her husband died she took in lodgers. She had four daughters and a son who was drowned as a young man, at Lulworth. Mr Dodds, one of the lodgers, married the eldest daughter. Shortly after the birth of a daughter, Violet Rosalie, Mr Dodds died. After a while, Violet's mother married again, this time to Mr Jack Jacobs who lived in East Chaldon; so she took Violet there. Violet's mother had two more girls by her new husband. When Theodore came to live in the village, Violet was about seventeen years old. She was married to Theodore on, I believe, the day before her eighteenth birthday. Violet and Theodore lived in a thatched cottage opposite the green at East Chaldon; but after the birth of their son, "Dicky", they moved to a house named, by Theodore, "Beth-Car", the House of the Pasture, or the House of Bread. This was a larger, red-brick house supposed to have been built by Thomas Hardy's brother. Francis, the younger son of Theodore and Violet Powys, was born there. The family later moved to Mappowder, another Dorset village, where Theodore and Violet brought up their adopted daughter, Susie Theodora.'

FRANCIS LLEWELYN POWYS (1908-) – the second son of Theodore Powys – went, like his uncles (but not like his father who went to the Wilkinson school at Aldeburgh) to Sherborne Prep. School, where he won a Classical Exhibition to King's School, Bruton. After leaving there, he worked in a bank till illness cut this short. He went to France for two years, and on his return worked at Foyle's Bookshop. In 1933, he married Sally Upfield, daughter of the Headmaster of Victory Place School, Walworth – one of the schools destroyed in the war. During the war, Francis served five years in the Army. After that, he worked at Better Books, and then he founded The Powys Bookshop in Hastings. He had by then taken up photography professionally, and he wrote articles on it, and on travel. In 1968, he sold the shop, and retired to Dorset to the cottage where his Aunt Katie had lived. Here he looks after the Powys Estate, with the help of his wife, Sally. Sally Powys transcribed and typed the *Diaries* of John Cowper Powys, two volumes of which were published by Greymitre Press and further volumes are to be published by Cecil Woolf. Francis and Sally Powys have the help of Gerald Pollinger, of Laurence Pollinger Ltd, who became John Cowper Powys's literary agent from the time Jack went to Wales.

Francis Powys has published volumes of poetry, including *At the Harlot's Burial* and *The Ghost of Marseille*.

ISOBEL POWYS (1906-) – daughter of Bertie and Dorothy Powys – was the third painter among the Powyses. Her aunt, Gertrude, had exhibited her pictures: Willie painted in water-colours. Isobel Powys is a Powys from both sides of her family, for her father married a distant cousin. She is now the key figure at Powys Conferences.

PETER POWYS-GREY (1922-1992) – was the son of Marian Powys. His father was not the mythical Peter Grey, whom Jack and Marian invented, but Ernest Angell, a man Marian thought the most suitable father for her child.

Peter Powys-Grey graduated from Philips Exeter Academy in 1940, and from Harvard College, Class of 1944, with graduation in 1947. In between those years he was in the U.S. Infantry, mainly in the Pacific. In 1948, he married Barbara Elizabeth Tyler, in East Chaldon, Dorset. The two children of their marriage are Christopher Hamilton and Catharine Philippa Powys. From 1951 to 1956, Peter Powys-Grey worked for the American Express Company, and travelled to Russia for them. Then, until 1973, he was a Public Relations Director of the New York Chamber of Commerce. He was responsible for many of the pocket parks and some of the housing projects in the Greater Metropolitan Area. Five years after his divorce in 1967, he married Matilda Lorenta. That marriage lasted ten years, but also ended in divorce. Peter Powys-Grey was the founder of many projects; the Downtown centre, the rehabilitation centre for drug users, the Wall Street Flower Shop, supplying trees, plants and shrubs for low income areas, the Friends of Tompkins Square Library, the American Commedia dell'Arte Institute. He was also Chairman of the Samaritans in New York. He was active in the Powys Societies of North America.

EZRA POUND (1885-1972)
There are innumerable books about Ezra Pound's life and work: *The Life of Ezra Pound* by Noel Stock; *Ezra Pound* by T.S. Eliot; *Ezra Pound, Poet and Sculptor* by Professor Donald Davie; etc. An account of Ezra Pound, 'H.D.' and Frances is given in Frank Wintle's documentary film, 'Hilda's Book', for Television South-West. There is an amusing and candid account in 'The Mystic Leeway' by Frances Gregg of the love and friendship between the three of them when they were young.

Ezra Pound brought greatness to others as well as to himself: he encouraged Yeats to adopt a maturer style of poetry: he edited some of T.S. Eliot's poetry. In his own work, Ezra Pound has been compared as an experimentalist in poetry with Picasso in the visual arts.

From 1912, Ezra Pound was working in Europe, as the London Editor of 'The Dial', when Alyse Gregory – later Llewelyn Powys's wife – was its Managing Director. Ezra Pound was also co-founder, with Wyndham Lewis, of 'Blast'. Margaret Anderson, in *My Thirty Years War*, describes Ezra Pound, in the Paris of 1923 – where he was acting as foreign Editor of 'The Little Review': 'He was dressed in the large velvet beret and flowing tie of the Latin Quarter artist of the 1830s . . . . . Photographs have given no idea of his height, his robustness, his red blondness . . . . . could have given no indication of his high Roosveltian voice, his nervousness, his self-consciousness. After an hour in his studio I felt that I had been sitting through a human experiment in a behaviourist laboratory . . . . .'

In 1914, Ezra married Dorothy

Shakespeare, who had been Yeats's mistress. Dorothy bore Ezra a son, Omar. Ezra and the distinguished violinist, Olga Rudge, had a daughter, Mary.

For his Fascist beliefs Ezra Pound was put in a cage by the United States Army in Italy, during the Second World War. A United States Court then shut him away, as insane, from 1945 to 1958. Ezra Pound's wife, Dorothy, and his mistress, Olga Rudge, agitated for Ezra's release; as did many others. In 1958, Ezra settled with Olga in Italy.

Ezra spent his last year in silence. He repented his 'suburban clap-trap' — as he called it — of his anti-semitism; and he felt he had wasted his gifts. He had, however, affected his times, and affected them greatly for the good; though the grim chaos of his politics had wasted many years.

ANN REID (1900-1932) — Louis Wilkinson's second wife — was as much under average height as Louis was over it. 'It was quite ridiculous to see them together,' writes Ethel Mannin in her *Confessions and Impressions*. '. . . . . the doll-like Ann looking like something out of a Russian ballet, with her smooth hair and pointed face; odd people to be married to each other, odd people to be married at all, you feel, and yet when you know them you couldn't imagine them being married to anyone but each other.'

Ann's early death was the tragedy of Louis Wilkinson's life. He was honest enough, though, to wonder, some years after Nan's death, whether the marriage would have lasted. She would probably have continued to write novels, though, and — judging by her *We are the Dead* and *Love Lies Bleeding* — have continued to develop as a novelist.

STEPHEN REYNOLDS (1881-1919) — for whose love Katie Powys went mad for a time, in 1912 — had been very much in love with Katie. As a young man, Stephen Reynolds had studied music and chemistry, and gained his B.Sc., with Honours. He went on to the Ecole de Mime in Paris, and became editor of a weekly critical review, living on next to nothing in an attic. Alyse Gregory, Llewelyn Powys's wife, says that, living like that, and with shoals of rejection slips for his writing, he fell ill and became a wreck, but he managed to get back to his home in Wiltshire. There he found that he could not even form letters, and had to learn the alphabet again. He moved to Sidmouth, Devon, but had another collapse. On his return home, the doctor told him that he would never work again. In 1903 he returned to Sidmouth, where he lived with the Wolseys, a family of fishermen. Stephen Reynolds worked with them. He determined to turn his back on his own middle class. Working as a fisherman restored his health.

The fishermen began to appreciate his education. They put him on their negotiating committees. He became a member of the Committees of Inquiry into the Cornwall Fisheries. He continued to write, encouraged by Edward Garnett, Thomas Secombe, Ford Madox Ford and Joseph Conrad. His book about the fishermen, *A Poor Man's House* (The Bodley Head, 1908) was a success. It was reissued in 1982 by O.U.P., with a foreword by Roy Hattersley.

It was through Katie Powys's own work with the fishing community that she met him. Lucy Penny writes that she thinks that Stephen Reynolds finally decided not to marry Katie, because he wanted to give all his time to writing. All that time, he was writing an article on the effects of neurasthenia.

Stephen Reynolds had other books published – including *The Holy Mountain* in 1909 – but none succeeded like *A Poor Man's House*.

PERCEVAL ROBERTS (1883-1923) – the young man who travelled across the Atlantic with Frances and Louis and Jack and May in 1912 – was a particular friend of Oswald Green, the founder of the Blue Tulip Club at Oxford, to which Louis Wilkinson, as an undergraduate, had belonged. Louis and most of the others were sent down, but Perceval Roberts escaped expulsion.

When he committed suicide it was after several attempts that had been thwarted by his friends. Louis Wilkinson had once walked him up and down, a whole night, to get poison out of his system.

WALTER RUMMEL (1887-1953) – the pianist and composer whom Frances and 'H.D.' met in Paris in 1911, at Ezra Pound's introduction – was twenty-four years old at the time. He was the son of Franz Rummel, the pianist; and he studied with Godowski; and Kann in Berlin; and was a student of Fabian in Washington. He collaborated with Debussy. He also collaborated with Ezra Pound in a musical work. Some of his compositions are now used as exercises for students.

G. ARNOLD SHAW (1875?-1937) – started The University Lecturers' Association at the suggestion of Louis Wilkinson. Arnold Shaw had been working in a New York music shop before that. He continued to work there till he earnt enough from the lecture commissions to support his family.

Phyllis Playter writes that Arnold

met his first wife, Lizzie, on the ship going over to the United States. Their daughter Edith married twice, and has two sons. Arnold Shaw and his second wife, Hattie, had one son, Armin, and one daughter, Patricia. This daughter, Patricia, was stricken with polio, but continued with her job, travelling about New York in a bath-chair. On Arnold Shaw's death, his second wife, Hattie, married a Mr Frank Waldo, who saved Arnold Shaw's family from the disasters that had plagued them in his later years.

The best account of Arnold Shaw is in the *Autobiography* of John Cowper Powys.

THE HONOURABLE RALPH SHIRLEY (1865-1947) – cousin of the Powyses – son of Philippa and Canon Shirley, Regius Professor of History at Oxford. Ralph Shirley had a sister, Alice, who married the Reverend W.R. Linton; and their daughter was the Marion Linton who went into a convent instead of marrying Llewelyn Powys. Ralph Shirley's brother, Walter, succeeded as the eleventh Earl Ferrers.

Ralph Shirley owned a controlling interest in the publishing house of William Ryder & Son, the firm that published Jack's early poetry, and that acted for the sale of Theodore Powys's *An Interpretation of Genesis*.

Jack called Ralph 'Trismegistus', the magic man, for Ralph edited 'The Occult Review', and wrote several books on occult topics. Ralph Shirley believed, nevertheless, that a study of occultism led to scepticism.

Shirley died in his eighty-second year after romping too vigorously with children at Christmas.

Louis Wilkinson said that Shirley was full of knowledge – general, classical and strange – and that he was always good company.

ELLEN VAN VOLKENBERG (1895?-?) — wife of Maurice Browne, and founder, with him, of the Chicago Little Theatre — was an actress, producer and manager. John Cowper Powys and Maurice Browne and Ellen suggested to Dreiser, Masters and to Frances and Louis Wilkinson, that they should all combine to write for the Little Theatre. Jack then wrote to Louis Wilkinson, '. . . . . The idea is that you and I and Maurice each write a play for three men and three girls — one girl to be Maurice's fiancée, Nelly Van Volkenberg. I like her, though she is a little plump — but she is very piquant and little-girlish.' Louis wrote back that he had no theatre experience.

Maurice Browne had met Ellen Van Volkenberg when she was with a party of Americans visiting Europe. He had fallen immediately in love with her and had followed her to the United States — after pawning the family silver to reach her. She was giving one-woman shows — one of the first women to do so. He also found that she watched a play with tears streaming down her face; whether it was comedy, romance or tragedy. Afterwards — writes Maurice Browne in his *Too Late to Lament* — she would dry her tears and, after some contemplation, act the whole play, adapting her voice and carriage and character to the various parts.

Maurice and Ellen started the Little Theatre in the storage place of the Chicago Fine Arts Building. Charles C. Curtis, the manager, let them have it for $3,000 a year. They built a stage, and installed equipment of the latest design. They even fitted in a little cafe and bookstall. The summer was the worst time for them because, with windows shut, it was stifling and, with windows open, the piano shop opposite deafened actors and audience.

When Ellen Van Volkenberg returned to Maurice Browne — after divorcing him twenty-five years earlier — it was to help him with his Maurice Browne Ltd productions in London. She returned to the United States; and generously made Maurice Browne an allowance, for the rest of his life.

LOUIS UMFREVILLE WILKINSON (1881-1966) was born at Aldeburgh, Suffolk. A good deal of his life up to 1941 is described in the Letters.

That there was an antagonism as well as a deep friendship between Louis Wilkinson and John Cowper Powys, *before* Louis married Frances, is shown in this letter of 1907 from Jack to Louis: 'Bernie O'Neill when he was down here [at Montacute] said, "You Powyses are always speaking as though Louis was a cunning sort of dog, as cunning a dog, in fact, as you are yourselves" — and then the word "worldly" as applied to you led on to an unaccountable outburst of fury on my part, in which I denounced you in so scandalous a manner that even those impenetrable psychologists were shocked. However, after this outburst with trembling lip and tearful eye was over, I speedily returned to my normal and rational condition and then was only anxious to find the explanation of this explosion of subliminal feelings — '.

Louis' feelings of love and hate for Jack were greater after Louis married Frances.

After the death of his second wife, Ann Reid, Louis married Diana Bryn, whose sister became the Duchess of Westminster. Finally, some time after he had divorced Diana Bryn, he married Joan Lamburn, who was older than Diana, but much younger than Louis. Joan Lamburn died before him, leaving Louis with worsening eyesight and increasing helplessness. He had so loved life that he longed for death. In 1963, he died on one of his visits to our family.

He had fought against evil conventions and laws. He was ruthless in some of his personal relationships, but ruthless, too, in fighting damnable prejudices.

He had loyalty to those he loved. He had interest in his family and in the family tree, too, but in his own way. He writes in a letter that his particular Wilkinson line can be traced back – on the male side – to Horsley in Northumberland, in the seventeenth century, and – on the distaff side – to 1139. 'But, good heavens, everyone goes back to 1139, and to the very beginning which is far more distant! – and thousands of people have ancestors of high rank: it is only that they have no record. In looking up family records, it interests me, of course, to see that a great-great-etc. grandfather was Duke of Norfolk, that another great-great-etc. grandfather was beheaded for high treason; also that another great-great-etc., when Ambassador to Venice, was poisoned by order of James II. . . . .'

For long Louis was the black sheep of his family. His success as a lecturer, and then as a writer, finally reconciled him to them.

Louis was elected to the Council of the Royal Society of Literature. Through him, John Cowper Powys was given a grant.

Louis was finally persuaded to give talks on the BBC; but only when told that he would be recorded as he sat at dinner with other guests.

When he stopped writing in extreme old age, he was still consulted about films with Edwardian background, or on works about Oscar Wilde.

Few men have appreciated wine, women and life more, or had such good health, or done so much good; and not many have got away with so much.

A list of Louis Wilkinson's publications is included in the Bibliography.

ERSKINE WOOD (1852-1944) – who lived with Sara Bard Field, and married her when he could – seems a somewhat staid figure in the Letters, but he was wild and romantic and, when needs be, practical. Peter Powys-Grey said that he was also unpredictable. Mark Twain showed Erskine Wood a pornographic book he had written – 'a scatological book', Peter Powys-Grey described it – which Mark Twain said could never be published. 'It *can!*' said Erskine Wood. He had the power to publish it on a U.S. Army press, and he did. That queered his pitch for ever with the U.S. Army.

Erskine Wood might have been invented by Walt Whitman, for he was a man of breadth, compassion and action. He was an adventurer and a poet.

He had served in the United States Army, had fought Indians, then had bitterly opposed the corruption of the Indian Ring in Washington (who were stealing the appropriations made for the Indians) and had resigned his commission. He practised law. In 1904 he had published *A Masque of Love*. In 1915 he had published *The Poet in the Desert*. In 1919 he had published *Circe*. With his blue eyes, thick white hair and grey white beard, he was a fine figure in the artists' circle of San Francisco. He and Sara were the champions of many causes.

He lived till he was ninety-two. Long before that he had become helpless, looked after by his wife, Sara Bard Field, who had shared his beliefs, and who was, like Erskine Wood, one of the figures of American idealism.

Index

Achilles 130, 195n
Acreman House (Sherborne) 19, 201n
Adams, Dr 216n
Adonais 71, 200n
Adrasteia 65, 199n
Adriatic, the 77, 103
Africa 204n, 208n, 214n, 219
Agricultural and Horticultural College, the 49
Alcazar, the 46
Aldeburgh (Suffolk) 5, 25, 54, 186n, 189-92n, 209n, 212n, 222n, 250n, 254n
Aldington, Richard 203n, 211n, 233n, 237n
Algiers 20
Alice Through the Looking Glass (Carroll) 57
Alleghany Mountains, the 2, 185n
Altoona 85
America xxiii, xxvi-vii, 1, 105, 114, 139, 190n, 194-5n, 198-200n, 202-3n, 206n, 210-13n, 215n, 220-23n, 226-7n, 230-31n
American Civil War, the xvi, 185n
American Commedia dell'Arte Institute, the 251n
American Express Company, the 156, 251n
American Tragedy, An (Dreiser) 202n
American Society for the Exten-
sion of University Teaching xxiii
Anderson, Margaret 118, 215n, 251n
Andreyev, Leonard 105, 209n
Angel Island (California) 124
Angell, Ernest 251n
Antwerp 76
Apologia Pro Vita Sua (Newman) 15, 188n
Arabian Nights, The 11, 100
Arcachon 220n
Aristophanes 97, 207n
Arnold, Matthew 130
Arrow of Gold (Conrad) 182
Ashcroft, Peggy 236n
Ashtead Heath (Surrey) 150, 224n
'Assumption of the Virgin' (El Greco) 210n
Atlantic, the 16, 44, 61
Atlantis, the Lost 44

Badingham (Suffolk) 155, 230-31n, 233n
Baltimore 144, 158
Balzac, Honoré de 45, 63, 195n
Barbey D'Aurevilly, Jules 63, 199n
Barry, Mrs 77, 201n
Barrymore, Mrs John 215n
Bath (Somerset) 122
Bay of Biscay, the 220n
Beaune 136, 213n, 218n, 220n

257